ROAD TRANSPORT
IN CUMBRIA
IN THE NINETEENTH
CENTURY

ROAD TRANSPORT IN CUMBRIA IN THE NINETEENTH CENTURY

L. A. Williams

Lecturer in Modern History
Dundee University

London

George Allen & Unwin Ltd

Ruskin House   Museum Street

First published in 1975

© George Allen & Unwin Ltd, 1975

ISBN 0 04 385062 6

Printed in Great Britain
in 10 point Times Roman type
by Unwin Brothers Limited
The Gresham Press
Old Woking   Surrey

Preface

The history of road transport has been a neglected topic of research. The reasons for this are not hard to find. Detailed documentary evidence relating to roads and their traffic is difficult to come by for most periods of British history, and when such evidence becomes somewhat more plentiful during the middle decades of the nineteenth century, roads are in the process of being superseded by railways as the main form of land transportation. It is only natural that railways should have received much more attention from economic and social historians. The impact which rail transport made upon the environment was more dramatic in its effects, and the records of the various railway companies often provide a wealth of information for the research worker.

However, there is to my mind ample justification for embarking upon detailed studies of road transportation. In the first place, until about 1840 roads carried a high proportion of the nation's passenger traffic and, together with canals and coastal shipping, an appreciable amount of freight also. Hence, their importance in the early years of industrialisation and rapid urban and population growth must not be overlooked.

Second, although after about 1840 railways clearly take over the bulk of this traffic, it is still worth having a close look at the way in which road transport interests reacted to the challenge posed by a faster, cheaper and generally more efficient form of transportation. In addition, during this later period of the nineteenth century, despite a marked decline in 'through' traffic upon the various main roads, short-distance traffic increased considerably especially in the vicinity of major towns and, of course, within the towns themselves. Hence, a study of the interaction of road authorities with the various railway, urban and rural interests in this period will, I hope, demonstrate that the study of road transportation, even in a more obscure phase of its history, can shed some light upon various aspects of economic and social development.

All historians of transport are indebted to Jackman. His pioneer *History of Transportation in Modern Britain* (first published in 1916) has not been superseded. It includes a number of illuminating chapters on the history of road transport, and the appendixes relating to travel costs are, to my mind, particularly valuable.

Unfortunately, Jackman's monumental survey stops at roughly 1850. Hence, historians of road transport for the latter half of the nineteenth century have to turn elsewhere for information. Perhaps the most valuable book covering this later period is the Webbs' survey entitled *The Story of the King's Highway*. This was written in 1913 and forms a volume in their study of English Local Government. The Webbs concentrated upon administrative developments rather than, say, on the nature of traffic using the roads. Nevertheless, their book is an indispensable guide for historians studying eighteenth and nineteenth century roads and their governing bodies.

More recent historical studies of road transport have usually fallen into one or other of three categories. The first group comprises histories of stage and mail coach firms, of which Edmund Vale's book *The Mail-Coach Men* (1960) is an outstanding example. In the second category, are studies of road engineers and administrators. In this respect, Telford has been fortunate in his biographers and there are two substantial studies of his contribution to road and bridge building: namely, Alexander Gibb, *The Story of Telford* (1935) and L. T. C. Rolt's book entitled *Thomas Telford* (1958). There is still not as yet, to my mind, a really satisfactory life of Telford's eminent contemporary J. L. McAdam, although the article by Robert H. Spiro, 'John Loudon McAdam and the Metropolitan Turnpike Trust' is a very informative analysis of one aspect of McAdam's activities.

A third group of writings has dealt with road transport as a whole in relation to the social and economic environment. Such studies have been relatively few in number but valuable in content. They include A. R. B. Haldane's two classic studies of Scottish road development: *The Drove Roads of Scotland* (1952) and *New Ways Through the Glens* (1961). It is also worth noting two more recently published works: one by John Copeland entitled *Roads and Their Traffic 1750–1850*; and a study of Turnpike Trusts by William Albert entitled *The Turnpike Road System in England, 1663–1840*.

Other studies along these lines have been more locally or regionally orientated and there are a number of illuminating local surveys of this kind. They include the following:

1 Percy Russell, *A Leicestershire Road* (1934)
2 Arthur Cossons, 'The Turnpike Roads of Nottinghamshire', *Historical Association Pamphlet*, No. 97 (1934)

3 W. B. Crump, *Huddersfield Highways down the Ages* (1949)
4 G. C. Dickinson, 'Stage Coach Services in the West Riding of Yorkshire between 1830 and 1840', *Journal of Transport History* (May 1959)
5 G. C. Dickinson, 'The Development of Suburban Road Passenger Traffic in Leeds, 1840–95', *Journal of Transport History* (Nov. 1960)
6 K. A. McMahon, 'Roads and Turnpike Trusts in East Yorkshire', *East Yorkshire Local History Society* (1964)
7 J. L. Hobbs, 'The Turnpike Roads of North Lonsdale', C.W.T. (1955)

It is clear that further local and regional studies of this nature will have to be done before any major re-consideration of road transport history on a national basis can be undertaken.

The historian of road transportation, unless he is unusually fortunate, has to accept that his source material will be scattered and incomplete. There is, of course, a good deal of centrally located material in the various Parliamentary Reports, Acts of Parliament and Statistical Returns on road transport, but, in the main, the researcher has to rely for his primary information upon local archives. Prominent amongst these are the various Turnpike Trust records: minute books, account books and miscellaneous correspondence. Another fruitful source is the Quarter Sessions records for individual counties. These include a good deal of information about parish roads, and county, parish and privately owned bridges. In relation to Cumbria this was an extremely useful source of information; particularly when a legal dispute over the responsibility for repairing a road or bridge threw a good deal of light upon local vested interests and administrative realities. However, Quarter Session records rarely commented upon the volume and nature of traffic using the various roads.

Turnpike Trust records were often more helpful in this respect. Records of toll gate receipts enable one to build up some sort of general picture of the volume of traffic making use of the various main roads. However, Turnpike Trust material was defective in other respects. In the first place, in Cumberland and Westmorland at least, the majority of Trusts were not well documented, at least in terms of what has survived, and material relating to the West Cumberland Trusts was particularly sparse. Hence, the picture I have given of Turnpike Trust history in this region has inevitably become rather more selective than I would have liked. Furthermore, even well-documented Trusts such as Cockermouth

—Penrith and Carlisle—Eamont Bridge do not contain very much information for the 1800–20 period of their history.

On the whole, the available records rarely provided the sort of information which would permit confident answers to basic questions about: the kinds of traffic using the various roads, the proportion of the Trusts' toll revenues which was made up of receipts from passenger traffic as opposed to freight, the extent of seasonal fluctuations in the volume of traffic using the roads, and the proportion of traffic which was short as distinct from long distance. It must be added that occasionally this last question can be answered more positively, since Trusts sometimes gave details of toll receipts for individual gates, rather than following the usual practice of simply providing toll receipts for the whole Trust without breaking down these figures more precisely. I found local newspaper records particularly valuable in giving me this more detailed information.

Perhaps the biggest disappointment from my point of view was that only a small number of Turnpike Trust Minute Books appear to have survived for the Cumbrian area. Most of this material would originally have been in the possession of local solicitors, and it is quite possible that there is still a certain amount of relevant material in solicitors' strong-rooms which has not yet come to light.

In view of these intrinsic difficulties, I was particularly fortunate in having a great deal of assistance from Mr Jones and Miss Macpherson, the respective archivists at Carlisle and Kendal Record offices. They and their staffs gave me every possible help in my search for relevant documents, and it is largely due to their efforts that a good deal of my source material has been rescued from the depths of solicitors' offices. I was also fortunate in being able to make use of the Tullie House library in Carlisle which contains an excellent collection of books and pamphlets on local history, in addition to an impressive sequence of local newspapers. I would like to thank the Librarian and his staff for their help in giving me access to these facilities. There are a great many other people in the Lake District to whom I also owe thanks for all their patient help and co-operation.

Finally, I am deeply indebted to Professor Simmons and the staff of the Leicester University History Department for all the help and encouragement which they have given me over the years. Professor Simmons, in particular, has given me a great deal of his time, and has stimulated and guided me throughout the writing of this book.

L. A. WILLIAMS, Dundee

Contents

Preface   *page* 7
Abbreviations   15
1 Introduction   17
2 Road and Bridge Administration   42
3 Road Transport Developments in the Pre-railway
   Period   76
4 Competition for Traffic   129
5 Some Problems of Urban Growth   163
6 Trust Dissolution and its Aftermath   178
7 Conclusion   202
Appendixes   214
Bibliography   238
Index   263

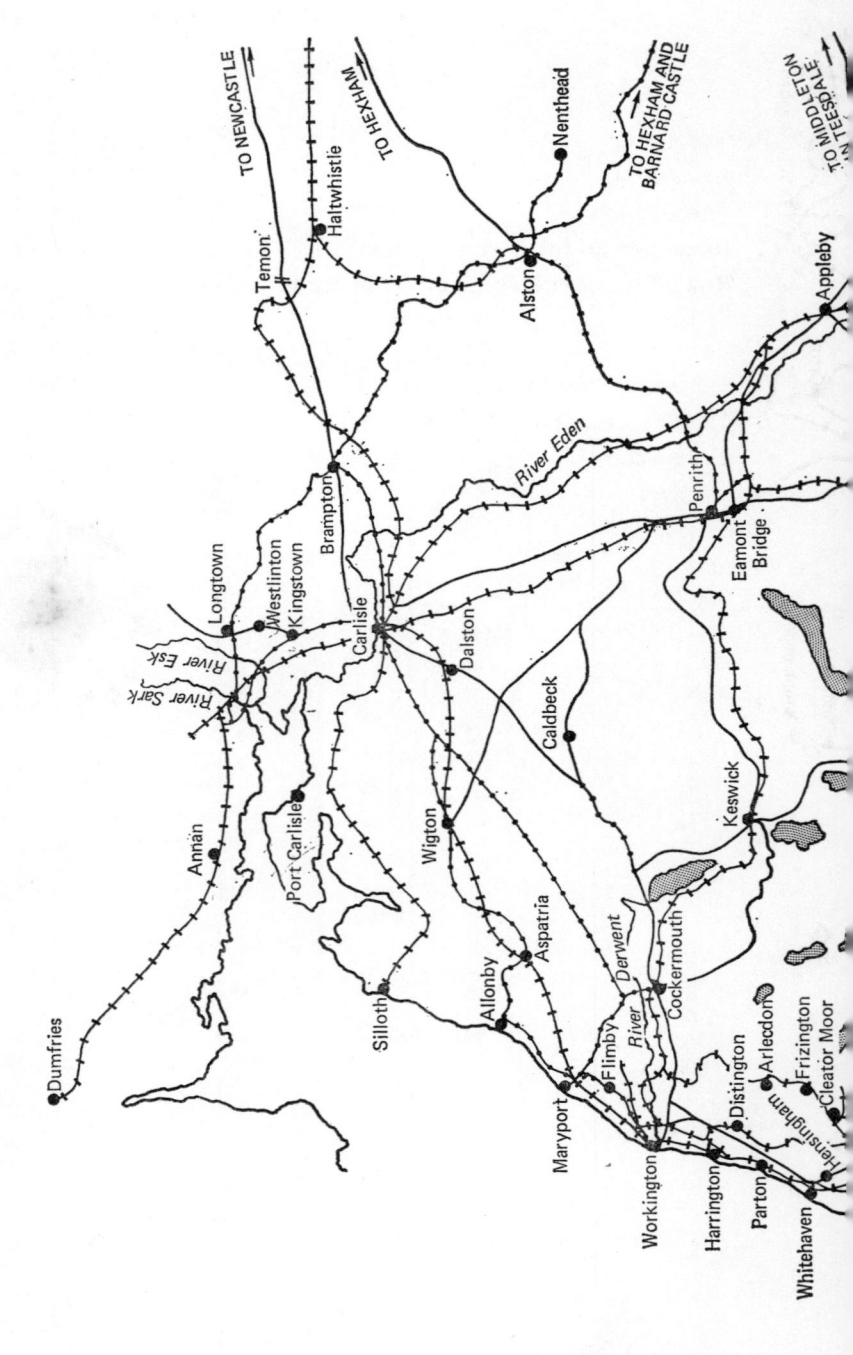

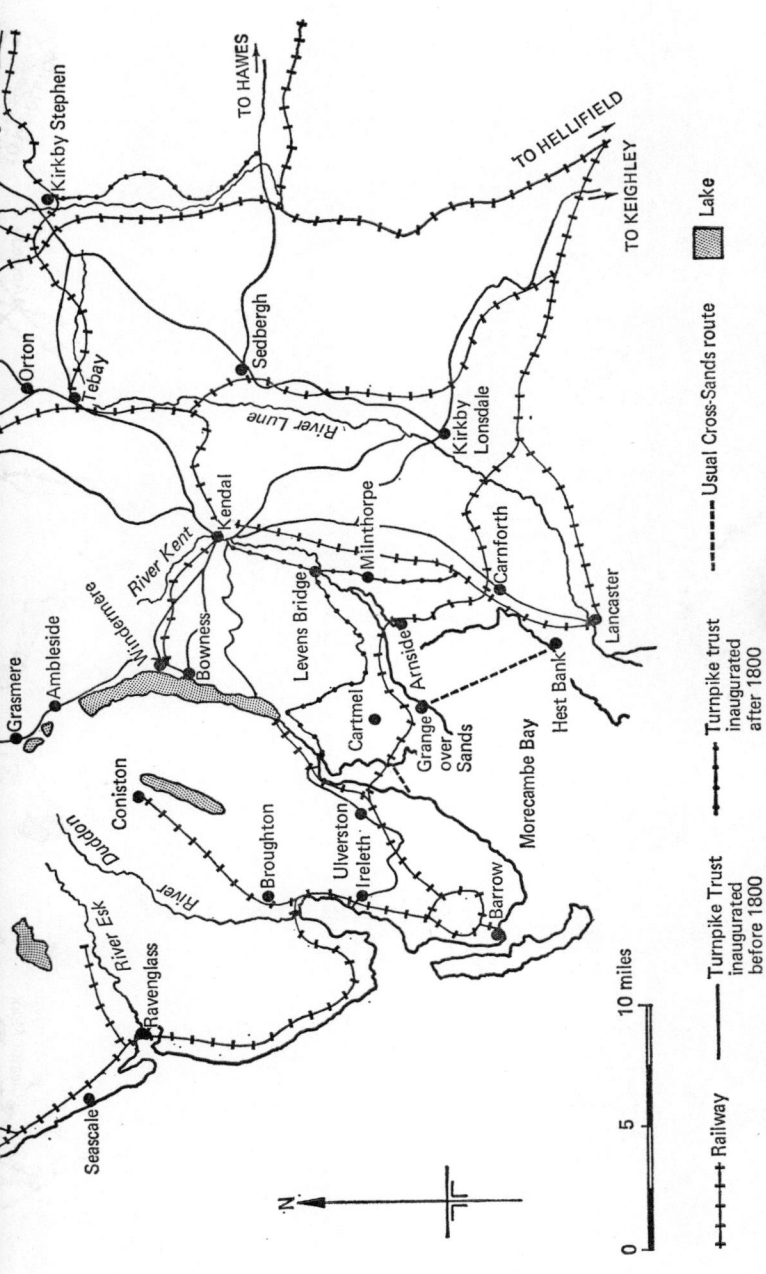

Frontispiece. Map of Cumbria outlining its road and railway network in the nineteenth century.

Railway

Turnpike Trust inaugurated before 1800

Turnpike trust inaugurated after 1800

Usual Cross-Sands route

Lake

N

0   5   10 miles

Abbreviations

1. C.W.T.   *Transactions of the Cumberland and Westmorland Antiquarian and Archaeological Society*
2. C.W.A.L.S.   *Transactions of the Cumberland and Westmorland Association for the Advancement of Literature and Science*
3. Q.S.   Quarter Sessions
4. L.R.O.   Lancashire Record Office
5. C.R.O.   Carlisle Record Office
6. K.R.O.   Kendal Record Office
7. T.H.C.   Tullie House, Carlisle
8. K.M.   Keswick Museum
9. H.L.R.O.   House of Lords Record Office
10. P.R.O.   Public Record Office
11. B.M.   British Museum
12. T.H.R.   Transport History Record Office, London
13. L.P.A.   Local and Personal Acts
14. H. OF C.   House of Commons
15. H. OF L.   House of Lords
16. O.S.   Old Series
17. EAMONT TRUST   Carlisle–Eamont Bridge Turnpike Trust
18. JACKMAN   *Transportation in Modern England* (1962)
19. S. & B. WEBB   Sidney and Beatrice Webb, *The Story of the King's Highway* (1913)
20. BAILEY & CULLEY   J. Bailey and G. Culley, *A General View of the Agriculture of the County of Cumberland* (1794)
21. W. PARSONS & W. WHITE   *History, Directory and Gazetteer of Cumberland and Westmorland* (1829)

Chapter 1

INTRODUCTION

Cumberland, Westmorland and the Furness district of Lanca-shire[1] form a distinct physical region of England. The area is bounded by the Pennine summits to the east and north-east, the Irish Sea to the west, and the waters and sands of Morecambe Bay to the south and south-west.

The region is an isolated one and, although modern methods of communication have made it very much more accessible during the last 150 years, the barrier of relief and its distance from large cities, London in particular, have been of very great significance in determining its historical development; its relative immunity to a good many outside influences giving it a distinctive social and economic structure in the eighteenth century.

Cumbria can be divided into two main physical regions: a highland area and a stretch of coastal lowland. The highland zone comprises the central lake district massif and the western fringe of the Pennines; the latter being partly separated from the lake mountains by the valley of the river Eden. The lowland plain embraces coastal or 'Low' Furness and then extends north-westwards up the West Cumberland coast in a narrow strip, finally broadening into a more extensive lowland area in North Cumberland where it comprises the flood plain of the rivers Eden, Esk and their tributaries.

The nature of this relief has made Cumbria difficult to penetrate and to cross. Therefore, one has also got to take into account the isolation of particular communities within Cumbria as a promi-nent feature of its social and economic development. The valleys of the Eden, and to a lesser extent the Lune, have, it is true, provided natural low level route-ways within Cumbria as far inland as Appleby and Sedbergh, respectively, but any penetration beyond or between these places involves crossing an arm of the Pennines. Also, the rivers and lakes of the region have had some share in its

---

[1] Hereafter referred to as Cumbria.

penetration and exploitation, but this does not seriously modify the overall picture. This study attempts to evaluate the extent to which, during the nineteenth century, improved road conditions reduced the isolation of this region and also helped to create a more integrated regional economy. In order to discuss nineteenth century road transport, it will be useful first to review transport conditions in an earlier period.

Road transport in this region can be traced back to Roman times. The Romans had built a network of roads in Cumbria in order to connect up their various military camps, and there is evidence that certain of these roads were still being used during the Middle Ages. For instance, a road from Carlisle to Appleby, via Sowerby, was in use at this time, as were stretches of Roman roads further south; comprising a highway from Burton to Holderstone, one from Farleton to Burton and a third road between Hincaster and Sedgwick.[2] The other medieval roads included the 'street' from Appleby to Tebay, the Brampton 'streitte' to Appleby and the North Road between Kendal and Shap. It is probable also that the expansion of monastic houses within the area and the accompanying extension of sheep rearing necessitated a good many roadways between the different monasteries, and also between individual religious houses and neighbouring market towns such as Egremont and Cockermouth.

In addition to this internal road system, there is some evidence of early penetration of the region from outside. For instance, on 28 April 1281, the Archbishop of York is recorded to have reached Burton-in-Kendal; four days later he was at Cartmel and on 10 May he had reached St Bees, before returning to Burton two days later. There are also records of Newcastle merchants buying Cumbrian wool for export in 1397 and again in 1423, 1427 and 1444.[3] Similarly, there is evidence that as early as the fifteenth century, Bristol merchants were shipping Kendal cloth to Spain.[4] Also, the Southampton Brokage books referred to Kendal traders by name in the autumn of 1442, and record that between November 1492 and March 1493, eleven Kendal traders made a total of fourteen journeys to Southampton, carrying packs of cloth. Subsequently, there are a good many references to Kendal wool traders in the various sixteenth century Southampton Brokage books, culminat-

---

[2] C. Bouch & G. Jones, *A Short Economic and Social History of the Lake Counties, 1500–1830* (1961), pp. 18–21.   [3] Ibid.

[4] M. Postan, *English Trade in the Fifteenth Century* (G. Routledge & Sons, 1933), p. 216.

ing in a peak year of 1536–7, when a total of fifty-three packs was brought in from Kendal.[5]

Despite this evidence of intermittent travel, the mountainous nature of much of the surrounding countryside must have almost inevitably made travelling particularly arduous in this northern region. Visitors to Cumberland and Westmorland had no doubt been ready to expect the worst and were not disposed to be charitable when relating the conditions which they encountered. For instance, three travellers between Penrith and Kendal in 1634 remarked that they went

'through such ways as we hope we never shall again, being no other but climbing and stony, nothing but bogs and myres, or the tops of those high hills so we were enforced to keep to these narrow, loose, stony, base ways, though never so troublesome and danger-ous . . . on we went for Kendal, desiring much to be released of those difficult and dangerous ways, which for the space of eight miles travelling a slow marching pace we passed over nothing but a most confused mixture of rocks and bogs.'[6]

John Ogilby recognised only four roads in Cumbria on his map drawn in 1675. One road from Kendal to Carlisle via Shap, and a second one from Egremont through Whitehaven to Workington, Cockermouth, Bothel to Carlisle. These two roads were linked by a crossroad from Cockermouth to Kendal via Keswick and Amble-side. Finally, he denotes a road between Newcastle and Carlisle; this route crossed the Eden at Corby and continued eastwards through Castle Carrock. It is unlikely, however, that any of these roads were usable by wheeled traffic at this time, and most goods were carried across country by pack horses.

These transport facilities might have sufficed at a time when there was a very limited demand for the carriage of people and commodi-ties, but they soon proved inadequate for the growing needs of the region during the eighteenth century.

During this period, Cumbria, in common with other areas of Britain, underwent considerable changes. In the first place, the population of the region appears to have expanded very markedly although it is difficult to obtain reliable statistics for this before the first national census of 1801. Two surveys of the population of Cumberland and Westmorland have, however, been recorded prior to this date: one by Denton in 1688 and another by Waugh in

5 B. C. Jones, 'Westmorland Packhorsemen in Southampton', C.W.T., LIX (1959), pp. 65–84. 6 B.M., Additional MSS 34754, pp. 19–20.

1747. On the basis of these two censuses and by an examination of parish registers, it has been calculated that the population of Cumberland in 1700 was about 60,000,[7] whereas the corresponding figure returned at the 1801 Census was 117,230.[8] This represents a 95 per cent population increase during the eighteenth century. It has been similarly calculated that the population of Westmorland in 1700 was about 27,000,[9] whereas it had risen to 40,805 by 1801,[10] an increase of 36 per cent. Parallel studies have also been made of some of the Furness townships. For instance, Broughton in Furness had a population of about 550 in 1700 and this figure had increased to 1,005 by 1801.

These figures are, of course, only approximate, but they do provide strong evidence that the population of Cumberland, Westmorland and Furness increased substantially during the eighteenth century. This rise possibly exceeded the national average increase in Cumberland, whilst falling somewhat below this figure in Westmorland.

A considerable proportion of this increased population lived in towns of over 1,000 by 1801; there being eight such towns in Cumberland, three in Westmorland and one, namely Ulverston, in Furness. The growth of such towns was usually the result of an expansion of mining operations in the locality or, alternatively, because of the growth of particular industries within their boundaries.

Economic developments were most rapid and widespread in West Cumberland. In the first half of the eighteenth century, the mining of coal was becoming increasingly important in the economy of the area; coalfields extending from Maryport to St Bees Head produced the greater part of a total Cumberland coal production of about 500,000 tons a year by the 1780s.[11] West Cumberland also possessed extensive resources of iron ore; notably in a seven mile strip of land between Knockmurton and Egremont, and also around Millom and in Furness.[12] However, these ores were not exploited so rapidly as was coal.

The initiative of local landlords played a large part in these mining and urban developments. The Lowther, Curwen and

---

[7] G. P. Jones, 'Some Population Problems Relating to Cumberland and Westmorland in the Eighteenth Century', C.W.T., LVIII (1958), p. 124.

[8] *Parl. Papers*, 1801–2, **VII**, p. 48.   [9] G. P. Jones, op. cit., p. 125.

[10] *Parl. Papers*, 1801–2, **VII**, p. 376.

[11] Isaac Fletcher, 'The Archaeology of the West Cumberland Coal Trade', C.W.T., **III** (O.S.) (1876–7), pp. 266–313.

[12] J. Nicholson and R. Burn, *History of Cumberland*, **II** (1777), p. 135.

Senhouse families, in particular, took advantage of the natural resources of the region and mobilised its increasing working population more effectively. For instance, the port of Whitehaven, whilst possessing a favourable coastal position and nearby mineral resources of coal and iron ore, also owed a great deal to the ambition, energy and resources of successive generations of the Lowther family. Sir John Lowther had been initially responsible for extending the collieries in 1666, at which time the town's population was negligible;[13] by 1755 local mining had developed very considerably and the population of Whitehaven had risen to about 11,000. By 1785 the town numbered 17,000 inhabitants.[14] Similar factors determined the growth of Maryport, Workington and Harrington. These three ports were also controlled to a marked degree by prominent local families: Maryport by the Senhouses, and Workington and Harrington by the Curwens. Maryport and Harrington expanded from small hamlets into towns of over 1,000 population during the second half of the eighteenth century; the majority of the people being employed in coal mining. The rise of Maryport is a particularly good illustration of the stimulus which expanding coal production could give to urban development. Workington, on the other hand, was an older development and the Curwen family were already operating four pits within a short distance of the town by 1750.[15] Carlisle also expanded considerably during this period. The town had suffered greatly in the past from endemic Border raids, and its rapid growth in the second half of the eighteenth century was undoubtedly aided by the more settled conditions which followed the capitulation of the Scottish army in 1746. Its recovery was not immediate and as late as 1759 a contemporary described it as 'A small deserted, dirty city: poorly built and poorly inhabited'.[16] Two years later, however, in 1761, a calico printing business was set up by the Newcastle firm of Scott Laird and Company. Shortly afterwards, Messrs Ferguson established their cotton spinning works,[17] and by 1800 Carlisle was a thriving textile town with a population of over 8,000. The growth of textile industries in Carlisle also stimulated similar developments in neighbouring towns. For instance, a firm began printing

---

[13] W. Whellan, *History of Cumberland and Westmorland* (1860), p. 440.
[14] Ibid., p. 441.
[15] I. Fletcher, op. cit., p. 297.
[16] R. G. Hutton, 'A Lakeland Journey, 1759', C.W.T., LXI (N.S. 1961), p. 292.
[17] W. Hutchinson, *History and Antiquities of Cumberland*, II (1794), p. 664.

calico at Wigton in 1790,[18] and in 1794 a large water powered cotton mill was built at Keswick.[19]

The growth of these towns during the second half of the eighteenth century also helped to encourage the increased exploitation of the more fertile agricultural areas of Cumbria. As early as 1750, clover, wheat and turnips were being grown in Cumberland; turnips being of particular importance in providing winter fodder for cattle. Further developments in agriculture, as in mining, owed a great deal to the direction of progressive local landlords. John Christian Curwen in particular was quick to recognise the increased possibilities of commercial farming, and with this in mind he set up an experimental farm at Schoose to pioneer more scientific methods. He was particularly interested in the selective breeding of stock to improve milk yields and beef production, and to this purpose he introduced short-horn cattle into Cumberland to replace the inferior Galloway stock. Furthermore, he was eager to disseminate the results of his findings and to encourage local activity generally. He formed an Agricultural Society and also organised shows and competitions in various aspects of stock breeding and in the manufacture of farm implements.

The organisation for long-term agricultural improvements was provided by the far-reaching changes in land ownership which stemmed from the Enclosure Movement. Enclosures had been sporadic for centuries in the form of strip consolidation, but became much more systematic towards the end of the eighteenth century. It has been estimated that 200,000 acres of land in Cumberland were enclosed between 1793 and 1816.[20] Crops were now grown for sale as well as for cattle fattening and domestic consumption. For instance, Bailey and Culley, in their survey of Cumberland agriculture in 1793, point out that potatoes were now cultivated 'by almost every farmer, not only for the use of their own families, but for sale, when the situation is not too distant from a good market'.[21]

Not all of these economic developments stemmed directly from improved roads, and the West Cumberland economy in particular relied primarily upon improved shipping and harbour facilities to

[18] W. Hutchinson, ibid., p. 467.

[19] P.R.O., A.D.M. 66/123, Out letters from the Receivers of the Northern Estates to the Greenwich Hospital Commission (1791–4).

[20] T. H. Bainbridge, 'Some Factors in the Development of Cumbrian Agriculture especially during the Nineteenth Century', C.W.T., XLIV (1945), pp. 84–5.

[21] See Bailey & Culley, p. 26.

cater for its expanding requirements. This region was doubly fortunate in that, in addition to extensive mineral resources it also possessed good harbour facilities within relatively easy reach of some of its principal mines. Consequently, the development of shipping played a large part in initiating and accelerating economic growth in this region. Whitehaven, Workington and Maryport all depended to a large degree upon overseas and coastal trade and, as a result, the growth of each town was closely linked to the development of its harbour.

Whitehaven was the first of the three ports to develop extensive trading links. By the close of the seventeenth century she had an interest in the colonial trade and as nearby coal resources were opened up, an export trade in coal to Ireland also developed. During the second half of the eighteenth century, Whitehaven's colonial trade declined; her tobacco imports suffering from the competition of Glasgow merchants and, subsequently, from the American War of Independence. Fortunately, this loss was more than offset by an increase in coal exports from local mines; only a small proportion of an estimated annual production of 160,000 tons being consumed in the area itself.[22] In addition, iron ore provided an increased source of export revenue for Whitehaven in the eighteenth century, particularly after the opening up of the Crowgarth mine at Cleator in 1789. Soon after this, Whitehaven was exporting an annual average of 20,000 tons of ore, the bulk of it going to the Carron iron works.[23]

In view of this expanding export trade, it is hardly surprising that there was a pronounced increase in the number of ships registered at Whitehaven harbour. Lysons estimated that between 1735 and 1785 the total increased from 46 vessels carrying 1,871 tons to 260 vessels of nearly 30,000 tons.[24] He was equally impressed by the expansion of shipbuilding locally. 'There are six shipbuilders yards at Whitehaven. Vessels built at this port are in great reputation.'[25] The Lowther family were predictably active in encouraging harbour expansion and shipbuilding, Sir James Lowther being expecially prominent in this field. Workington and Maryport, although a little slower to develop, were nevertheless equally dependent upon shipping facilities for the export of local mineral resources. Thus the Curwen and Senhouse families emulated the Lowthers in financing harbour improvements at their respective ports, and the Wood family of shipbuilders were operating in both

[22] I. Fletcher, op. cit., p. 289.   [23] W. Hutchinson, op. cit., p. 30.
[24] D. Lysons, *History of Cumberland* (1815), p. 24.   [25] Ibid.

Maryport and Workington towards the end of the eighteenth century.[26]

The region's lakes were also utilised more frequently during the eighteenth century and played a useful part in the transport of slate from the various quarries at Langdale,[27] Tilberthwaite and Coniston. Coniston Lake was particularly useful as a routeway, since the local lead mines increased their output quite considerably in the second half of the eighteenth century. Copper was also produced locally and likewise exported mainly through Ulverston.[28]

Similarly, cattle droving and trade by pack horse was essentially cross-country and did not depend very much upon improved road conditions. The Northern Pennines in particular were crossed by a number of great Drove roads during the eighteenth century. 'From Westmorland a variety of roads lead to the south, some cross the country by Richmond or Ripon to join the eastern Drove road at Northallerton or Boroughbridge, whilst others lead south to Kirkby Lonsdale, to Settle and to Skipton.'[29] Large numbers of cattle passed along these roads every year to the various fairs and markets; notably Carlisle, Brough Hill, Penrith and Roseley. It has been estimated that there were 40,000 beasts shown at Appleby Fair in 1781.[30] At the same time, Highland cattle were constantly passing through this northern Pennine region on their way south to Norfolk where they were fattened prior to their slaughter at London. A large proportion of these cattle passed through Carlisle itself during most years of the eighteenth century.[31] Cattle drovers were unhampered by the paucity of good roads and, in fact, preferred the unmetalled tracks, since the latter were less likely to injure the feet of their animals.

Cross-country pack horse traffic played an important part in the early development of parts of this region. This trade had become highly organised by the middle of the eighteenth century, individual carriers often owning a considerable number of horses which together made up the 'pack train'. This consisted of about thirty animals all moving in single file. These trains travelled across the hills by a regular series of routes, the softer portions of the tracks being set with large stones to consolidate their surfaces. Large

26 Oliver Wood, 'Development of the Coal, Iron and Shipbuilding Industries of West Cumberland, 1750–1914' (Ph.D. Thesis, University of London, 1952), p. 86.   27 S. Leigh, *Leigh's Guide to the Lakes* (1830), p. 44.
28 W. G. Collingwood, 'The Keswick and Coniston Mines in 1600 and Later', C.W.T., XXVIII (1928), pp. 5–6.
29 A. R. B. Haldane, *The Drove Roads of Scotland* (1952), p. 178.
30 *Cumberland Pacquet*, 26 June 1781.
31 W. Hutchinson, op. cit., p. 662.

quantities of goods were conveyed in this way; each horse carrying from 2 to 3 cwt.

Many of the more remote Pennine dales relied exclusively upon pack horses for the carriage of necessary food and fuel during the greater part of the eighteenth century. One writer recalls that in Cumbria in 1750

'only yeomen and the larger occupiers could boast of carts; the produce of the farms; hay, corn and peat being brought in on railed sledges and the more portable articles on pack horses. Coal and lime were conveyed by the last method across the miry moors and commons, where tracks instead of roads existed till near the end of the eighteenth century; and many persons now living remember the very common use of the pack horse both as the general carrier from town to town and the vehicle in transit for grain to the mill or market, and for manure, etc., on the farm.'[32]

In addition to serving local subsistence needs, pack horses also had considerable commercial utility during this period; woollen goods and lead ore being the most important commodities carried. The lead industry was centred around Alston in East Cumberland. This area was remote both from the coast and from the main centres of population, and the mines were thus dependent upon the organisation of a pack horse service carrying ore down to Newcastle for export and importing necessary foodstuffs from the Vale of Eden to feed the local mining population. Thus a relatively well organised carrier service undoubtedly played a large part in the development of mining in this area, and by 1767 the local lead mines were producing a total of 24,500 bings[33] a year.[34]

The woollen trade was centred on Kendal, and initially local carriers here, like their counterparts further north, concentrated on providing a cross-Pennine service. This soon became a valuable link between the early West Riding woollen industries and the hand-loom weavers and sheep rearers of East Westmorland and North Yorkshire. By the second half of the eighteenth century, however, the Kendal merchants also began to provide a wider service. For instance, their London trade appears to have been well established by 1750 when Robert Dawson was making regular journeys up and down the Great North Road on his way between Westmorland and London. Unfortunately, his accounts give few

[32] William Dickinson, *Essays on the Farming of Cumberland* (1853), p. 39.
[33] A 'bing' is equal to 8 cwt (O.E.D.).
[34] P.R.O., A.D.M. 66/117, Out letters from the Receivers of the Northern Estates to the Greenwich Hospital Commission (1777–80).

details of what he was carrying apart from isolated references to 'Hairs' and more frequent ones to 'Boxes of Oysters'. It is probable, however, that woollen goods comprised the bulk of the outgoing traffic from Kendal to London. Whatever its nature, the volume of Dawson's trade was considerable. For instance, on 24 February 1752 he carried—'2 Barrels, 3 cases, 1 Tub, 2 articles described as "frail", 10 unspecified articles, 2 Trunks, 9 Chests, 6 Trusses, 6 Boxes, 4 Bags and a Box of Oysters.'[35]

By the 1770s the Kendal pack horse trade was both large and wide ranging. Nicholson and Burn, in their history of the two counties, acknowledge its important role in the economy of the region and incorporate into their survey details of contemporary weekly traffic to and from Kendal.

'One gang of pack horses to and from London, every week, of about 20 horses.

do.		from Wigan weekly about	18 horses
do.		Whitehaven	20 horses
do.		Cockermouth	15 horses
Two Gangs	do.	from Barnard Castle	26 horses
	do.	from Penrith twice a week	
		about 15 each gang	60 horses
One gang about 15		from Settle twice a week	30 horses
do.		from York weekly	12 horses
do.		from Ulverston	5 horses
do.		from Hawkshead about	
		6 twice a week	12 horses
		from Appleby do.	12 horses
		from Cartmel do.	12 horses
		from Sedbergh, Kirkby Lonsdale, Orton, Dent	

and other neighbouring villages about 20 horses besides 24 every 6 weeks from Glasgow.'[36]

Thus, on the basis of these figures, it would appear that about 230 pack horses were regularly entering and leaving Kendal each week during the 1770s.

It is clear, therefore, that Kendal's central position on the various pack horse routes had a good deal to do with its early growth. It was a centre of local trade and had a flourishing domestic textile industry by the middle of the eighteenth century. It is also worth noting that stage coach services were probably operating

---

[35] C.R.O., Lowther MSS, Accounts of Robert Dawson (1750–8).
[36] J. Nicholson and R. Burn, op. cit., I, p. 266.

between Kendal and London as early as 1658.[37] However, it is unlikely that such services would be very regular or frequent at this early date, and any major increase in the size of the town must inevitably depend upon improved road conditions. Pack horses were a fairly reliable and conveniently flexible form of transport but far too slow: a journey from Kendal to London usually taking up to eighteen days.

The Kendal local authorities appear to have appreciated the potential importance of road transport at quite an early date. In 1669, the Westmorland Quarter Sessions ordered that owners of land on either side of the North road should 'cut and flash their hedges hanging into the way under pain of 10/– each'.[38] Again, in 1703, the Sessions maintained that the surveyors of the Barony of Kendal 'do sufficiently repair the highways and enlarge the same where necessary and cut bushes or boughs of trees or hedges that hang into and are troublesome to passengers, as so to make them good and sufficient for the passage of coaches, carts and carriages before the 11th October next'.[39] A little later in the same Order Book, warrants were issued to Petty Constables to cause surveyors of highways to erect signposts at every cross lane.

These measures do not appear to have brought about much improvement, and the two recorded surveys of Kendal Ward by Benjamin Browne, in his capacity as High Constable, reveal the local roads in a very unfavourable light. Browne's first survey was made in 1712 and in this he mainly concerned himself with the bridges in the Ward. He points out the need for repairs to a number of bridges including Stramongate, Bannisdale, Elterwater, Colwith and Brathay, but does not suggest any rebuilding at these sites and is generally moderate in his criticisms. In his survey of the highways in 1730–1, however, Browne is much more severe and does not have a single word of praise for any of the roads in Kendal Ward; they all being referred to as 'Bad' or 'Narrow' or 'covered with ye hedges'.[40]

Nevertheless, despite Browne's strictures, it is significant that two comprehensive surveys were made at such an early date, and this fact at least suggests that the Kendal authorities were concerned about the condition of their roads and were making some attempts to improve them despite obvious difficulties in implementing their policies. It is also reasonable to suppose that there may well have

[37] Jackman, p. 119.
[38] K.R.O., Kendal Order Book (1669–96).
[39] K.R.O., Kendal Order Book (1696–1724).
[40] K.R.O., Browne MSS, I, p. 220.

been contemporaneous surveys made of other Cumbrian districts, but no records have survived to throw any further light on this point.

Despite such scattered evidence of improvements, road conditions were far from adequate even for the more limited needs of this early period. A correspondent in the *Agreeable Miscellany* for 1749 noted 'the particular necessity there is for the roads being mended in Westmorland wants no demonstration to those that even travelled a few miles in any part of the country . . . I believe it is universally allowed by all parties that the roads are excessively bad and in some places dangerous to be passed'.[41]

In short, there was a growing recognition that the existing parochial authorities were an inadequate basis for road administration. It was to meet this demand for a more sustained and systematic concentration of administrative resources, capital and professional skills that Turnpike Trusts were set up to administer the more important roads. It was hoped that, by taxing people according to their use of the main roads, the various Trusts would collect sufficient revenues in toll payments to enable them to subsidise large scale road improvements.

The Trusts could then be dissolved and the roads could revert to the control of the parochial authorities; all outstanding repair and constructional expenses having now been met. Most important of all, the setting up of Turnpikes signified a growing recognition that, on important 'through' routes, it was unfair to expect parishioners to contribute substantially to the repair of a road which most of them had little cause to use.

The first Turnpike Act was passed as early as 1663 entitled 'An act for repairing the highways within the counties of Hertford, Cambridge and Huntingdon'. This measure had become necessary because 'the ordinary course appointed by the laws and statutes of this realm is not sufficient for the effectual repairing and amending' of the road. Consequently, the justices in each of these three counties were to appoint annually three surveyors who were in turn authorised to consider what repairs were necessary to the highways. A toll gate was to be installed along the road in question to meet these expenses. However, no provision had as yet been made for the appointment of Turnpike Trustees; their function being at present assumed by the highway surveyor. It was not until 1695–6 that a second act was passed; for the repair of part of the post road between London and Colchester. This act was similar to the

[41] *Agreeable Miscellany*, 23 December 1749.

previous legislation of the 1660s, but on this occasion the nominated surveyors were also allowed to borrow money on the credit of
the tolls.

During the early years of the eighteenth century the number of
Turnpike Acts increased. At first, the justices continued to be
responsible for administering the main roads, but in 1706 the first
body of Turnpike Trustees was established, and in 1711 the justices
were finally relieved of their responsibility for toll administration,
although they frequently continued to have an interest in road
policy as members of Turnpike Trust boards.

The first Cumbrian Trust was inaugurated in 1739 and embraced
a number of roads radiating outwards from Whitehaven. This was a
significant development, and indicates that, despite this area's
dependence upon shipping facilities, road transport also had a part
to play in shaping its economic growth. Minerals had to be carried
to the coast for shipment and, although the distances involved were
rarely more than about ten or twelve miles, it was important that
this 'feeder' service between mine and harbour should be an
effective one. Hence waggonways were built, carrying trucks down
to the harbour wherever gradients proved suitable, and there was
also every incentive to improve the road network in the hinterland
of the main coastal towns. Whitehaven as the principal port was
foremost in pioneering road building in the region, and the town's
activities in this field pre-date the inauguration of the first turnpike. In particular, there is evidence that Sir James Lowther
displayed a marked interest in local road improvement from 1709
onwards. Defoe records that prior to this time the roads in the
hinterland of the port 'were becoming ruinous and bad by the
great use made of them since the improvements in the harbour, for
before that time they were very narrow and seldom made use of by
carts and wheeled carriages'.[42]

The Whitehaven Harbour Improvement Acts of 1709, 1712 and
1739 provided for an almost complete reconstruction of the roads
leading into the town, and this in turn led to a substantial improvement in travelling conditions in the vicinity of the harbour, with a
corresponding increase in short distance cart traffic carrying coal
from the mines to the harbour for export. By 1746 the Whitehaven
roads were asserted to be 'Every day improving . . . equal to the
best Turnpikes around London'.[43] These improvements therefore
seem to have been well received by contemporaries and to have
given a decided impetus to short distance traffic between the

[42] Daniel Defoe, *Tour of England and Wales*, **III** (1748), p. 266.
[43] *Gentleman's Magazine* (1748), p. 5.

various coal mines and Whitehaven harbour. More generally, they provide the first evidence in Cumbria of systematic highway construction on a relatively large scale with a clearly defined end in view.

The inauguration of the Whitehaven Trust set a precedent for the creation of a considerable number of Turnpike Trusts in different parts of Cumberland and Westmorland during the 1750s and 1760s, and by the close of the eighteenth century there was a total of fifteen Turnpike Trusts in Cumberland, Westmorland and Furness.[44]

During this period Kendal became the centre of a network of Turnpikes just as it was already the centre of the various pack horse routes. The town benefited accordingly. The inauguration of the Heron Syke Trust over Shap Fell and the Cockermouth–Keswick–Kendal Trusts helped to promote through traffic to and from Kendal, whilst branch Trust roads to Appleby and Kirkby Lonsdale[45] were, no doubt, equally important in stimulating local traffic. Kendal was now able therefore to consolidate and expand its position as a market and woollen manufacturing town. Wool was carried increasingly along improved roads by cart and by waggon, as well as by pack horse along the traditional cross-country routes. This trade had its headquarters in the various inns along Stricklandgate in the centre of Kendal. Most of these inns, such as the *Woolpack*, have survived all 'improvements' and still retain their characteristically wide yard entrances through which the cumbersome waggons loaded high with wool used to pass.

It is more difficult to estimate the contribution of road improvements to the contemporaneous growth of Carlisle. The building of the Military Road between Carlisle and Newcastle in the middle years of the century, no doubt improved communications between the two towns, and the activities of Scott Laird and Company in the 1760s reflect growing commercial links between them. On the other hand, the Military Road does not appear to have been very well made. It was not designed primarily for commercial traffic in the first place, but rather 'for the passage of troops and carriages from the city of Carlisle to the town of Newcastle on Tyne'. As such, it might well have been an improvement on previous routes, but it certainly failed to satisfy some expectations. Contemporary comments on its condition were almost invariably disapproving, and both Arthur Young and Bailey and Culley single it out for condemnation in their respective surveys of the region. Thus,

---

[44] See Appendix A for further details.   [45] Ibid.

although the building of the Military Road no doubt helped to encourage industrial developments within Carlisle, it may not have been a very decisive factor. North and East Cumberland in general, probably benefited as much, if not more, from the contemporaneous improvement of the Stainmore road. Nicholson and Burn attributed its good condition to the passage of a Turnpike Act.

'The badness of the road (which perhaps was indeed the worst hard road in England) contributed to render all the rest more dismal, and in stormy weather it was the more vexatious as the traveller could make no speed. But now from one of the worst, it has by reason of the Turnpike Road carried that way became nearly as good as the best road in the Kingdom and (to note the importance of commerce and correspondence) instead of twice a week the post goes six times a week to and from Brough.'[46]

The road was important also as a carrier of agricultural commodities, especially butter. Nicholson and Burn noted that some of the more enterprising Dalesmen 'make a considerable advantage by the sale of butter especially since the Turnpike road was made over Stainmore whereby a communication by land carriage is opened to the seaport towns from whence they supply the London markets'.[47] It is quite possible, however, that the authors exaggerated the importance of this Turnpike Act as a factor in the improvement of the Stainmore road, since the road had already been commended by the surveyor John Harper in 1751 as 'the finest road in England'.[48] This was before the road was turnpiked. Nevertheless, the Turnpike Act seems to have provided a basis for further improvements even if it did not initiate them.

Improvements to the Stainmore road were particularly timely in view of the poor condition of the alternative main through route into Cumbria: the road over Shap. The Shap road was the most direct route for travellers and goods passing between Lancaster, Kendal and Carlisle and there was every incentive to improve its condition. However, the nature of the surrounding countryside presented formidable and expensive engineering problems to contemporary road makers. The road was particularly treacherous in winter time, and Prince Charles had great difficulty in moving his troops along it during the winter of 1745.

'On the 16th (December 1745) the main body of the army marched for Shap, but the rearguard were obliged to stop at a farm four

---

[46] Nicholson and Burn, *History of Westmorland*, I (1777), p. 577.
[47] Ibid., p. 11.   [48] C.R.O., Lowther MSS, Plan of Military Road.

miles from Kendal by reason that a great number of the carriages and particularly the four wheeled waggons in which was part of the ammunition could not be forwarded because of the badness of the road.'[49]

After the inauguration of two Turnpike Trusts between Kendal and Carlisle there is some evidence to suggest that the condition of the road improved, and by 1763 a stage coach was running over Shap for the first time. A few years later, the Shap road satisfied the exacting requirements of Arthur Young. Young was a notoriously caustic critic of poor road conditions wherever he encountered them, but he was quite favourably impressed with the stretch of road between Kendal and Shap; describing it as 'exceeding hilly and some very steep, but the road itself excellent'.[50] Nevertheless, the journey over Shap was still a very difficult one and the Stainmore road continued to be the main route out of Cumbria for London-bound traffic in the eighteenth century.

A notable feature of Cumbrian road history in the eighteenth century is the extent to which local landlords were active in agitating for road improvements. Some of the most prominent Cumbrian families invested quite considerable sums in the various Turnpike Trusts which were set up during the eighteenth century. The Lowther family were conspicuous from the start in the affairs of the Whitehaven Trust as has already been noted, and their initiative was copied by the Senhouse, Curwen and Graham families amongst others. Local landed participation in Turnpike improvements was to be an equally conspicuous feature of nineteenth century road history as later discussion will show.

No doubt the motives of these improving landlords were mixed. To some, Trust investment might simply be a speculation at a time when there appears to have been a good deal of surplus capital available for investment purposes in the North of England.[51] However, other landlords were becoming increasingly aware of the economic advantages and personal convenience to be derived from swifter and more comfortable travel facilities. Thus Sir James Lowther, when promoting a branch road to Caldbeck, maintained that it was 'desired of so many for the good of trade which is the

[49] J. F. Curwen, *Records Relating to the Barony of Kendal*, III (1923), p. 6.

[50] Arthur Young, *A Six months Tour through the North of England* (1770), p. 427.

[51] Cf. Edward Hughes, 'North Country Life in the Eighteenth Century' *History* (1940–1).

main thing aimed at in these numerous Turnpike Bills that have been passed'.[52]

Not all landlords were equally aware of the value of good roads, however, and Sir James Lowther had also cause to complain about early antagonism to Turnpikes. 'It is so difficult to get forward a Turnpike Bill when there is a very great length of road to mend.'[53] Mannex and Whellan echo the same note when recalling the inauguration of the earlier Cumbrian Trusts. 'When local acts were obtained for their improvement, the exaction of tolls gave rise to much popular fury, the people then not clearly seeing that the advantages obtained by good roads greatly counterbalanced the amount of tolls levied for their formation and repair.'[54] This opposition did not often prevent the ultimate passage of an Act, but the obstructive action of landowners might well affect the alignment of a particular stretch of road and compel it to follow a traditional route which did not encroach upon new land but which was not always very suitable for future needs. Subsequent attempts to divert or widen Turnpikes and to reduce their gradients often proved equally difficult in the face of local hostility. For instance, the Tebay to Kirkby Stephen road followed the line of an old pack horse track, as did the Kendal to Ireleth Turnpike. The latter, in particular, was very unwisely aligned as far as Penny Bridge, and incorporated two very steep hills: one over Underbarrow Scar and a second over Staveley Brow.

Thus the commercially minded landlords were more likely to appreciate the need for better road conditions, whilst their less adventurous counterparts preferred low rates to improved roads. The conflict between these two elements in Cumbrian society was destined to become more widespread in the course of the nineteenth century.

Another potential source of conflict was over the Trusts' placement of Turnpike gates. A judicious positioning of these gates was necessary if most Trusts were to gain the maximum financial advantage from this increased traffic on the roads. It was particularly important that short distance traffic should not escape toll payments. Hence there was a high concentration of toll gates along heavily used sections of road. For instance, two of the four gates on the Kendal–Ireleth Trust road, at Lowfield House and at Holme Green, were sited on a relatively short stretch of the road,

---

[52] C.R.O., Lowther MSS, Misc. Letters on Cumberland Roads (1748–56), Lord Lonsdale to Richard Radcliff, 17 February 1753. [53] Ibid.
[54] P. J. Mannex and W. Whellan, *History, Gazetteer and Directory of Cumberland* (1847), p. 38.

B

between Ulverston and Ireleth. This reflected an attempt by the Trustees to capitalise upon the short distance iron ore and slate traffic around Dalton and Ireleth.

Relations between the central government and local builders and coach proprietors were also becoming strained by the end of the eighteenth century. Official government policy towards road improvements was somewhat negative. In general, it was felt that traffic should be regulated in order to preserve the roads in their existing condition. The demand for positive improvements in road conditions to meet new requirements met with scant favour in official circles. Thus, early Trust Acts were characterised by a mass of complicated legislation relating to the width and shape of wheels, and also defining limits to the weight of such vehicles. Regulations against narrow wheels dated from 1662, and by the second half of the eighteenth century a complex of confusing and often contradictory legislation had accumulated on this subject. There had been a long-standing dispute in this period over the relative virtues and defects of broad and narrow wheels. Some people maintained that broad wheels did greater damage to the road surface by virtue of their greater weight, whilst others held that narrow wheels were more likely to cut ridges into the road and thus cause it to deteriorate rapidly. By the beginning of the nineteenth century, however, opinion appears to have hardened against narrow wheels, and measures were introduced in an attempt to compel a minimum wheel width for all vehicles using the Turnpikes.

Most Trusts discriminated against narrow wheeled vehicles by charging their owners a higher rate of toll payments. Likewise, Trusts often installed weighing machines in order to penalise overweight vehicles. Provisions of this kind were incorporated into a great many of the late eighteenth and early nineteenth century Trust Acts, and help to account for their great length and complexity.

Hence, although roads were undoubtedly providing an improved transport service in Cumbria by the close of the eighteenth century, they still had very distinct limitations. In the first place, not all parts of the region were equally well served by road transport, and South-West Cumberland, Furness and Cartmel in particular were still very remote from the main lines of communication.

There were two approach routes to South-West Cumberland. The first route was a pack horse track from Langdale into Eskdale over the Wrynose and Hardnott passes. This journey was short and direct; advantages which were appreciated by John Wesley when journeying between Kendal and Whitehaven on his missions. However, the track was unsuitable for wheeled traffic throughout this period and was hence unlikely to become a very popular thoroughfare. The alternative route was by the coastal road from Ulverston across the Millom sands and then northwards through Bootle and Ravenglass. Wesley also used this route on occasions, and in 1759 he wrote a graphic account of his journey up the Cumberland coast. It took him from 8 a.m. until midnight to travel from Bootle to Whitehaven. One senses that he would think twice before repeating the experience. 'I can advise no traveller to go this way, he may go round by Kendal and Keswick, often in less time, always with less expense and far less trial of his patience.'[55] Furness and Cartmel were equally isolated. They were approached from the south across Morecambe Bay Sands; the only alternative route being along the Turnpike road between Kendal and Ireleth. The latter was seldom used by wheeled traffic during the eighteenth century because of its very steep gradients. In this case the turn-piking of a road had failed to effect a substantial improvement in its condition. Consequently, the cross-sands route was the one most generally used by travellers to Furness, and there is evidence that chaises travelled 'oversands' between Lancaster and Ulverston as early as 1781.[56] Despite occasional spectacular accidents, this route was considered by many authorities to be a relatively safe one, guides being appointed by the Government to direct people across the sands.[57]

However, despite the relative popularity of the 'oversands' route, there was little travelling within Furness itself, apart from the short distance carriage of minerals from the mines around Dalton and Ireleth to the coast for export; some of these roads being built by the mining companies out of slag from the various pits. Cartmel was even more remote, and Stockdale pointed out that 'there was not until some little time before the end of the last century, a four wheeled carriage of any kind in the whole parish of Cartmel, excepting at Holker Hall and Bigland Hall'.[58]

The remoteness of this region undoubtedly retarded its economic development during the eighteenth century. It had considerable natural resources: rich agricultural land south of Egre-

---

[55] *Journals of John Wesley*, **IV** (1909), p. 313.

[56] *Cumberland Pacquet*, 11 September 1781.

[57] The guide was given a house at Sandside and a salary of £22 a year, payable from the revenues of the Duchy of Lancaster—cf. John Fell, 'The Guides over the Kent and Leven Sands, Morecambe Bay', C.W.T., **VII** (1883).

[58] Stockdale, *Annals of Cartmel* (1872), p. 572.

mont and large reserves of iron ore around Millom and in Furness, but these were not fully exploited in the eighteenth century because of the area's poor roads and inadequate harbour facilities. Had the region been less remote from the main lines of communications, it is likely that there would have been more investment in harbour building and economic development generally. This is almost certainly the case in Furness as later discussion of Barrow will demonstrate.

West Cumberland north of Egremont, and North Cumberland had less direct cause for complaint in view of the proliferation of Turnpikes in these areas, but the prolonged agitation for the building of a canal linking Newcastle with Carlisle and Maryport would suggest that Whitehaven, Workington and Maryport in addition to Carlisle were far from satisfied with the existing main roads. In particular, as we have seen, there seems to have been fairly general agreement amongst contemporaries as to the poor condition of the Cumberland section of the 'military road' between Newcastle and Carlisle. In an attempt to remedy this deficiency, serious suggestions were made during the 1790s as to the feasibility of linking the east and west coasts by canal. It was felt that such a venture would help to promote cross-country traffic and thus reduce the economic and social isolation of West Cumberland. William Chapman, a noted surveyor, was asked to make a survey of the possibilities of such an undertaking, and in his report of 1795 he drew particular attention to the desirability of encouraging Baltic and Dutch trade and to disseminating the various Irish agricultural imports of beef, pork and raw hides. He also pointed out the benefits which would accrue to Cumbrian manufacturers if this canal was built. 'The facility of communication with both seas and various intermediate parts of the Kingdom may probably cause new manufactures to arise at the already flourishing town of Carlisle, and at Hexham, Brampton and other interior places.'[59] Chapman followed up these recommendations by suggesting the possible extension of this canal from Maryport south along the coast to Workington. The well-known surveyor, William Jessop, was also in favour of such a canal and produced a similar report in the same year.[60] In 1807 Chapman wrote a further report on the subject[61] but, despite this publicity, the canal project was never

[59] C.R.O. Senhouse MSS, Chapman's Report on the proposed Newcastle–Maryport Canal (1795).

[60] C.R.O. Senhouse MSS, William Jessop's Report on the proposed Newcastle–Maryport Canal (1795).

[61] C.R.O., Senhouse MSS, Mr Chapman's Report on 'The means of obtaining a safe and commodious communication from Carlisle to the sea' (1807).

realised, although a shorter canal was eventually opened in 1819 linking Carlisle with Port Carlisle.

Other contemporaries criticised road transport on the grounds of its expense. The carriage of bulky goods, even over short distances, proved very costly. Thus, when Lord Harley made his tour of the north of England in the 1720s he found that the carriage of coal into Darlington from mines ten miles distant from the town more than doubled the cost of fuel.[62] There is evidence to suggest that carriage rates were somewhat lower by the end of the eighteenth century, but they still remained high, particularly for heavy commodities such as coal and iron ore. The failure of successive attempts to develop an iron industry in West Cumberland and Furness during the eighteenth century provides a good illustration of the limitations of contemporary road transport. Both areas lacked suitable coking coal and Durham was the nearest source. Under these conditions it was clearly impossible for the existing carrier services to transport coal into West Cumberland in sufficient quantities at economic rates. Attempts were made to build furnaces at Millom in 1752, at Seaton in 1762 and at Lowca in 1790, but by the end of the century only the Seaton furnace was in operation. Apart from this, the only iron industry of any consequence was in Furness and this, significantly, was based upon charcoal and water power rather than upon coke. The industry here dated from 1711 when William Rawlinson and Stephen Crossfield built a furnace at Backbarrow. Soon afterwards a second blast furnace was built at Leighton.[63] These operations were given a further impetus by the prohibition of trade with Sweden and the consequent withdrawal of competition from Swedish haematite. The Furness iron industry continued throughout the eighteenth century but it never became a large scale development and it is doubtful if there were ever more than six furnaces in blast simultaneously.[64] Charcoal could not form the basis of an expanding iron industry, and West Cumberland continued to export the bulk of its ore until the middle of the nineteenth century.

In general, from the limited evidence available it does appear that roads in Cumbria underwent some improvement during the second half of the eighteenth century. The passing of 15 Turnpike Acts might not have instantaneously triggered off an improvement in the condition of each road, but it does reflect an overall increased

[62] Edward Hughes, op. cit.
[63] J. D. Marshall, *Furness and the Industrial Revolution* (1958), p. 22.
[64] Ibid., p. 30.

interest and investment in road improvements. There were also improvements in the construction of vehicles using the roads. Pack horses were being superseded in many areas by carts and waggons, and stage coaches were less cumbersome by 1800. Thus the carriage of people and goods was facilitated and travelling times were reduced. By 1773 the *Flying Machine* coach was performing the journey from Carlisle to London in 3 days,[65] and this time had been further reduced to $51\frac{1}{2}$ hours by 1788.[66] These times compare very favourably with the 9 days taken by the advertised coach of 1734,[67] and an average time of 12 to 18 days taken by contempory pack horse trains.

This improved passenger service illustrates the importance of roads as agents of social as well as economic change. As early as 1777, Nicholson and Burn noted that few people now made their own clothes. 'In the article of clothing they have departed of late years from their ancient simplicity. Their forefathers were wont to clothe themselves with their own wool manufacture at home, which wool is now bought up for the use of manufacturers at Kendal and in the West Riding of Yorkshire'.[68] The two authors rather regret this change, and the same theme is taken up by Bailey and Culley in their survey of 1794. 'The Turnpike roads have brought the manners of the capital to the extremity of the Kingdom. The simplicity of ancient times has gone. Finer clothes, better dwellings and more expensive viands are now sought after by all.'[69] The region also appears to have had some quite advanced educational facilities by the close of the eighteenth century. For instance, Kendal was quite prominent by the 1790s in the field of adult education; in 1787 and again in 1791 John Dalton was giving courses there in Natural Philosophy.[70] One educational historian has noted of Cumbria that 'at the close of the century (eighteenth) there were few illiterates and the superiority of the northern peasant in general knowledge was a common observation in diaries of travel'.[71]

This apparently high level of literacy amongst the local population would appear to indicate that Cumbria was by no means backward and isolated in all respects during this period. The improved distribution of news by this time, was, no doubt,

65 *Cumberland Pacquet*, 3 October 1776.
66 C. G. Harper, *The Manchester and Glasgow Road*, I (1907), p. 9.
67 *Cumberland Pacquet*, 9 May 1734.
68 J. Nicholson and R. Burn, *Westmorland*, op. cit., p. 11.
69 Bailey & Culley, p. 212.
70 Thomas Kelly, *George Birkbeck* (1957), pp. 58–9.
71 A. E. Dobbs, *Education and Social Movements, 1700–1850* (1919), p. 67.

another factor encouraging people to learn to read. The first Cumbrian newspaper, the *Cumberland Pacquet*, dates from 1775, and Wordsworth, writing at a later date, also commented upon the increasingly rapid conveyance of both news and people. For instance, he compares the rapidity with which news of the Battle of Trafalgar reached the more remote parts of the Lake District with the time taken by the corresponding news of the 1745 Jacobite Rebellion to penetrate the area.

'At that time, news such as we have heard might have been long in penetrating so far into the recesses of the mountains, but now, as you know, the approach is easy, and the communication in summer time almost hourly; nor is this strange, for travellers after pleasure are become not less active, and more numerous than those who formerly left their houses for purposes of gain.'[72]

Thus the passage of Turnpike Acts, increased investment in road improvements, reduced travelling times, and economic and social changes all provide evidence of improved roads. Cumbria was certainly fortunate in that her most valuable mineral deposits lay close to her seaboard. Hence, she could make maximum use of her shipping facilities and was not nearly so dependent upon land transport as were more inland mining areas. However, there seems little doubt that developments in road transport during the eighteenth century facilitated, reflected and were stimulated by economic growth. Contemporaries certainly saw it this way. Members of the Lowther family, as we have seen, were conspicuous investors in Turnpike Trusts, and the family was not given to wasting its money. The fact that the Lowthers and other prominent landlords in the region invested in road improvements illustrates the faith which they had in the expanding utility of road transport.

Despite these developments, surviving contemporary comments upon the region as a whole in the late eighteenth century suggest a more balanced and critical view of the area's achievements and future needs. There is an overall acknowledgement of progress made during the previous half century in a good many branches of local economic development, but a corresponding realisation by some observers that a great deal of the resources of Cumbria were, as yet, still unexploited.

The potential of the region was recognised by Sir James Lowther as early as 1752 when he noted that 'there is hardly any

72 W. Wordsworth, *Guide to the Lake District* (1835), p. 120.

county in England more capable of considerable improvement than the county of Cumberland is'.[73] A little over fifty years later, in 1808, Thomas Harrison, in a letter to the Select Committee of the Cumberland Navigation Canal, was able to echo these sanguine expectations, and at the same time point to the positive achievements of the last few decades within Cumberland. 'There is reason to believe that it will soon be the most flourishing, fertile and highly cultivated county in England. Different kinds of manufacturers are constantly established at Carlisle and the neighbouring towns, and industry promotes the greater multiplicity of them.'[74] This sensation of living in the midst of a period of social and economic upheaval is colourfully conveyed in an article by James Drigg, a South Cumberland contributor to the *Gentleman's Magazine*, who writes in 1790 that

'at the beginning of this century, the inhabitants were in a state bordering on extreme poverty. Large families on small estates could but with difficulty earn a subsistence for themselves; they lived barely on the products of their little farms without either a hope or desire of raising fortunes . . . they were generally very superstitious. . . . But things are now assuming a new appearance. The rust of poverty and ignorance is now gradually wearing off. Estates are bought up into fewer hands; and the poorer sort of people move into towns, to gain a livelihood by handicrafts and commerce . . . the houses (or rather huts) of clay which were small and ill-built are mostly thrown down, instead of which strong and roomy farmhouses are built.'[75]

Bailey and Culley, on the other hand, are somewhat more critical of contemporary developments in the region. They pay tribute in their survey to the energy and initiative of a good many of the Cumberland gentleman farmers and acknowledge that it is to them 'that this region owes the introduction of any of the modern improvements in agriculture; and we are glad to find a spirit of enterprise arising amongst them, for the adoption of new forms of culture and improving breeds of stock'.[76] However, at the same time, the two authors castigate the agricultural conservatism of the smaller landowners or 'statesmen' of Cumberland who collectively owned a high proportion of the land. 'These

[73] C.R.O., Lowther MSS, Misc. Letters on Cumberland Roads (1748–56).
[74] C.R.O., Senhouse MSS, Misc. Correspondence, Thomas Harrison to the Select Committee of the Cumberland Navigation Canal, 19 August 1808.
[75] *Gentleman's Magazine*, I (1790), pp. 505–6.
[76] Bailey & Culley, p. 209.

INTRODUCTION

"Statesmen" seem to inherit with the estates of their ancestors
their notions of cultivating them, and are almost as much attached
to the one as the other. They are rarely aspiring and seem content
with their situation.'[77] The conclusion of Bailey and Culley's
report was that constructive changes were being made but there
was a great deal more still to be done if the economy of Cumberland
and Westmorland was to be transformed upon a profitable basis.
For instance, they estimated that there were at least 150,000 acres
of 'Improvable Common" within Cumberland.[78]

Another contemporary, Jonathan Boucher, was particularly
concerned with drawing attention to the unrealised potential of
the area and was unimpressed by past achievements and present
attitudes. 'I am persuaded a county cannot be named more
abounding in natural advantages than Cumberland nor more
deficient in all these advantages which are the result of human
ingenuity and human industry.'[79] Perhaps Boucher was unduly
severe in his indictment but his comments on the unexplored
potential of the region were quite justified. Mineral wealth was not
yet sufficiently exploited, nor had there as yet been any real
progress made towards the establishment of an iron industry in
Cumberland. Furthermore, much valuable land had yet to be
cultivated and large parts of the region were in many respects
undercapitalised and isolated.

Thus there was a clear need for further improvements in inland
transport if the full potential of Cumbria was to be realised.

[77] Ibid. The word 'statesman' in this region was often used synonymously
with 'yeoman'.
[78] Ibid., p. 202.
[79] C. M. L. Bouch, 'Jonathan Boucher', C.W.T., XXVII (1927), pp. 148-9.

Chapter 2

ROAD AND BRIDGE ADMINISTRATION

THE PARISH

This was the basic unit of road administration throughout most of this period. Prior to the setting up of Turnpike Trusts the parish was responsible for the repair of all roads. Subsequently, it limited its attentions more strictly to roads which were not deemed sufficiently important to be turnpiked. However, turnpike legislation did not necessarily result in any major reduction of parochial responsibility. In the first place, most roads were not turnpiked and were, therefore, still directly under parochial control and, second, it was generally accepted that the parish should continue to be ultimately responsible for the repair of all roads, including turnpikes, in the event of the Trusts in question being unable to fulfil their responsibilities.

Highways were maintained by means of the unpaid compulsory labour or 'Statute Duty' of the parishioners who were obliged to work for six days of every year upon the roads in their parish. In addition, any inhabitant who owned a cart and three or more horses was expected to send his horse team accompanied by two able men to maintain the roads for the statutory length of time. If this labour proved insufficient to repair the roads adequately, the justices in Quarter Sessions were given power by the Act of 1773 to authorise the township surveyor to levy an additional assessment upon the parish in order to subsidise further repairs. The machinery of Statute Labour was quite inadequate, however, to maintain the roads. It could hardly be expected that unpaid parishioners would have either the knowledge or inclination to form a competent labour force upon the highways. In addition, this labour was unlikely to be directed adequately by the local surveyor of roads.

The office of surveyor of a parish or township was an annual appointment which was allocated to the various parochial landowners in rotation. Consequently, the holding of this office was no indication of the occupant's fitness for the work which he was expected to perform. Despite the haphazard nature of his appointment, however, a surveyor's duties were complex and onerous; involving an understanding of parochial finance and book-keeping and, also, the active supervision of road repairs. Most parishioners would have been quite incapable of fulfilling these duties competently even assuming a high degree of conscientious application. When one considers that the appointment was unpaid and that it also involved the holder in much local unpopularity by virtue of his levying highway rates and enforcing Statute Duty, it is hardly surprising that most surveyors attempted to avoid their duties whenever possible. Few people would have accepted the office in the first place but for the threat of legal action by the justices in the event of refusal.

No doubt on occasions individual surveyors were sufficiently talented and public-spirited to discharge their duties satisfactorily. For instance, a surviving surveyor's Account Book for Ravenstonedale parish, covering the years 1779–1800, suggests that accounts at least, were kept in some detail during these years in this particular parish.[1]

Nevertheless, the general picture of eighteenth century parochial administration is of unskilled and unwilling labour under unskilled and unwilling supervision. If a parish unduly neglected its roads it was liable to be 'presented' by the justices and, if found guilty, it was fined at the discretion of the Court and ordered to repair the highways complained of. The device of 'presentation' proved a useful way of indirectly enforcing a compulsory levy upon the parish, over and above its statutory obligations. However, when parishes were presented, the legal processes involved were quite often very prolonged; in the meantime the condition of the highways deteriorated further.

It appears that in most parts of Cumbria it was rare for highways to be presented during the early and middle years of the eighteenth century. For instance, when the highway from Low Cark to High Newton was presented in the middle of the century, Stockdale, the historian of Cartmel, records that 'this at that time was a very unusual proceeding and gave rise to great complaints on the part of the rate payers of the township through which the road passed, they universally declaring that the cost of carrying out the work would beggar them'.[2] This was a justifiable complaint

1 K.R.O., Surveyors' Payment Book—Ravenstonedale Parish (1779–1800).
2 J. Stockdale, *Annals of Cartmel* (1872), p. 296.

for many parishes. They possessed neither the administrative resources nor the capital to finance extensive road improvements. Parishes which were dissected by main roads had particular cause for complaint. The wear and tear on these roads was normally greater and a high proportion of the traffic concerned was non-local and hence did not contribute towards the costs of repairing the damage caused. These considerations helped to precipitate a movement for the setting up of toll gates along roads of this kind.

The establishment of Turnpike Trusts undoubtedly relieved the parishes of a considerable burden by transferring their busiest roads into other hands. However, this did not absolve them from all maintenance responsibilities on these roads, and they were still obliged to provide labourers for Statute Duty at appropriate times of the year. Indeed, in the long run, many parishes found that their road repair obligations continued to mount. One reason for this lay in the continuous expansion of wheeled traffic during the late eighteenth and early nineteenth centuries. This traffic was not wholly absorbed by the recently created Turnpikes, and local travellers in particular often used their knowledge of the various side roads to good effect in an attempt to avoid toll payments. Furthermore, the business of successive Quarter Sessions during this period suggests that local Justices were now more vigilant in inspecting parish roads and in administering fines where necessary. However, roads were rarely 'presented' unless their condition had deteriorated and, consequently, although this system helped to preserve existing standards of road maintenance, it did little to promote and encourage new and improved standards. In fact the county did not always succeed in enforcing even these minimum regulations. Its authority to issue a particular presentment was sometimes disputed by the parish concerned, and, as a result, necessary repairs were further delayed.

The North Lonsdale Hundred of Lancashire seems to have had particular difficulty in asserting its authority over the rather remote parishes and townships of Cartmel, during the first quarter of the nineteenth century. The usual pattern in this area was for the parish, when indicted, to claim that the responsibility lay with the individual township through which the neglected road ran, rather than with the parish as a whole. Alternatively, parish or township might attempt to argue that the Cartmel Enclosure Commission had altered the alignment of the road in question and hence ought to be responsible for at least part of the cost of its subsequent repair. One such stretch of road, between Stribers and Low Wood village, gave rise to a 21-year dispute involving the parish of Cartmel, the Cartmel Enclosure Commission, and the townships of Upper and Lower Holker.

The dispute began in 1805 when the Quarter Sessions for North Lonsdale Hundred judged the parishioners of Cartmel guilty of neglecting the road in question and fined them £900.[3] The parish's first step when confronted with the bill was to appeal to the Cartmel Enclosure Commission. The Commission admitted that 'several roads in the parish had been repaired by the Commission for the Enclosure of the Common, but as the road in question is carried through ancient enclosures, they at present refuse to apply any part of their funds in repairing it'.[4]

In the meantime, a certain Thomas Maychell had been given the unenviable task of collecting the £900 from the Cartmel parishioners. By July 1807, Maychell was able to report that he had collected the full £900, but that, as a result of further neglect, the road would now cost more than this amount to repair. Having said this, Maychell seems to have realised the implications of his remark, and began to emphasise the difficulties which he had encountered in collecting the initial £900 'and begs to decline any further concern in any subsequent fines which may be necessary, it being entirely contrary to his habits and disposition'.[5]

Maychell was accordingly replaced by William Wilkinson who undertook to collect a further £300. Wilkinson was less successful than his predecessor, and the parish in the meantime attempted to shift the responsibility for further road repairs on to other shoulders. They again approached the Enclosure Commission and also the townships of Upper and Lower Holker through which the road ran. After further delays, a compromise was reached in 1813 when it was decided that the parish as a whole should raise £350 to put the road into an adequate state of repair, whilst all future maintenance responsibilities should be divided between the two townships.[6] However, this does not seem to have settled the issue, and during the next few years the road continued to be neglected. The townships of Upper and Lower Holker were now held responsible, but they argued in their turn that the parish had not kept its side of the bargain, as the roads had not been adequately repaired as yet. It was not until 1826 that parish and township settled their differences. The parish finally repaired the road to the satisfaction of both the Quarter Sessions and the two townships, whilst the

[3] L.R.O., Q.S.P., Lancashire Q.S. Petition Rolls, N. Lonsdale Hundred, October 1805.   [4] Ibid.

[5] Ibid., Midsummer 1807.

[6] J. Stockdale, op. cit., p. 363.

latter agreed to take over responsibility for all future maintenance work.[7]

Statute Labour, in common with the system of presentation, also survived into the nineteenth century, although magistrates were often quite flexible in the way they enforced this requirement. For instance, the parishioners of North Lonsdale Hundred were allowed to set aside three months of every year, during which time no Statute Labour need be performed. This ensured that local farmers would have full use of their labour force and horse teams during the busiest part of the year.

In areas where there was a surplus of local labour, Statute Duty as a requirement by the parishioners became less necessary and individuals tended increasingly to make a fixed payment to the Turnpike Trust or parish surveyor in lieu of their traditional repair obligations. Such payments were often quite substantial; a farmer who normally contributed a horse team during the period of Statute Duty would be expected to pay between 3s and 6s daily instead. By the 1820s, cash payments in lieu of Statute Duty had become the normal pattern in the Cumbrian counties, and this procedure was particularly appreciated by Trusts whose toll receipts alone were not always sufficient to meet their maintenance commitments. Such Trusts had clearly not derived satisfaction from parochial Statute Labour in the past, and no doubt preferred to make their own arrangements. Other Trusts could afford to be more complacent at times. Thus the Ambleside Trustees resolved in July 1825

'That it appears to us that the Turnpike Roads from Kendal to Raise (Dunmail) and from Kendal to the Lake of Windermere are in such a state and condition with regard to repairs and revenues that the Statute Duty required to be paid by the said townships through which such Turnpike roads run, may for the present be wholly dispensed with, and employed more advantageously for the benefit of the other public highways within the said townships liable to the said Statute Duty and that such Statute Duty do wholly cease on the 8th day of October next.'[8]

In 1835 Statute Duty was abolished together with the present-ment of highways. The new Act[9] gave the parish vestry powers through their nominated surveyor to levy a rate for the main-tenance of parish roads. This specification had little effect upon some parishes, as they were already accustomed to collecting

7 Stockdale, p. 364.   8 K.R.O., Ambleside Trust Minutes, 30 July 1825.
9 5–6 William IV, cap. 50.

fixed composition payments, but an additional clause in the Act which abolished composition payments to Trusts had more important repercussions for the poorer Turnpike Trusts as regular composition payments had been a necessary supplement to their toll revenues. It can also be argued that the ending of these payments to the Trust was equally disadvantageous to the parish itself in the long run, since, in the event of the Trustees having insufficient capital to maintain their roads, the responsibility would fall, often belatedly, upon the parishes concerned and thus involve them in very heavy maintenance expenses. James McAdam recognised this danger and informed the Select Committee upon the Highway Rates Bill that, 'I am quite sure it is in the interests of the parishes that Turnpike roads pass through under these circumstances that they should contribute some portion of their rates annually, rather than allow the roads to get into such a state as to be indictable and require a large sum to put them again in any decent state of repair'.[10]

The principal significance of the 1835 Act, however, was that it gave the newly constituted parish vestries the power to appoint salaried surveyors. It appears that some of the Cumberland parishes were quick to act upon this injunction and by 1837 the parish of Sebergham and the township of Kirkbampton were allowing their surveyors a salary of £12 and £5, respectively.[11] By 1863, the Highway Committee appointed for Cumberland under the new Act noted that 'There is a very considerable outlay for establishment charges in the shape of surveyors' salaries as appears by the annexed return'. This return reveals that the annual salaries of the surveyors in each of the Cumberland Wards were as follows:

Allerdale Ward above Derwent	£117 10s 0d
Allerdale Ward below Derwent	£52 13s 6d
Bootle Division	No returns available
Cumberland Ward	£42 1s 2d
Derwent Division	£130 7s 0d
Eskdale Ward	£26 5s 0d
Leath Ward	£43 11s 6d
Longtown Division	£42 7s 7d[12]

This amounts, therefore, to a total expenditure on surveyors'

[10] *Parl. Papers*, 1837, **XX**, p. 356.
[11] C.R.O., Misc. Papers re Appointment of Surveyors (1837–8).
[12] C.R.O., AH/6/2, Q.S. Highway Papers for Cumberland, Report of the Committee on Highway Administration, April 1863.

salaries of £454 15s 9d for the county as a whole, excluding Bootle ward. Thus it appears that a good many townships were now taking their responsibilities for road repairs rather more seriously, although paying a surveyor did not necessarily result in any substantial improvement in highway workmanship. There was still a need for more competent surveyors and the 1863 Committee complained that 'The highways would be better and more economically managed by the employment of skilful surveyors'.[13] On the other hand, adverse comments about road conditions in this period should not automatically be equated with similar complaints made at the beginning of the century. Standards had risen and expectations were higher by this time.

The Committee made the above observation in the context of an argued need for larger units of highway administration, and the failure to provide this latter requirement was the principal defect of the 1835 Act. This legislation confirmed the authority and independence of the parish vestry. However, the parish subsequently proved too small a body to provide an adequate basis for the organisation of road repair, and it is doubtful if many parochial authorities could afford to employ surveyors with the requisite specialised knowledge to cope with their increasing responsibilities. The 1835 legislation did make some provision for the formation of 'highway districts', but such combination was to be voluntary on the part of each group of parishes. The Government, in this respect as in others, would suggest but not compel. Few Cumbrian parishes took advantage of this freedom to combine, although there is at least one instance in Cumberland of the early formation of such a highway district: this comprised the parishes of Kirkbampton, Burgh by Sands and Bowness which applied to the Michaelmas Sessions of 1841, 'to unite the said parishes into a District for the purpose of having one sufficient person to be the Surveyor of the Highways of such District'. Permission was granted, and Chris Brown of Abbey Holm Cultram was recommended for the post of 'District Surveyor' at an annual salary of £35. This sum was to be provided for out of a highway rate levied upon the several parishes and townships within the newly formed 'district'. However, in other respects each of these parishes was still independent and levied its own money to be expended upon its own highways.[14]

It was not until 1862 that the legislation of 1835 was seriously

13 C.R.O., AH/6/2, Q.S. Highway Papers for Cumberland, Report of the Committee on Highway Administration, April 1863.
14 C.R.O., Cumberland QS Petition Rolls, Mich. 1841.

amended. The Act of that year empowered justices in Quarter Sessions to combine parishes compulsorily into highway districts under highway boards. Thus the parish vestry lost some of its power and was now responsible only for the levying of its own particular contribution to a district highway rate. However, a failure on the part of the Home Office to enforce and clarify this legislation gave rise to many delays in the formation of highway districts and also some confusion as to the area covered by each such district. Leath Ward was the first highway district to be created in Cumberland after the passage of this act. It comprised sixty-five parishes, and was constituted in 1865. This initiative was followed by the setting up of Longtown, Brampton and Wigton wards in 1867; a little later in 1871, the Whitehaven Poor Law Union became a 'highway district', and in the following year the nineteen parishes of Bootle Ward were similarly combined.[15] Thus the 1862 Act was adopted with considerable caution in this county; in fact it was never fully implemented, since the three parishes of Alston, Garrigill and Penrith refused to be incorporated into Leath Ward in 1865,[16] and the first named went on to form its own highway district from a single parish.[17]

Westmorland was considerably more obdurate and was one of seven or eight counties in England which retained its parish management in undiluted form until 1878.[18] There was already a certain amount of pressure for larger administrative areas within Westmorland, however, and a speaker at a meeting of the Kendal Farmers' Club in May 1871, complained of the inadequacy of the township as an administrative unit for road repair and its 'almost indiscriminate appointment of anybody as surveyor'. The meeting went on to urge that the existing Poor Law Unions should be made the basis for highway administration.[19]

Westmorland was not typical in this respect, but the relatively slow and uneven application of the 1862 Act in many parts of Cumberland appears to have reflected the national pattern. Thus the Webbs in their book acknowledge that the provision of larger areas of administration in 1862 was a distinct improvement upon previous highway practice, but they lament the general slowness of its implementation and also argue that the county would have been a much more rational administrative unit.

---

[15] C.R.O. AH/6/9, Q.S. Highway Papers (1863–90), Return of Particulars of Highway Districts in Cumberland to the Local Gov. Board, 1871.
[16] Ibid. [17] S. & B. Webb, p. 209.
[18] K.R.O., Westmorland Highway Committee Papers (1888–1905).
[19] *Westmorland Gazette*, 27 May 1871.

THE COUNTY

The county was a larger administrative unit but had a more limited field of responsibility. It was originally only concerned with the maintenance of the larger bridges within its limits, plus 100 yards of road on either side of each bridge. The smaller bridges, in common with the roads, were a parochial responsibility. County bridges were few in number at the beginning of the eighteenth century and were usually under the direct supervision of the justices; a bridge master being seldom appointed at this early date.

The unskilled nature of much bridge repair and its inadequate supervision became a serious problem during the eighteenth century, when the increase of wheeled traffic led to a demand for new bridges under county control to replace the old fords and pack horse bridges. The county was thus made responsible for an increasing proportion of all newly-built bridges during this period and a good many older ones as well. This was a consequence of the increasing application of the 1555 Act, by which the county was deemed liable for the repair of all bridges where the liability could not be definitely proven to rest elsewhere. This practice had increased to such an extent in Cumbria that by 1753 the region possessed a total of 293 county bridges.[20] This list included practically all identifiable bridges with the exception of such as were clearly in private hands.

The county authorities generally were in the difficult position of being burdened with greatly increased responsibilities for bridge building and repairs at a time when their other administrative obligations were also increasing in scope and complexity. Bridge repair was an important responsibility, but the justices were also responsible for the keeping of the peace by the employment of constables, and also for the administration of the Poor Law. It is true that, by the end of the eighteenth century, it was usual for the justices to appoint bridgemasters, but it is doubtful if many authorities had either the time or the professional knowledge to supervise the work of such officers. There is little evidence in this period to suggest that very much thought or money was devoted to bridge construction or repair, and these deficiencies were reflected in the poor condition of a great many Cumbrian bridges at the close of the eighteenth century.

[20] H. S. Cowper, 'Ancient and County Bridges in Cumberland and Westmorland; with Some Remarks upon the Fords also Including Lancashire North of the Sands', C.W.T., XV (1899).

During the following century, however, the administration of county bridges became increasingly regularised and centralised. An examination of the Westmorland county accounts reveals the development of some facets of this movement towards a more centralised authority for bridge administration. In 1826 the county was divided up into four wards for bridge repair; each ward being controlled by a bridgemaster who also acted as treasurer and high constable. There does not appear to have been any provision at this time for a single authority to co-ordinate the policies of the different areas. In addition, each ward bridge-master had other responsibilities and was thereby unable to devote his full attention to the bridges in his area. However, in 1828, the east and west wards of the county were amalgamated under one full-time official, George Robinson. In 1838, Robinson was appointed bridgemaster for the whole county and in the following year Kendal and Lonsdale wards were likewise combined.[21] Consequently, by 1840 the structure of the Westmorland bridge administration had undergone a considerable change. The county was now divided into two wards for bridge repair; each ward being under a part-time surveyor and both surveyors being supervised by a county bridgemaster who was a full-time official.

The equivalent accounts for Cumberland reveal that there was one bridgemaster for the whole county by 1830[22] and, prior to this time there were two such officials.[23] There do not appear to have been any officially recognised subordinate ward bridgemasters at this period and this is somewhat surprising in view of the greater extent of this particular county. However, the county bridge-master did not directly control the whole area, since the four baronies of Millom, Holm Cultram, Dalston and Crosthwaite maintained their own bridges throughout this period and were accordingly reimbursed by the county at the end of each year.[24]

As county bridgemasters assumed greater responsibilities, it became necessary for the magistrates to supervise their activities more closely. Hence, successive Cumberland bridgemasters were obliged to report four times a year to their employers on the work done in the previous quarter. These Quarterly Reports have all survived,[25] and collectively provide a valuable summary of county expenditure on bridge repair in this period. In addition, they contain a good deal of interesting information about the

21 K.R.O., Westmorland County Stock Accounts (1826–78).
22 *Parl. Papers*, 1834, **XIV**, p. 207.   23 Ibid.
24 C.R.O., Cumberland County Stock Accounts (1838–78).
25 C.R.O., Q.S. Petition Rolls.

changing techniques of bridge repair. No comparable reports for
Westmorland have survived although details of bridge expenditure
in this county were incorporated into the Annual General
County Accounts between 1826 and 1878. The Lancashire
Sessions displayed a similar eagerness to be kept regularly
informed about bridge expenditure, and in 1848 they appointed a
Committee 'to make an investigation into the whole management
of and expenditure upon County and Hundred Bridges and to
consider the propriety of consolidating the management'.[26] This
further supervision was becoming increasingly necessary in view
of the rising costs of bridge repair during this period. For instance
in the year 1841–2, bridge maintenance in Westmorland was more
than double any other single item of county expenditure, and in a
good many other years it surpassed all other heads of expenditure
in both Cumberland and Westmorland.[27] The duties of the North
Lonsdale bridgemaster, however, appear to have been considerably less onerous than those of his counterparts in Cumberland
and Westmorland. In October 1866, the Lancaster District
Finance Committee recommended to the Quarter Sessions 'that
the whole of Lonsdale Hundred should be placed in the hands of
one bridgemaster in consequence of the light duties to be performed'.[28]

    None the less, most bridgemasters had arduous duties to fulfil
and in view of this it was becoming increasingly important that
they should be well qualified. Considerable care was therefore
taken over their appointment. The Cumberland Finance Committee, in their report of 1850, recognised the importance of the
bridgemaster's office and the need for its occupant to be amply
remunerated.

'From the sudden damage to which all bridges are necessarily
exposed, they require constant and vigilant attention, as well as
considerable scientific knowledge for their proper repair as well as
construction. No doubt persons may be found ready to undertake
this important office at a very reduced salary, but when your
Committee weigh the number and great expense of building and
repairing these bridges in former times, the good order in which
they are now kept, and the small expense at which they are main-

26 L.R.O., Q.A.V. 3/1, Report of the General Financial Committee on
Public Bridges in the County of Lancashire, 1849.
27 K.R.O., Westmorland County Stock Accounts (1826–78).
28 L.R.O., Report of the Lancaster District Finance Committee, October
1866.

tained compared with what was formerly expended for very insufficient work, your Committee cannot but come to the conclusion that Mr. Milton's superintendence has been attended with very beneficial results.'[29]

In consequence, the Committee resolved not to reduce Milton's salary of £450 a year. This report may have been occasioned by protests from other county officials against the very high remuneration of the bridgemaster. However, there is no further evidence which throws light upon why a reduction in Milton's salary should have been contemplated at this time. It must also be remembered that Milton's salary included his travelling expenses which were almost certainly considerable.

The majority of the Cumbrian bridgemasters during this time held office for long periods and this fact, together with their increasing salaries, implies that they were probably competent men who gave satisfaction to an increasingly vigilant county authority. For instance, George Robinson was bridgemaster of Westmorland for at least twenty-nine years and his successor, Joseph Bintley, did not retire until 1919 on the completion of fifty years of service.[30] Similarly, William Field, the bridgemaster of North Lonsdale, assumed office in 1816 and was not replaced until his death in 1860, by which time he must have been ninety-one years old.[31] Field's long tenure of office may well have been more the result of the justices' low estimation of the importance of the office than of any positive merit on his part, but he does appear to have been a quite remarkable man and to have been particularly prominent in Cartmel which, according to Stockdale, was 'governed by him'. He was originally a shopkeeper, but then expanded his activities and was eventually High Constable, Stamp Distributor, Vestry Clerk and Will Maker.[32] It is doubtful if these multifarious duties left him much time for the supervision of the seventy-nine 'hundred' bridges for which he was responsible. In fact, it was observed by the 1848 Committee that some of these bridges had not been seen in the last twelve years. However, whatever reservations one has about Field, all the evidence points to the merits of his counterparts in Cumberland. Milton's quali-

[29] C.R.O., Report of the Cumberland Q.S. Finance Committee on County Expenditure, 1850.
[30] K.R.O., Westmorland County Stock Accounts (1826–78).
[31] Field was seventy-nine years old in 1848, Stockdale, *Annals of Cartmel*, p. 574.
[32] J. Stockdale, *Annals of Cartmel*, (1870), p. 575.

ties have already been emphasised, and his successor, John Cory, appears on the basis of his Quarterly Reports to have been a fair minded and painstaking official who was always prepared to work in close conjunction with the county justices and their appointed committees.[33]

Although the Cumbrian bridgemasters had overall responsibility for bridge repairs in their respective counties, they did not, as a rule, direct the actual repair work. Instead, they were mainly concerned with the general supervision of county bridges and the inspection of completed repairs; necessary repairs being usually let out by contract. However, bridge contractors did not always give satisfaction and there are several notable recorded examples of bad workmanship. For instance, in 1873 the assistant bridgemaster of Cumberland, Mr Meyers, informed the Quarter Sessions of the suspension of all work at Bowerhouse bridge on account of the wilful disobedience of the contractor who refused to obey his instructions as to how the bridge should be repaired. 'The fact is, the Contractor was completely out of his element, he told me that he had never built a bridge before and had never worked in granite and the wonder is that he should have entered into the contract to repair the bridge under such circumstances.'[34] It was no doubt partly as a precaution against such failings that the justices appointed sub-committees to superintend the larger bridge repairs, such as at Harraby where £5,000 was spent in rebuilding the bridge in the late 1820s under the supervision of an appointed sub-committee.[35]

The appointment of such committees does not necessarily reflect any official dissatisfaction with the quality of supervision exercised by county bridgemasters. It was recognised generally that these officials did not have the time to supervise all bridge repairs themselves. Bridge repair was not their only duty. In particular, they were responsible also for the maintenance of the various county buildings. For instance, successive county bridgemasters in Cumberland until 1881 were responsible for the maintenance of the Court House, a Lunatic Asylum, an Industrial School, 13 Sessional Courthouses and 22 'Lock-ups'; as well as a multitude of bridges and bridge roads scattered all over the county.[36] This situation was scarcely satisfactory. Bridge maintenance was a specialised and exacting occupation and as such

[33] C.R.O., AH/6/26, Cumberland County Surveyors Reports (1857–80).
[34] Ibid., June 1873.
[35] C.R.O., Cumberland Q.S., Petition Rolls, July 1830.
[36] C.R.O., CCH/3/1, Cumberland Highway Committee Papers (1879–84).

should have been the responsibility of a separate official free from other distractions.

In general, the authority of the county over bridge repair in this period was more extensive in theory than in practice. As we have noted, the introduction of county bridgemasters, although clearly producing beneficial results, did not enable these officials to exercise sufficient oversight over most bridge repairs on account of their other commitments. Also, the justices' authority to enforce parish amalgamation from 1862 onwards, did not always produce the desired effect in Cumberland and produced no effect at all in Westmorland, although it is not clear how far the latter phenomenon was a product of parochial hostility to amalgamation, and how much a product of the Justices' reluctance to enforce the Act in the first place. It is also worth noting that for most of the nineteenth century the county had no control over road repair, except for the area of road on either side of the various bridges. The Act of 1823[37] which compelled Turnpike Trust clerks to submit annual returns to the Clerk of the Peace appeared to point the way to some measure of county control over the administration of main roads, but nothing further was done in this direction until the last two decades of the century. By this time, the dissolution of the majority of Turnpike Trusts had paved the way for some measure of integrated administration for both roads and bridges.[38]

TURNPIKE TRUSTS

Turnpike Trusts differed from the other administrative bodies we have noted in several important respects. In the first place, they were the only authority which specialised exclusively in road maintenance. Also, they did not carry comparable responsibilities. In the event of a Trust being unable to attend adequately to the repair of its roads, the parishes and not the Trust would bear the ultimate responsibility. Furthermore, Turnpike Trusts were set up as temporary institutions which would be dissolved as soon as the roads themselves were sufficiently improved and Trust creditors had been repaid. The toll gates would then be dismantled and the detailed supervision of main roads would revert to the parish.

The temporary nature of Trust institution was emphasised every twenty-one years when the Trustees had to apply for an

---

[37] 4G4, cap. 16.
[38] See Chapter 6 for a detailed discussion of events in this period.

extension of their powers in a 'Renewal Act'. This in theory could prove an expensive exercise in self-justification in which they pointed out the increasing traffic on their roads, resulting in increasing maintenance costs and their consequent need to raise toll charges or to borrow more money to meet these expenses. However, in practice, by the beginning of the nineteenth century, the renewal of Turnpike Acts had become fairly automatic in most cases and this fact was openly recognised by the Select Committee of 1820. This Committee stated that they wished

'to remove a mistaken notion, founded perhaps on obsolete practice or opinions, that the existence of some debt is absolutely necessary for establishing a claim before parliament for the renewal of such Acts. On the contrary an extinction of debt must be taken as strong proof of good management, and therefore as an additional reason for entrusting the maintenance of the roads to the same hands.'[39]

Nevertheless, even if the final result was rarely in doubt, Trusts still had to go through all the legal processes of securing Renewal Acts, and this continued to be a drain on their resources. In fact, the Select Committee of 1833 estimated that, on average, a quarter of the debts of Turnpike Trusts in England and Wales could be accounted for by the cost of obtaining Renewal Acts.[40]

This element of centralised control inherent in the procedure by which Trusts sought Renewal Acts, also manifests itself in the detailed stipulations of these Acts respecting the degree of authority which trustees could exercise during each 21-year period of the Trust's life. For instance, although each Trust had the right to erect toll gates there were usually restrictions placed upon the number of gates which could be erected along any given stretch of road. Similar restrictions were placed upon the number of tolls which could be levied upon any given vehicle in the same day; most categories of traffic being allowed to make a return journey without further toll payments. The rates of toll for different categories of vehicles were also carefully outlined in consecutive Acts, and Trusts had no authority to alter these rates, although they might be revised when a new Renewal Act was granted to the Trust concerned.

Each Trust was administered by a Committee of Trustees drawn from the area. The number of Trustees varied considerably from one Trust to another, but was seldom less than about

---

[39] *Parl. Papers*, 1820, **II**, p. 301.   [40] *Parl. Papers*, 1833, **XV**, p. 409.

fifty and frequently more than 100. It was intended that Trustees should be recruited from the more substantial landowners and professional people in the area. Hence, as a safeguard to ensure this, it was specified that all prospective Trustees should be in possession of an estate with a rental value of at least £100 a year. This property qualification was justified by James McAdam on the grounds that 'other parties in the towns, particularly possessing considerable personal wealth, frequently attend these meetings, not having that personal interest in the road which landed proprietors most naturally possess'.[41]

There is little doubt that a considerable proportion of the more important Cumbrian landowners took an interest in road improvements within their localities during the eighteenth century. Their loans helped to finance early road improvements whilst their co-operation was necessary in cases where such improvements encroached upon adjacent enclosed farmland. This pattern continued during the first half of the nineteenth century and local landlords featured prominently on the subscription lists of newly formed Trusts in this period. Hence, it is not surprising that Trusts in this position were interested in acquiring the services or at least the names of such men as Trustees. For instance, when the Cockermouth to Carlisle Trust was inaugurated in 1824, it included six members of the Lowther family, Sir Philip Musgrave, Sir James Graham of Netherby, John Christian Curwen and Humphrey Senhouse of Netherhall amongst its original Trustees.[42]

The support of such men is significant, but there is little evidence to suggest that, as a rule, they played a very big part in the detailed working out of Trust policy. In practice, Trust administration was usually in the hands of local townsmen of whom quite a high proportion were solicitors. It is quite likely, in fact, that certain of these members would not fulfil the property qualification for Trust membership, but this point would probably be overlooked in view of their general usefulness. Hence prominent legal families such as Halton, Bowman, Bleaymire, Broach, Heelis and Mounsey dominated the administration of successive Cumbrian Trusts. They were constant attenders at meetings and held a high proportion of the official positions on the various Trust bodies. A remarkable instance of the domination of a Trust by a single family is provided by the history of the Brougham Bridge Trust which was administered solely by members of the

Hutchinson family for at least thirty years, between 1827 and 1858, and probably for an even longer period altogether.[43] Similarly, the clerkship of the Cockermouth–Penrith Trust was held by a member of the Fisher family from 1803 to 1857.[44] Another conspicuous feature of nineteenth century Turnpike administration, as revealed by a study of the surviving Minute Books, is the almost uniformly low attendance at Trust meetings. Also most meetings were attended by the same nucleus of people. Some Trustees may have had little interest in any aspect of road building and administration, and might simply be members of a Turnpike Trust for reasons of social prestige. Alternatively, a large landowner might feel that nominal membership of such committees came within the category of discharging his public obligations. Such a man would not necessarily feel obliged to take an active interest in the work of the committee he joined. Other Trustees probably had a selective interest in road administration, and would attend meetings only when a particularly important issue was being discussed. At any rate, whatever their motives for joining, the majority of Trustees stayed away from Trust meetings and it often proved difficult for Trusts to secure the attendance of the three or four necessary to form a quorum. Little business was conducted, for instance, by the Cockermouth–Penrith Trust during the early years of the nineteenth century, and between June 1804 and February 1824 a total of fifty meetings had to be adjourned owing to the lack of a quorum.[45] The absentees do not seem to have missed much, however, since the business of the remaining meetings of the Trust in this period was of a very perfunctory nature and, more often than not, simply involved the appointment of new Trustees or the letting of toll gates. Even the Trustees of the Carlisle–Eamont Bridge road, who were responsible for the important stretch of road between Carlisle and Penrith, were reluctant to attend meetings. Their apathy does not appear to have been seriously disturbed by the prospect of the opening of a connecting railway along this particular route in 1846. This event made the mid 1840s the most critical period in the Trust's history and yet only 33 Trustees out of a total membership of 137 attended the meetings of the Northern Division of the Trust between 1843 and 1847.[46]

There is no evidence of any increased interest in Trust affairs

43 See Appendix E.   44 Ibid.
45 K.M., Cockermouth–Penrith Trust Minute Book (1804–24).
46 C.R.O., Carlisle–Eamont Trust (Northern Division) Minutes, 28 July 1849.

later in the century. For instance, out of 275 scheduled meetings of the Carlisle to Temon Trust between 1855 and 1877 only 63 had a quorum, and the Trust did not meet officially at all between 28 February 1863 and 11 November 1865.[47]

However, this apparent lack of involvement on the part of most Trustees did not prevent a small minority of conscientious members introducing fairly radical changes in Trust management during the first half of the nineteenth century. The first and probably the most important of these changes concerned the methods and conditions of appointment of Trust officials. Surviving records suggest that Trust officials were very poorly paid during the early years of the nineteenth century. For instance, the Sedburgh Trust only gave its surveyor £5 in 1800[48] and the Carlisle-Skillbeck Trust made £5 2s cover all its staff salaries in this period.[49] This latter Trust seems to have kept its salary expenses down to this level by dispensing with the services of a surveyor and making use of the various township surveyors along this line of road. There is no record of how the respective townships reacted to this added burden, but contemporary criticisms of transport conditions in this area, suggest that the Turnpike itself did not benefit from this arrangement.

By the 1820s abuses of this kind were infrequent, and a growing number of the Cumbrian Trusts were offering more attractive salaries to their prospective officials. This was in line with the contemporary recommendations of John Loudon McAdam. McAdam laid especial stress upon the importance of the surveyor's office and the need for this to be filled by technically competent and conscientious officials who would devote their full time to their duties. In order to attract people of the requisite calibre on these terms it was necessary to attach a substantial salary to this particular post. McAdam was, of course, concerned with the reform of Trust management throughout the country, but his connection with Cumbria was closer than with most areas. He was adviser to at least eight Cumbrian Trusts during the 1820s and 1830s, and was personally involved in a number of road making operations within the region during this period. Hence, it is likely that his recommendations would carry a good deal of

[47] C.R.O., Carlisle–Temon Trust Minute Book (1855–77); although this Trust specified that seven people were to constitute a quorum—a rather high figure by contemporary standards.
[48] K.R.O., Westmorland Q.S. Petition Rolls, Mich. 1801.
[49] T.H.C., Account book of George Blamire, Treasurer of the Carlisle–Skillbeck Trust (1790–1827).

weight in this region and help to persuade at least some of the Cumbrian Trusts to implement his proposals respecting the appointment of officials.

McAdam had no cause for complaint about his own salary as surveyor during this period. He was greatly sought after by many Trusts in England and Wales and could command a high fee in consequence. His fee for superintending the building of the Alston roads was £500 a year,[50] and as such reflects the resources of his employers, the Greenwich Hospital Commission, as well as his own reputation. Other surveyors could not hope to command this kind of salary but McAdam's appointment did establish a pattern whereby most Cumbrian Trusts began to pay their officials much more generously than in the past. For instance, McAdam's successor as surveyor of the Alston Trust received £150 a year[51] as did the Superintendent Surveyor of the Whitehaven Trust.[52] Similarly the surveyor of the Cockermouth–Penrith Trust was being paid £110 a year by 1856[53] and this compares most favourably with the £15 which one of his predecessors received in 1807.[54]

These examples are by no means typical, however, and officials of smaller Trusts received considerably less than this; the general average salary for this category of surveyor being between about £15 and £30, whilst the corresponding allowance for clerks and treasurers was marginally less as a rule. After about 1830, the allowances of all three officials remained, on the whole, fairly static until the late 1860s by which time a good many Trusts were beginning to reduce their commitments in an attempt to accelerate the repayment of their mortgage debt.

In general, therefore, it would appear that the larger Cumbrian Trusts were paying their surveyors a substantial salary by the 1830s. A salary of over £100 a year in this period could reasonably be expected to attract a fair range of applicants whilst at the same time ensuring that the holder of this office could afford to look upon his post as a full-time one. The smaller Cumbrian Trusts are rarely specific as to whether their surveyors served full-time or not, but it seems likely on the basis of the salaries they offered that in most cases such appointments would be on a part-time basis. None the less, these Trusts also were allocating a

[50] P.R.O., Greenwich Hospital (Northern Estates) Minutes, 20 October 1827.
[51] C.R.O., Cumberland Q.S. Petition Rolls, Easter 1836.
[52] Ibid., Easter 1842.   [53] Ibid., Easter 1857.
[54] K.M., Cockermouth–Penrith Trust Minutes, 20 October 1807.

markedly higher proportion of their income to official salaries by the 1830s and in this sense they were attempting to put into practice at least some of McAdam's recommendations.

The value which the Cumbrian Trusts were now attaching to their surveyor is also illustrated by the increased care which they took over his appointment. For instance, the Northern Division of the Carlisle–Eamont Trust appointed a sub-committee of three Trustees to examine the seven applications for this post upon the death of the previous occupant, Andrew Patterson, in 1865. A short list of three persons was then selected for interview. It was also emphasised in the course of the nomination, 'that the surveyor be required to devote his whole time to the duties of his office'.[55] In addition to this latter proviso, the prospective surveyor of a Trust was sometimes required to comply with a number of more detailed and specific instructions before his appointment was confirmed. For instance, George Theobalds, the newly appointed surveyor of the Ambleside Trust, guaranteed to the clerk, John Collinson,

'that I will diligently and carefully go and examine the whole line of the Turnpike road from Ambleside to Dunmail Rays once in every fourteen days between the 1st November and the 1st day of May in each year and once in every seventeen days between the 1st of May and the 1st of November in each year; and at such other times as the case may seem to require or the said John Collinson may order me.'

He made a similar promise to examine the remainder of the Trust road between Kendal and Ambleside each week of the year and to report upon his findings to Collinson within two days of each examination.[56] Once a surveyor had agreed to conditions of this kind and taken up his appointment, he was normally obliged to present annual reports upon the state of all roads under his supervision, and to submit detailed estimates of all proposed improvements to the Trustees. Also as a further check, several Trusts appointed sub-committees to inspect his road making and book-keeping. The first committee of this kind which I have been able to trace was established by the Ambleside Trustees in 1803.[57] However, this appears to have been an unusual development for this period and the majority of these sub-committees were established during the 1850s and were accorded formal status in the

[55] C.R.O. Carlisle–Eamont Trust (Northern Division) Minutes, 4 November 1865.   [56] K.R.O., Ambleside Trust Minutes, 3 February 1829.
[57] K.R.O., Ambleside Trust Minutes, 1 March 1803.

Trust Renewal Acts of this period.[58] Thus most Trust surveyors in Cumbria appear to have been closely supervised in addition to having been carefully appointed in the first place. In return for their increased salary and responsibilities they had to account for all that they did.

Trustees had more time to devote to the supervision of road maintenance once they ceased to be responsible for the actual collection of toll receipts. During the early years of the nineteenth century many Cumbrian Trusts continued to appoint and supervise their own toll collectors, but this was rarely a very satisfactory arrangement. Unless Trustees had the time or the inclination to keep a continuous watch on each gate, it was difficult to eliminate the possibility of fraud on a considerable scale over the years. Certainly, it was relatively simple in most instances for the collector to withold a proportion of the tolls which he received. These considerations prompted a growing number of the Trusts to 'let' their toll gates at a public auction, and by the late 1820s this appears to have become the normal procedure in Cumbria, there being few subsequent references to the appointment of toll collectors by the various Trusts. As soon as the toll auction was over, the agreed rent would be incorporated into the Trust's financial statement for the coming year. Hence, most Trust toll receipts simply indicate the rent which the lessee had agreed to pay the Trust upon his undertaking charge of a particular gate. They are not necessarily an accurate reflection of the volume of traffic which passed through the toll gate during the year. In addition, since the lessee was eager to make a profit, he would naturally expect to receive more money in toll revenues than he had given the Trust in his annual rent. Consequently, unless the lessee's estimate was over-optimistic, the traffic on a Turnpike road during any one year as expressed in toll receipts, would normally be higher than the figure quoted in the Trust's annual financial statement.

The reluctance of individuals to rent gates usually reflects an anticipated decline in the revenues of the Trust concerned. Thus, both divisions of the Carlisle–Eamont Bridge Trust were unable to lease their gates between 1846 and 1851[59] on account of the

[58] For instance, The Heron Syke Trust in 1850 (L.P.A., 13–14V, cap. LXIV); The Appleby Trust in 1851 (L.P.A., 13–14V, cap. XIII); and the Kendal–Kirkby Lonsdale–Milnthorpe Trust in 1854 (L.P.A., 17–18V., cap. CXLV).

[59] C.R.O., Carlisle–Eamont Trust (S. Divis.) account book (1844–79) and Northern Division Minute Book (1840–59).

lessees' concern as to the effect which the newly-opened Lancaster to Carlisle Railway might have upon the receipts of their respective gates. Similarly, the appointment of 'Toll Collectors' by the Cockermouth and Carlisle Trust during 1843 and 1844[60] and the earlier substitution of collectors on the Cockermouth–Workington[61] and Cockermouth–Maryport Trust roads[62] between 1838 and 1844, may have reflected the lessees' concern about the effects of the Maryport and Carlisle railway upon the traffic using these roads.

The practice of leasing tolls became highly organised during the first half of the century, and a small group of professional 'Toll Collectors' began to control an increasing proportion of the gates of several Cumbrian Trusts. Several of these 'collectors' lived outside Cumbria, and, having appointed sub-collectors to officiate at their gates, they were content to supervise their employees from a distance. The Hunslet partnership of Charles Winn and Joshua Bower, with assistance from Enoch Blackburn as 'surety', collaborated in the leasing of a great many Cumbrian toll gates during the middle years of the nineteenth century. They were collectively involved in the affairs of at least six Cumbrian Trusts between 1838 and 1877[63] and were perhaps actively concerned in the affairs of several other Trusts which are less well documented.

Their attention ranged from Ulverston to Brampton and they were equally prominent in the East Riding of Yorkshire and in Lincolnshire in the years between 1823 and 1866. Joshua Bower appears to have been a particularly interesting personality with a very varied background; before becoming a toll lessee he was successively a carpenter, glass manufacturer and colliery owner.[64] Other prominent lessees who came from outside the Cumbrian area include Richard Bailey from Preston, and the Varty family of drapers from Newcastle.

Many local men also leased toll gates; such families as Scholick, Simpson, Wood, Hodgkinson and Forster feature quite frequently in the surviving Trust records. Several of these lessees were listed in the local Directories as 'Toll Collectors', although they

[60] C.R.O., Cumberland Q.S. Petition Rolls, Easter 1844 and 1845.
[61] Ibid., 1838–44.   [62] Ibid., 1841–4.
[63] These Trusts were: Ambleside, Carlisle–Brampton, Carlisle–Eamont (Northern Division), Carlisle–Eamont (Southern Division), Cockermouth–Penrith and Ulverston–Carnforth.
[64] K. A. McMahon, 'Roads and Turnpike Trusts in East Yorkshire', *East Yorkshire History Society* (1964).

usually appear to have had other occupations as well. Thomas Thomson, for instance, was a 'shoemaker' of Grasmere,[65] whilst George Forster was a 'bookseller' established in Penrith.[66]

It appears, therefore, that the leasing of a good many Cumbrian toll gates was the result of careful organisation on the part of a small, well integrated group of professionals who were often members of the same family, and who collaborated in bidding for a selected group of potentially profitable toll gates. As individual groups of lessees became more powerful, it became increasingly necessary for the Trusts to prevent them abusing their authority. In the first place, there was the very great danger that organised bidding for the gates would bring down the rent to a figure which was uneconomic for the Trust concerned. It was usual, therefore, for most Trusts to attach a minimum price to each gate and to relet the same at a future date if the proposed rent did not meet this 'reserve' figure. Trusts were also entitled to accept private bids in the event of the bidders combining at toll auctions.

The Carlisle–Eamont Trustees took full advantage of their liberty in May 1842, when it was decided 'that the Treasurer have power to relet the Hesket Gate by private contract for one year for any sum not exceeding £743, or to put a suitable and proper person to collect the Tolls at the said gate, such person not being likely to become a Lessee of the said Tolls on any future occasion'.[67] This last provision was, no doubt, a precaution against a toll Collector being deliberately negligent in his duties in order that he could subsequently have the lease of the gate at a suitably low figure.

Once the lessee had been appointed, the Trustees listed the conditions of the appointment in his contract in order to deny him any legal pretext for evading his duties. Usually the lessee would be asked to advance a month's rent to the treasurer upon taking possession of the toll house and to continue one month in advance with his payments until the expiration of his period of tenure. Similarly, the lessee was obliged to name two sureties in support of his claim. If these conditions were not complied with, the gate was relet and the lessee forfeited his deposit. In a further attempt to prevent the lessees becoming too independent, the Trust imposed a three-year limit upon the tenure of all leases although this limit was often circumvented when lessees renewed their control over particular gates at successive auctions.

[65] Parsons & White, p. 619.   [66] Parsons & White, p. 506.
[67] C.R.O., Carlisle–Eamont Trust (Northern Division) Minutes, 28 May 1842.

The efficient collection of tolls was becoming increasingly necessary for most Trusts if they were to repay their mortgage debt. Many Trusts had not cleared the debts which they had contracted during the eighteenth century, whilst others accumulated new debts and increased old ones during the early decades of the nineteenth century. During this period in Cumbria, as elsewhere in the country, new Turnpikes were set up and a good many other Trusts borrowed extensively to finance further road improvements. The greater part of this money was lent upon the security of the Trusts' anticipated toll revenues.

Although the great landowners and mining magnates such as the Lowther family, the Dukes of Portland and Devonshire and the Earl of Carlisle were inevitably important creditors of the Trusts, a great many tradesmen, professional men and smaller landowners also made significant contributions. In fact, one of the most interesting facets of Trust history during this period is the light which the mortgage lists throw upon the relatively wide range of Cumbrian society which had money to invest.[68] Thus the Earl of Lonsdale's contribution of £4,201 to the Cockermouth–Penrith Trust[69] was matched by another substantial loan of £3,000 by John and James Gandy, two Kendal merchants, to the Heron Syke Trust in 1821. The same Trust also borrowed £300 on mortgages from Edmund and William Thompson, two 'yeomen' of Kendal parish. Several schoolmasters also figure in these mortgage lists: Samuel Marshall, a Kendal teacher, took over the Gandy mortgage of £3,000 in 1826, whilst John Taylor, another Kendal schoolmaster, lent the Heron Syke Trust £150.[70]

Various charitable, ecclesiastical and educational organisations also invested in Turnpike Trusts. For instance, the Huntingdon Charity Trustees lent the Cockermouth–Penrith Trust a total of £500,[71] whilst the Churchwardens of Brigham and Cockermouth each subscribed £50 to the Cockermouth and Workington Trust.[72] Similarly, the Governors of Sedbergh School subscribed £210 to the Sedbergh Trust, and their counterparts at Lorton School lent £100 to the Cockermouth–Penrith Trust.[73]

Most Trusts debts usually consisted of a few large single

68 See Appendix G.
69 K.M., Cockermouth–Penrith Trust Minutes, 16 April 1856.
70 K.R.O., Heron Syke Trust, Misc. Mortgage Agreements (1821–39).
71 K.M., Cockermouth–Penrith Trust Minutes, 16 April 1856.
72 C.R.O., Cockermouth–Workington Trust, Misc. Papers.
73 K.M., Cockermouth–Penrith Trust Minutes, 16 April 1856.

C

loans and a great many smaller contributions, the proliferation of which complicated the course of their ultimate repayment by the Trust. It is difficult to discern the motives of these multifarious creditors. Some, no doubt, looked upon their loan purely as an investment which would yield them a regular rate of interest of 4 or 5 per cent. For instance, much of the total principal debt of the Cockermouth–Penrith Trust in 1824 was reported to be owed 'to people who have no property along this line or bene-fited by the road, but who lent it either as an investment or for the benefit of the public; and the bonds have in many cases been transferred and now belong to persons totally unconnected with the County'.[74] Even the Earl of Lonsdale, despite his extensive landownership, did not actually own any property along the line of the Cockermouth–Penrith Trust road and was attested by Mr William Bleaymire to derive no benefit from this Turnpike 'except when he has to travel over it going between Lowther and Whitehaven'.[75] However, the Lonsdale family were the Trust's principal creditors and it is doubtful if their interest was purely speculative. The ramifications of their economic interests were so wide ranging that the improvement of any main road must ultimately benefit them, even if it did not directly affect their property. Thus it is probable that a good many of the larger Trust creditors looked upon their investment as a means to a wider end: the economic development of the region as a whole. By financing improved communications, both landowners and tradesmen would share in the region's growing trade and productivity.[76]

It is noteworthy that, £3,500,000 out of a total national Trust debt of £7,785,171 was lent without any security for interest or principal repayments.[77] This fact could point to the relative lack of speculative interest on the part of some creditors, although it is more likely that, in a great many cases, failure to obtain such security was the result of ignorance rather than intention on the part of the creditors. Many people undoubtedly were misled into thinking that the Government had provided security for their debt and that consequently there was no need for them to make any separate agreement with a particular Trust. Robert Fuge admitted before a Select Committee that the Government's policy on this subject could be easily misconstrued. 'With respect to the borrowing of money: the law is inequitable and oppressive,

---

[74] Ibid.   [75] Ibid.

[76] See Chapter 3 for an extended discussion of this particular theme.

[77] *Parl. Papers*, 1836, **XIX**, p. 386.

it might almost be said to be fraudulent because it induces persons to lend money as a supposed Parliamentary security which is no security at all.'[78]

These alleged ambiguities in some mortgage settlements proved to be a particular grievance of many of the creditors of the Ulverston–Carnforth Trust. The disgruntled mortgagees of this Trust claimed that they had subscribed a total of £9,650 towards the making of the Turnpike before the inaugural Act was passed in 1818. This sum was lent on the expectation that its repayment would be duly secured by an appropriate provision inserted in the subsequent Act. After the Act had been confirmed, the money subscribed was still considered insufficient to complete the building of the Trust road and, in consequence, the Trustees borrowed a further £8,150 under the powers of the Act and granted mortgages for this sum bearing interest at $4\frac{1}{2}$ per cent. The Trustees then claimed that, since no written agreement had been made with respect to the original debt of £9,650, no interest payments were due upon this sum. They also recognised that it would be politic to disregard the original creditors in order to encourage future investment.[79]

After prolonged litigation it was determined in the Trust Renewal Act of 1850 that the repayment of the later creditors should take precedence, but that the Trust should pay $3\frac{1}{2}$ per cent interest upon both debts.[80]

The Ulverston Trust was by no means unusual in distinguishing between its creditors in this way, and a good many other Cumbrian Trusts adopted a like practice in order to encourage further loans. Therefore it is hardly surprising, in view of the declining revenues of most Trusts, that, by the middle of the nineteenth century, many creditors had lost all confidence in the Trusts' ability to redeem their debt.[81]

It appears that this lack of confidence was shared by the 1840 Select Committee which reported on roads in England and Wales.[82] The conclusions of this Committee are well worth noting, since they were based upon evidence produced by the most comprehensive national survey ever undertaken of Turnpike Trusts and their management. The main theme of the Committee's conclusions was the need for Trusts to consolidate upon a regional

[78] *Parl. Papers*, 1836, XIX; p. 386.
[79] L.R.O., T.T.K 12, Ulverston–Carnforth Trust, Miscellaneous Papers.
[80] L.P.A., 13–14 vic, cap. LXV.
[81] See Chapter 6 for a development of this theme.
[82] *Parl. Papers*, 1840, XXVII.

basis in order to reduce their expenses and increase their efficiency. This argument was supported by an impressive battery of criticism directed at contemporary Trusts, most of which had not yet seen the wisdom of consolidation.

'The Reports and evidence to which we have referred, exhibit the evils of the present system of Turnpike management arising from the number of Trusts, the expense of renewing Acts of Parliament, the great amount of law charges, the number of officers and aggregate amount of salaries, the number and frequently unjust position of Toll Gates, the high rate of toll, the vast amount of Bonded Debt, the high rate of interest, the necessity of paying the interest with the Toll revenue and leaving the burden of maintaining the roads on the parishes through which they pass, the total absence of all control over the power of the Trustees to borrow and expend money, the want of sufficient check, and of authority to compel the keeping of regular, correct and just accounts of the receipts and expenditure of the funds and the employment of incompetent and unskilful and inefficient persons as Surveyors—and all reports express an opinion in which we fully concur, that, in order to obtain a more economical and efficient management of the roads it is absolutely necessary to resort to some system of consolidation. In proof of the advantages of adopting that course we would refer to the Metropolitan Trusts and the systems established in Scotland and the Isle of Wight.'[83]

This is, of course, a highly generalised picture and does not apply in all its fullness to most of the Cumbrian Trusts in this period. For instance, very few Cumbrian Trusts had as yet shown signs of abandoning their road repair duties to the parish. On the other hand, it is fair to say that the case for Trust consolidation met with little response in the Cumbrian counties during this period, although local advocates for such a measure were not lacking.

Sir James Lowther had recognised the importance of economising on Turnpike Acts as early as 1753 when, in a letter to a Mr Radcliffe, he pressed the citizens of Cockermouth to incorporate the Caldbeck and Keswick branches of the proposed Cocker-mouth–Penrith Trust into one Bill rather than go to the expense of drawing up separate Bills.[84] However, this initiative did not

[83] Ibid., **XXVII**, p. 10.
[84] C.R.O., Lowther MSS, Miscellaneous Correspondence on Cumberland Roads (1748–56), Lord Lonsdale to Richard Radcliff, 17 February 1753.

meet with success and was not repeated so far as I know during the eighteenth century. There was a further attempt in the early nineteenth century to amalgamate the Brougham Bridge Trust and a branch road from Penrith to Wigton, with the Carlisle–Eamont Bridge Trust,[85] but this scheme was abandoned in 1830.[86]

The leading advocate of Trust consolidation in Cumbria, as elsewhere, during the early part of the nineteenth century, was John Loudon McAdam. McAdam had achieved some measure of success in other parts of England and Wales when arguing the case of Trust consolidation. His greatest single achievement in this direction was to secure the consolidation of the fourteen Middlesex Trusts into a single metropolitan authority. This entailed the appointment of 46 commissioners to administer, under the supervision of McAdam, 172 miles of road yielding a total toll revenue of £60,000 to £70,000. This 'Metropolitan' Trust was to become the wealthiest and most important road authority in England.[87] Similarly, McAdam took over the control of 148 miles of Trust road in the Bristol area and, under his guidance, the Bristol Trust was often cited as a model of well integrated and economical administration.[88] Other large consolidated Trusts of this period included Worcester which incorporated 160 miles of Turnpike road, and Exeter and Hereford which were 156 miles long and 146 miles long, respectively.[89] McAdam was less successful in imposing these views upon the various Cumbrian Trusts he worked with during this period. His one success in this field was to persuade his principal employers, the Greenwich Hospital Commission, to group all the roads to their lead mines together under a single Trust. As a result, the newly created Alston Trust was of an unprecedented size for this region and had responsibility for 130 miles of road when it was inaugurated in 1824.[90]

However, Alston was exceptional, and the general tendency in this period was for large Trusts to subdivide rather than to combine their resources. For example, in 1811 the 'Military

---

85 C.R.O., Carlisle–Eamont Trust, Misc. correspondence re Road Bill of 1830.
86 Ibid., letter Edward Bleaymire to William Sisson, 11 March 1830.
87 R. H. Spiro, 'John Loudon McAdam and the Metropolis Turnpike Trust', *Journal of Transport History*, II (1955–6), pp. 210–11.
88 S. and B. Webb, p. 174.
89 Ibid., p. 180.
90 See Chapter 3 for further details.

road' from Carlisle to Newcastle was subdivided into two sections: the Cumberland section being subsequently known as the Carlisle to Temon Trust. This latter body became a quite separate organisation, having its own Trustees and a distinct rate of tolls.[91] Similarly, the Cockermouth–Keswick–Kendal Trust was split into two halves in 1824: a new Trust being created to administer the section of road between Keswick and Kendal.[92] Shortly afterwards, in 1830, the Carlisle–Eamont Trust was also divided but in this case the rupture was not so complete. The 1830 Act provided for two Divisions: one for the northern part of the road and one for the southern half. However, although the two Divisions had separate sets of Trustees and officials, there was scope for future co-operation since the two Trusts retained their common debt and hence had to pool their resources in order to repay creditors.

In spite of these divisions, some of the Cumbrian Trusts remained quite large by national standards. The Cockermouth–Penrith Trust still covered almost 62 miles of road, whilst the Cockermouth–Maryport and Appleby–Kendal Turnpikes measured 42 and 41 miles, respectively. In general the average mileage of the 24 Cumbrian Trusts was $24\frac{2}{3}$ miles, and as such compared quite favourably with the national average of just over 19 miles. However, it must be remembered also that many Cumbrian Trust roads ran through sparsely populated countryside and that the average was boosted by the exceptional size of the Alston Trust. At the other end of the scale, the Kingstown–Westlinton Trust measured just over 3 miles in length, whilst the Brougham Bridge Trustees had the onerous task of administering $1\frac{1}{2}$ miles of road.

In general it seems that whilst Cumbrian Trusts were reluctant to amalgamate, there was nevertheless in practice a good deal of overlap between them. J. L. McAdam was responsible for supervising at least eight Cumbrian Turnpikes[93] and this in itself must have imposed a certain degree of uniformity, both of administration and road making techniques. Similarly, the involvement of certain families in the affairs of several Trusts must have added to their common interest. Thus the Mounsey and Graham families featured in all the North Cumberland Trusts, whilst the Lowthers and Senhouses were equally prominent in West.

[91] L.P.A. 51G3, cap. XIV.   [92] L.P.A. 5G4, cap. XIV
[93] These Trusts comprised the following: Alston; Cockermouth–Penrith; Ambleside; Heron Syke; Milnthorpe–Levens; Whitehaven; Appleby–Kendal; and Carlisle–Eamont.

Cumberland as a unifying force in Trust policy. It was also usual for several neighbouring Trusts to share the same officials. For instance, John Bowman was treasurer of four Trusts and clerk of one. Similarly, Edward Steel and Edward Waugh were successive clerks of the Cockermouth–Carlisle, Cockermouth–Maryport and Cockermouth–Workington Trusts.[94]

Such Trusts were prepared to unite to defend their common officials against outside hostility, and when Emanuel Demaine was so threatened, the Carlisle–Brampton Trust determined 'that if any action be brought against the Surveyor of the Penrith or Military road, the Trustees of this road will join in an equal degree to defend such action'.[95]

The principal reason why such Trusts did not take the next step and amalgamate was that the richer Trusts did not want to inherit the debts of their poorer neighbours. James McAdam argued that it would not be necessary for rich Trusts to subsidise poorer ones since the debt of each Trust could be kept separate and, as a result of the economies wrought by consolidation, all Trusts would be established upon a more viable footing and thus be enabled to clear off their debts independently.[96] None the less, most wealthy Trusts appear to have shared an apprehension about increased mortgage commitments. For instance, when the heavily indebted Kirkby Stephen–Hawes Trust suggested an amalgamation with its more affluent Sedbergh neighbour in 1851, the Kirkby Stephen agent admitted, in a letter to John Flower, the clerk of the Sedbergh Trust, that the latter had little to gain from the proposed amalgamation, 'as they appear to be paying their interest in full and gradually discharging the principal sums owing on mortgage', whereas 'the advantage to the Kirkby Stephen creditors would be great without it being any considerable hardship upon the inhabitants'.[97] James McAdam favoured this amalgamation and concluded that 'the expense incurred is but a trifle compared to the advantage likely to accrue to the mortgagees since the expense of separate management will be saved if the Trust is united'.[98] The Sedbergh Trust rejected this proposition on the grounds that 'Our Debt will be all paid off in ten years—the Sedbergh Trust is the most prosperous in

[94] See Appendix E for further details.
[95] C.R.O., Carlisle–Brampton Trust Minutes (1828–63).
[96] *Parl. Papers*, 1839, IX, p. 416.
[97] K.R.O., Kirkby Stephen–Hawes Trust, Misc. correspondence, Browne & Son to John Flower, 9 March 1852.
[98] Ibid., James McAdam to John Flower, 2 December 1851.

England and will not improve itself by a union with Hawes'.[99]
The Ambleside Trust, significantly another wealthy organisation,
shared these views and held a meeting on 25 February 1836,
'for the purpose of taking into consideration the provisions of a
Bill now before the House of Commons for consolidating the
Turnpike Trusts in Great Britain and of the necessity and
propriety of petitioning the House that the said Bill may not
pass into Law'.[100]

The Bill which gave such concern to the Ambleside Trustees
did not pass into law, and in this respect it shared the same fate
as the recommendations of the Select Committees of 1830 and
1840. We have already noted the comprehensive proposals of the
1840 Committee, but it is also worth looking at the recommendations of the 1830 'Select Committee on Northern Roads'[101] in
view of its particular relevance for the Cumbrian area. This
committee was set up in response to complaints by mail coach
contractors regarding the condition of the roads between Carlisle
and Glasgow and Edinburgh respectively. The Committee's
report concluded that 'the improvement of these roads might be
best accomplished by a Board of Commissioners constituted in a
similar manner and invested with similar powers to those of the
Commission for the improvement of the roads between London
and Holyhead'.[102] It was felt that a commission of this kind would
be in a good position to advise the local road authorities, 'thus
assisting the Trustees of the several roads gradually to adopt,
under the authority of their own Acts, a more perfect and a
more economical system of road management than at present
prevails'.[103] I have found no evidence to suggest that any such
commission was set up following these proposals.

It is unlikely that successive governments were opposed to the
principle of Trust consolidation, but it is clear that they preferred
the initiative to come from the locality rather than from Whitehall.
This is in keeping with official policy towards road transport in
general during the first half of the nineteenth century, but this
is not to say that the State's role was altogether insignificant or
passive during these years. For instance, governments were
prepared on occasions to make grants or loans available to
individual road and bridge authorities.

[99] Ibid., John Flower to Fawcett, 19 October 1852—No accounts appear
to have survived for the Sedbergh Trust in these years, but the main purpose
of such a statement was probably rhetorical.
[100] K.R.O., Ambleside Trust Minutes, 25 February 1836.
[101] *Parl. Papers*, 1830, X.   [102] Ibid., X, p. 193.   [103] Ibid.

State grants were given very selectively within Cumbria, the only roads to be so favoured being the Military Road and certain sections of the roads leading from Carlisle in the direction of Glasgow and Portpatrick, respectively. The Military Road was built in the aftermath of the 1745 Jacobite rebellion and, as such, reflects the concern of the Government of that time to promote the stability and economic recovery of the Border area. The Carlisle–Portpatrick road was surveyed for the Government by Rennie and Telford in 1808 and again in 1811. Their reports were then studied by a Select Committee.[104] The Committee approved of the reports submitted by the two surveyors and recommended that three major bridges should be built along this line of road: one over the river Sark; a second one over the Esk at Garistown; and finally a new bridge to replace the existing one over the Eden at Carlisle. The Government accepted that there was a need for these bridges, and by 1821 a total of £35,000 had been advanced by the Exchequer to meet the costs of their construction.[105] The road between Carlisle and Glasgow also required a great deal spending on it in the opinion of Telford who had surveyed extensive sections of this route in the course of his northern travels during this period. Telford considered that improvements costing at least £76,000 would be necessary if the road was to satisfy the requirements of the mail service and travellers generally in this area.[106] The Government promptly advanced £50,000 to be divided amongst the various authorities along this line of road.[107]

It would seem that in making these particular grants, successive governments were influenced primarily by a concern for mail communications with both Scotland and Ireland, whilst the need to facilitate the passage of troops to Ireland via Portpatrick when necessary, was a considerable factor in prompting government interest in the Carlisle–Portpatrick road. It is worth remembering also that this repair work was being undertaken contemporaneously with the more spectacular improvements carried out on the Welsh section of the London to Holyhead route under Telford's direction. In this instance also the Government was prepared to subsidise road building in order to improve communications with the Irish ports.

The roads to Holyhead, Portpatrick and Glasgow were of

---

104 *Parl. Papers* 1810–11, **III**, p. 789.
105 C.R.O., Sales and Conveyances of Land Adjoining Turnpike Trusts.
106 *Parl. Papers*, 1814–15, **III**, pp. 331 et seq.
107 C.R.O., Sales and Conveyances of Land Adjoining Turnpike Trusts.

special concern to the Government, but most other road and bridge authorities could not expect state aid on this scale. It was more usual for state assistance to be given in the form of Exchequer loans. The Exchequer Bill Loan Commission was established in 1817 to provide credit facilities for public works schemes which, it was hoped, would afford 'Employment for the labouring classes of the community.'[108] These loans were only made available under certain conditions: the project concerned must be approved by the Government; the repayment of the Exchequer loan must take precedence over any other debts which the organisation had contracted; and, finally, the Trustees were often required to give their personal bonds that the money would be repaid at the specified rate. Despite these stringent conditions a good many road and bridge authorities contracted Exchequer loans, and by 1833 in England and Wales 109 Trusts had borrowed a total of £401,850.[109] The Longtown Trust was quick to take advantage of this facility and borrowed a total of £500 from the Exchequer in 1817,[110] the year in which the Loan Commission was first established. However, this example was not followed by other Cumbrian Trusts and I have only been able to trace one further instance of an Exchequer loan being made available within Cumbria. This was during the 1820s at a time when the Westmorland Quarter Sessions was faced with unusually heavy expense on account of flood damage to several of the bridges over the river Eden. On this occasion, a government loan of £7,000 was most timely.[111]

The majority of state grants and loans appears to have been made during the first three decades of the nineteenth century. After about 1830, successive governments were more concerned with scrutinising Trust finances and administration, and Trust officials were now required to communicate more frequently with the Home Office. For instance, after 1833 Trust clerks were obliged to submit copies of their Annual Accounts to Whitehall, thus giving the Government a continuous record of Trust income and expenditure after that date.[112] Trust officials were also obliged to fill in questionnaires from time to time on selected aspects of turnpike administration. However, the main instrument of enquiry, in this as in other fields, was the Select

108 57G3, c. 34.   109 *Parl. Papers*, 1833, **XV**, p. 409.
110 Ibid.   111 Parsons & White, p. 116.

112 Unfortunately, these Returns have not survived amongst the Home Office papers, and hence there is no way of knowing whether or not most Trusts complied with this particular requirement.

Committee. Forty-one such Committees were set up to review various aspects of road building and administration during the first half of the nineteenth century.

Thus by about 1850, the Government was much more comprehensively informed about road transport than at any previous period. It is significant also that the bulk of these enquiries took place during the period of early railway expansion. The information gained by successive governments during this period may not have been put to immediate use, but it did provide a basis for working out the mechanics and timing of Trust dissolution during the third quarter of the nineteenth century.[113]

This latter period saw the state exercising greater control over road administration, but at no time did governments take positive steps to enforce Trust amalgamation. There is little doubt that such a policy would have been in the interests of most Trusts and road users. Larger Trusts would have been able to economise upon some of their administrative expenses and to employ more highly paid surveyors. These surveyors in turn would be responsible for larger areas of road and this would tend to produce more uniform conditions of road maintenance along through routes. This criticism can be extended to road and bridge administration as a whole both in Cumbria and elsewhere during the greater part of the nineteenth century. Units of administration were too small and there was not enough co-ordination between them as a rule. Bridge and road repair were quite separate responsibilities. Some roads were maintained by parishes some by Trusts, and the Trusts themselves rarely administered more than about 25 miles of main road in any one direction.

However, in spite of these deficiencies, significant administrative developments had taken place both nationally and within Cumbria. In particular, the introduction of a growing number of salaried and more specialised officials by county, Trust and parish to supervise road and bridge building was of great importance. It suggests that during the nineteenth century the various authorities, whilst emphasising their separatism, were beginning to share a common concern for the state of their road communications.

[113] See Chapter 6.

Chapter 3

ROAD TRANSPORT DEVELOPMENTS IN THE PRE-RAILWAY PERIOD

Improved transport facilities were of the utmost importance in initiating and accelerating the widespread economic and social changes which took place in England and Wales during the nineteenth century. Agriculture became more intensive and an increasing proportion of land was now under cultivation, largely as a result of the increased momentum of the enclosure movement towards the end of the eighteenth century. Also, a considerable proportion of this enclosed land was converted to arable farming. Similarly, mining and industrial operations were gradually becoming more widespread and towns were growing in size and influence. These developments had their origin in the previous century and had been, to some extent at least, stimulated by road improvements during the second half of this period, but the increased pace of social and economic change during the early part of the nineteenth century revealed the need for further repairs to roads and bridges.

This was recognised by the Select Committee of 1836 which recommended that priority should be given to road construction rather than traffic regulation and that the 'mass of impolitic and vexatious restrictions which are laid upon traffic in many parts should be abandoned'.[1]

The Cumbrian authorities were not backward in promoting road improvements. An additional eleven Turnpike Trusts were inaugurated during the first three decades of the nineteenth century, and the period marked a second phase of turnpike development in Cumbria, following the original spate of Trust Acts, between 1750 and 1770. The setting up of new Trusts is significant in several respects. In the first place, it usually indicates that an increased proportion of the traffic using the road concerned was non-local and hence more likely to incur the displeasure of

[1] *Parl. Papers*, 1836, **XIX**, p. 348.

the local parishes charged with maintaining the road. The establishment of a Trust usually relieved the parishes of the greater part of this burden, and in doing so normally triggered off a greater level of expenditure on road maintenance and improvement, financed by toll payments. This increased expenditure often entailed widening and straightening sections of the existing roads and reducing the gradients of steep hills where possible. On occasion, completely new roads were built, notably by the Alston and Ulverston–Carnforth Trusts, but this was exceptional and Trust officials normally concerned themselves with improving the roads they had inherited. It is important also not to overlook the activities of older established Trusts during this period; the Carlisle–Eamont, Heron Syke, Cockermouth–Penrith, and Whitehaven Trustees all being conspicuous road improvers during the early part of the century. Also, the condition of many of the parochial highways underwent a corresponding improvement as a result of the activities of the various Enclosure Commissioners and 'improving' landlords.

This second period of road building activity probably made a greater impact upon the region than its eighteenth century counterpart had done. Techniques of road and bridge construction had improved markedly during the intervening period, and the various road authorities were now taking increasing pains to ensure that their revenues were spent judiciously and that repairs to roads and bridges should be of lasting value. During the eighteenth century, there had been numerous complaints about the unscientific construction of roads and bridges. Bailey and Culley, for instance, noted in 1793 that, whilst Cumbria had 'excellent' road making materials in its plentiful supplies of limestone, these stones were 'in almost every instance not broken small enough by one half'.[2] John Houseman made the same point when writing of Cumberland's roads in 1800. 'We find few places where they are judiciously made or kept in good repair. . . . The great errors in making roads in this county are, not breaking the stones small enough, and laying them on too thin; by which the road is never good, constantly wearing into ruts and always wanting repairs.'[3]

John Metcalfe of Knaresborough is generally considered to be the first man to take a scientific interest in road engineering.

[2] Bailey & Culley, p. 256.
[3] John Houseman, *A Topographical Description of Cumberland, Westmorland, Lancashire and part of the West Riding of Yorkshire* (1800), pp. 42, 43.

Metcalfe constructed many roads in Lancashire and Yorkshire during the second half of the eighteenth century, and Jackman considers that with him 'We have the first application of scientific principles in the construction of highways'.[4] Metcalfe laid particular emphasis upon the necessity for firm, well-drained foundations for any projected road; this to be overlaid by a smooth convex surface which would allow water to flow off both sides of the road.

The greatest names associated with road and bridge improvements, however, are Thomas Telford and John Loudon McAdam, both of whom were active in Cumbria during the early decades of the nineteenth century. Telford paid especial attention to solid foundations when constructing his roads; broken rock providing a covering for larger masses of foundation stone. In addition, he insisted that his roads should be as level as possible, and he took enormous pains to avoid steep gradients. These principles were manifested in his construction of the Carlisle–Glasgow and Holyhead roads, both of which were very great achievements by any standards. Telford was also, of course, a bridge builder of the highest class, and an emphasis upon detailed specifications was equally pronounced in this aspect of his work. However, Telford's work was costly and most Turnpike Trusts could not afford to employ him very frequently. McAdam, on the other hand, whilst also insisting upon the building of well-drained roads from carefully prepared materials, did not pay so much attention to road foundations. He maintained that the subsoil could support any weight if it was first carefully drained, and then rendered impervious by a covering of broken angular stones. McAdam's method proved cheaper and, in view of this and also because of his considerable administrative ability, he was much sought after by the various Turnpike Trusts.

The first record of any such intervention by McAdam in Cumbria occurs in 1823, when the Cockermouth–Penrith Trustees invited him to recommend them a competent surveyor to undertake certain road improvements.[5] In the following year, McAdam was personally responsible for the making of ten miles of new road between Keswick and Penrith and four miles of road between Keswick and Cockermouth.[6] By this time he was also responsible for supervising the Ambleside, Heron Syke, Milnthorpe and Carlisle–Eamont Trusts and was just beginning his extensive

---

4 Jackman, p. 268.
5 K.M., Cockermouth–Penrith Trust Minutes, 12 October 1823.
6 *Whitehaven Gazette*, 5 June 1824.

Alston operations.[7] His interest in Cumbria during this period is reflected by the fact that he had a house at Keswick from which he could supervise these various activities.[8] In view, of the range of McAdam's activities by 1824, it is probable that his interest in Cumbrian road improvements pre-dated 1823, although there is no evidence to confirm this conjecture.

McAdam's achievements at Alston have tended to overshadow his other activities in this region, but surviving detailed surveys of the Penrith–Greta Bridge Road[9] and, in particular, the Carlisle–Penrith Road in 1825,[10] illustrate his meticulous attention to detail and his continual emphasis upon the need to reduce gradients wherever possible. His achievements upon the Heron Syke Trust were equally notable, and in 1835 the *Cumberland Pacquet* noted in its editorial of 8 December that, 'We do not remember to have seen a stronger proof of the excellence of the system of road making practised by Mr McAdam than the following paragraph furnishes—The Heron Syke Road, previous to coming under Mr McAdam's care cost an average of £37 a year, now costs no more than ⅓ of that sum; and in addition to this, there is the great superiority of the road to be taken into account'.[11] One can also discern McAdam's influence at work in the increasing care which was now being taken when appointing Trust officials.

Telford's only direct intervention in Cumberland was in the building of the Carlisle–Glasgow and Carlisle–Portpatrick Roads, but the extent of his influence must have been considerable in helping to promote a more scientific approach to road and bridge building. The surveyor of the Brough–Bowes Trust openly acknowledged his debt to Telford in 1835, when surveying a proposed deviation to the road at Maiden Castle. 'It will be necessary to use every precaution to obtain a firm and sound foundation. To effect this, the proper mode is to lay a foundation of rough pavement of the kind always used by Mr Telford, for which purpose the coarse sandstone scattered along the whole line is very well suited.[12] It is more difficult to assess Telford's influence on bridge building in Cumbria. However, bridge

---

[7] See Appendix E.   [8] *Whitehaven Gazette*, 5 June 1824.

[9] Heelis' Solicitors Office, Appleby, Plan of the Turnpike Road from Penrith to Greta Bridge (1824).

[10] C.R.O., Lowther MSS, Plan of Improvements to the Penrith–Carlisle Turnpike Road, 1825.

[11] *Cumberland Pacquet*, 8 December 1835.

[12] Heelis' Solicitors Office, Appleby, 'Report on the proposed deviation from the Brough and Bowes Turnpike Road at Maiden Castle' (May 1835).

construction undoubtedly became an important item of county expenditure during the nineteenth century; narrow wooden bridges being gradually replaced by wider stone built structures. In 1795, the Court of Kings Bench made a ruling that in future all bridges should be made sufficiently wide to permit the passage of carriages, and this initiative was soon taken up by the county authorities of both Cumberland and Westmorland during the early decades of the nineteenth century. In 1810, Netherhall Bridge over the river Ellen near Maryport, was rebuilt after having been severely damaged by a flood in the previous year.[13] Two years later, work was begun on a new bridge over the Eden under the supervision of Telford. This bridge was designed by Robert Smirke and the whole operation was estimated to cost £9,126.[14]

Bridge building was also a prominent activity in Westmorland during this period; 'a good bridge' being built over the Eamont near Brougham Castle in 1813, whilst in 1815 the *Westmorland Advertiser* announced the completion 'of that long wanted accommodation, a carriage bridge over the River Eden, at Blandswath between Kirkby Stephen and Appleby'.[15]

Bridge repairs were equally brisk in both counties during the 1820s. Between 1820 and 1829 new bridges were built over the rivers Caldew and Petteril at Carlisle.[16] Kendal was a second centre of bridge construction at this time; Millers Close Bridge which had stood since 1743 was rebuilt upon a large scale in 1818,[17] and Nether Bridge was enlarged in 1822.[18] Parsons and White record that the Carlisle bridge building operations 'rank amongst the most useful improvements that have been effected during the present century for the accommodation of the public'.[19]

There were also important bridge improvements in West Cumberland at this time; in 1822 a new bridge was built over the Derwent at Cockermouth at a cost of £3,000[20] and in 1828 a 160 foot long bridge costing £2,600 was built over the River Cocker.[21] These improvements culminated in the completion of

13 C.R.O., Senhouse MSS, Letter from S. Saul to Joseph Barriskill (n.d.).
14 *Parl. Papers*, 1815, **III**, p. 350.
15 *Westmorland Advertiser*, 18 February 1815.
16 Parsons & White, p. 148.
17 J. F. Curwen, *Kirkbie Kendall* (1900), p. 380.
18 Ibid., p. 18.
19 Parsons & White, p. 148.
20 Whellan, *History of Cumberland and Westmorland* (1860), p. 301.
21 Parsons & White, p. 184.

another new bridge over the Derwent at Workington. This latter erection cost a total of £3,797.[22]

The late 1820s and the 1830s marked a particularly active period of bridge building. Between 1827 and 1833 the county of Cumberland spent an average of £3,082 a year upon bridge repair,[23] whilst Westmorland was even more extravagant between 1838 and 1841, spending an average of £5,854 a year on its county bridges during this period.[24] Finally, in 1850, the investigating committee into county expenditure gave its official approval to the heavy bridge expenses of the preceding decades, and commended the work of the Cumberland bridgemaster in effecting such a substantial improvement in bridge conditions.[25]

These roads and bridge improvements received considerable acclaim from contemporaries. J. Briggs, writing of Westmorland in the 1820s, noted that 'it was only of comparatively recent date that there was a good road in Westmorland. Now this County is only surpassed by few'. He drew particular attention to the Heron Syke improvements and also noted that 'The new Ulverston road is scarcely less surprising. Carriages and the heaviest waggons now pass safely over 4 or 5 miles of morass where, a few years ago, except in very dry weather, the human foot could not tread with security. The excellence of the roads in this county is not attributable to the materials alone, but to a superior method of constructing them.'[26]

Nevertheless, in considering these improvements, one must not overestimate the influence of Telford and McAdam. In the first place, both surveyors had many commitments all over the country and, in consequence, they were frequently unable to superintend road and bridge building operations because of their other duties. It appears, in fact, that McAdam usually confined himself to surveying a road at the request of the local Trust and was then content to delegate his authority to others who were in turn responsible for implementing his proposals. Thus 'sub-surveyors' were appointed under him, as at Whitehaven.

In addition, neither Telford nor McAdam was immune from criticism. Telford's standards were high but his services were costly. McAdam also had somewhat mixed relations with various

[22] K.R.O., Westmorland County Stock Accounts, 1822.

[23] C.R.O., Cumberland County Stock Accounts (1827–33).

[24] K.R.O., Westmorland County Stock Accounts (1838–41).

[25] C.R.O., Hodgson MSS, Q.S. Committee Report on Salaries and Expenditure of the County of Cumberland, 1850.

[26] J. Briggs, *Letters from the Lakes* (1825), p. 251.

interests within Cumbria. For instance, the Greenwich Hospital Commissioners were constantly complaining that he exceeded his estimates for road building operations. Also, farmers sometimes alleged that their horses would be 'lamed beyond recovery' by the sharp stones used upon his roads. Similarly, certain citizens of Kendal, writing to the *Westmorland Gazette* of 27 January 1827, pronounced themselves 'disgusted with McAdam's road making and wish it had been tried on Shap Fell instead of Strickland Gate Kendal'.[27] Also, improvements which pleased road users were not necessarily popular with pedestrians and householders. One Lancashire observer, writing in 1809, had a good deal to say upon this latter point. She acknowledged that sections of McAdam's roads in the Liverpool area were 'better for carriages and easier for draught horses', but she also maintained that they had marked disadvantages.

'For human beings in dry weather they are almost beyond endurance; for they are one continual cloud of dust, blinding to the eyes, filling the nostrils, going down the mouth and throat by quantities to suffocation and completely ruinous to all decent clothing. Houses by the road are inundated with dust, and all cleanliness destroyed and useless. The fields are so covered on each side, according as the wind blows, that they are of much less value an acre than those more distant from it.'[28]

Furthermore, some of the ideas of the two surveyors were being used by other authorities at an earlier date. There are, for instance, detailed bridge specifications for the first decade of the century, and early surveys such as that for the Ellenhall Bridge in 1803,[29] reveal a considerable knowledge of bridge construction, a sense of detail and a marked emphasis upon deep foundations. Similarly, the Enclosure Commissioners displayed quite advanced ideas on road construction as subsequent discussion will show.

The Enclosure Commission was one of several bodies which took a keen interest in road building in Cumbria during the first half of the nineteenth century. Mining and industrial magnates showed a corresponding concern for good roads, and collectively these various economic interests played a major part in the improvement of the region's road transport network during this

[27] *Westmorland Gazette*, 27 January 1827.
[28] R. J. A. Berry, 'Ellen Weeton, 1776–1850', *Historical Society of Lancashire and Cheshire* (1954).
[29] C.R.O., Q.S.R. Cumberland Q.S. Petition Rolls, July 1807.

period. In view of this, it is worth looking more closely at these economic activities.

Agricultural developments were particularly marked during the early decades of the nineteenth century. The war-time inflation of corn prices encouraged landowners to farm along more commercial lines, and the total corn acreage of Cumberland and Westmorland was approximately doubled between 1792 and 1814.[30] There was a corresponding increase in the acreage of land enclosed during this period: this rose in Cumberland from a total of 470,000 acres in 1794[31] to 670,000 acres by 1815.[32] Subsequently, enclosure proceeded at a slower rate; a further 80,000 acres being enclosed between 1815 and 1850.[33] The average size of these parliamentary enclosures was about 1,500 acres, but some of them were much more extensive. For instance, the Inglewood Forest enclosures embraced a total area of 28,000 acres.[34] There were a similar number of private enclosure agreements during this period although they affected smaller areas and perhaps accounted for about one third of the total acreage enclosed in Cumbria.

Thus a substantial proportion of Cumbrian wasteland was reclaimed, and the employment of improved techniques both in stock-rearing and in arable cultivation was thereby facilitated. The influence of the work of John Christian Curwen at Schoose Farm has already been mentioned in this context, and an increasing number of the more influential landowners began to adopt his practices during the early part of the nineteenth century. Sir James Graham was perhaps the most notable 'improving' landlord. He succeeded to a 24,000 acre estate at Netherby in 1824, and subsequently spent about £2,000 a year for the next twenty-five years in draining his lands. At the end of this period there were forty-two tileries in the Netherby region for land drainage

[30] D. Berry, 'The Social and Economic Development and Organisation of the Lake District 1750–1814' (unpublished M.A. Thesis, Univ. Manchester), p. 349.   [31] Bailey & Culley, p. 202.

[32] T. H. Bainbridge, 'Some Factors in the Development of Cumbrian Agriculture during the Nineteenth Century', C.W.T., XLIV (1943), p. 82.

[33] W. E. Tate, 'A Handlist of English Enclosure Awards', C.W.T., XLIII (1943), 175–98: The corresponding enclosure figures for Westmorland were 150,000 in 1794 (D. Berry as cited in n.30, 292). 210,000 acres in 1815 and 280,000 acres by 1850 (ibid.). The area of enclosed land in Furness and Cartmel increased from 50,000 acres in 1794 to approximately 85,000 acres by 1850 (ibid.).

[34] W. E. Tate, 'A Handlist of English Enclosure Awards', C.W.T., XLIII (1943), p. 189.

purposes.[35] Graham's example in Cumberland was followed by that of Sir William Lowther in Westmorland. Lowther's activities were concentrated upon the Shap Fell region where large areas of land were drained and enclosed; tileries and lime kilns being established at Lowther and Wetheriggs.[36] Other leading agriculturalists in these two counties included the Senhouse family and Lord Muncaster. These extensive drainage operations made possible the subsequent employment of new fertilisers such as guano, nitrate of soda and superphosphate. In 1861 the Kendal Farmers Club was formed, one of its avowed objectives being 'the analysing of artificial manures'.[37] There was a parallel development also in the manufacture of agricultural machinery, and it was estimated that by 1849 there were 306 threshing machines being used in West Cumberland,[38] whereas it is probably fair to assume that there were no such machines in existence at the beginning of the century, since they are not referred to by Bailey and Culley in their Survey of 1794. Seed drills were also distributed rather more widely by this time, and almost every parish had its plough maker.

Thus it became increasingly important that, as commercial agriculture developed, farmers should have readier access to neighbouring markets and also adequate facilities for exporting their produce from the area. It was natural therefore that they should show an interest in road improvements. In fact, the Glamorgan Agricultural Society even went so far as to offer premiums of £1 1s to the best and most active Highway surveyor in each 'hundred' of their county. These prizes were first offered in 1778 and were subsequently donated annually for at least the next forty years.[39] This policy of encouraging road improvements in the interests of agriculture received official support from the Government when the Board of Agriculture was set up in 1793. The Board was quick to criticise contemporary methods of road construction, and emphasised the need for improved standards to facilitate the marketing of agricultural produce and the transport of fertilisers. It was hoped that the more progressive farmers together with the Enclosure Commissioners in each

---

[35] T. H. Bainbridge, 'Some Factors in the Development of Cumbrian Agriculture, especially during the Nineteenth Century', C.W.T., XL (1945), pp. 84–5.

[36] Ibid., p. 85.   [37] Ibid., p. 87.   [38] Ibid.

[39] D. E. Fraser, 'The Development of the Road System in Glamorgan up to 1844, with special reference to Turnpike Roads' (M.A. Thesis, Univ. Wales, 1940), p. 218.

locality would use their resources and influence to bring about higher standards of road construction.

On the whole, these expectations were fulfilled in Cumbria during this period, and the major Cumbrian landlords, in addition to being prominent mortgagees of Turnpike Trusts, took an active interest in road and bridge improvements in general. Sir James Graham and John Christian Curwen, both advanced agriculturalists, were also, hardly surprisingly, notable advocates of improved conditions of road transport. As early as 1806, the Editor of the *Carlisle Journal* commended their efforts in this field and went on to say that the road and bridge improvements which they had promoted were 'now going ahead with great spirit. The plan of the new bridge at Carlisle is actually determined on and the dangerous hill at Eamont Bridge has been reduced and made perfectly easy and commodious for travellers, at a great expense principally advanced by Lord Lowther'.[40] The Lowthers also displayed a conspicuous interest in the Cockermouth–Penrith Turnpike road. We have already noted the size of their loan to this particular Trust, but it appears that in addition they took a detailed interest in the way in which their money was utilised. The family's labours in this respect were acknowledged by the Penrith solicitor, William Bleaymire, in front of the Select Committee of 1856. Bleaymire considered the present Lord Lonsdale to be 'a great improver of roads and he brought Mr McAdam down and he was very anxious about this road and took a great interest in getting it made'.[41] Members of the Senhouse family also were concerned in road and bridge improvements in the Maryport area, and offered in 1858 to make a 'considerable improvement to Maryport Bridge'.[42] A landlord such as Sir James Graham was particularly useful to the neighbouring Turnpike Trusts since, by virtue of his position in the House of Commons, he was thereby in a position to ease the passage of Turnpike Renewal Bills through Parliament. He was instrumental, for instance, in guiding the Carlisle–Eamont Trust Renewal Bill through both Houses with the minimum of delay in 1808.[43]

---

[40] *Carlisle Journal*, 10 May 1806.

[41] C.R.O., Bleaymire and Shepherd Collection, Miscellaneous Papers relating to the Cockermouth–Penrith Trust Renewal Bill of 1856.

[42] C.R.O., AH6/26 Cumberland County Surveyors Reports (1857–80), June 1858.

[43] C.R.O., Carlisle–Eamont Trust, Miscellaneous Papers relating to Trust Renewal Bill, 1808.

The Enclosure Commissioners were in an especially good position to influence contemporary roadmaking, as their work frequently necessitated the rebuilding of sections of road to correspond with the changing alignment of individual fields. The evidence suggests that the Enclosure Commissioners within Cumbria made full use of their opportunities to promote improved road conditions.

William Dickinson, writing of the extensive enclosures in East Cumberland between 1790 and 1820, noted that

'the first great advantage felt to follow these enclosures was the substitution of stone-made roads for the miry and dangerous tracks over the Commons. These gave facility of transit for lime and for the abundant crops produced on the fresh soils. They also afforded freer and easier access to markets, and gradually opened out resources and communications of which the inhabitants had no previous idea and of which they began to feel the benefits.'[44]

The Inglewood Enclosure Commissioners in this region paid particular attention to road improvements and constructed a total of sixty-six public carriage roads.[45] Cartmel Enclosure Awards contain similarly extensive evidence of road building operations, and their activities were of particular significance in view of the marked isolation of this region. The Cartmel enclosure involved about 9,000 acres of land and the appropriate Act of 1796 provided for the construction of twenty-four public highways linking Grange, Newton, Newby Bridge, Witherslack, Crosthwaite, Bigland and Holker. In addition, a total of seventy-nine 'private carriage ways' were constructed by the authority of the Commissioners. Stockdale was greatly impressed by their achievement. 'Under the Enclosure Act too, there were formed and made many excellent roads covered throughout with small broken stones in the place of ruinous old clog-wheel cart and pack horse tracks; many wide and useful bridges built where previously there were merely unsafe fords and slippery stepping stones.'[46]

Other bodies which effected notable road improvements included the Crosthwaite and Hutton Roof Enclosure Commissioners; the former completing a total of fifteen public highways in 1848[47] whilst the latter authority had made a number of

44 W. Dickinson, *Agriculture of East Cumberland* (1853), p. 10.
45 C.R.O., RE/135, Inglewood Forest Enclosure Award.
46 J. Stockdale, *Annals of Cartmel* (1870), p. 326.
47 C.R.O., Cumberland Q.S. Petition Rolls, Mich. 1848.

road diversions totalling 4,194 yards of new road by 1824.[48] These roads were each built 30 ft wide and, on occasions, even greater widths were stipulated. For instance, the Stapleton Enclosure Award of 1801 authorised the Commission 'to build carriageways through the enclosed lands when they think fit but each road must be at least forty feet wide between the ditches and the fences'. The Dalston Enclosure Commissioners also insisted on their road being at least 40 ft wide. In 1807 they authorised the construction of twenty-four new stretches of highway, two of which measured 66 ft in width'[49] Such measurements were exceptional, but most Commissioners insisted upon an average road width of at least 30 ft, and as such, their roads were substantially more commodious than any which had hitherto been constructed by the parochial authorities; the latter did not usually exceed 15 ft in width at the beginning of the century.

Most of these new roads were also built as straight as possible and great care was usually taken in their construction. The Cartmel Enclosure Commission, for instance, gave detailed instructions to their appointed surveyor regarding the surface of their projected highways. The new road leading over Bank Moor was to be

'regularly formed and covered with stones not less than twelve feet wide and nine inches thick in the middle or crown of the road, and five inches at the hem or skirt, exclusive of a covering of three inches thick in its whole breadth of good samel or small gravelly substance, and the stones to be well broken and none of them to exceed the size of a goose's egg. After the road shall be formed, the same shall be viewed by James Stockdale Esq. and Mr John Gibson before any stones are permitted to be broken upon it, and the like view to be had after the stones are broken and before any gravel or covering be laid thereon.'[50]

Similarly, the Dalston Enclosure Commissioners emphasised the importance of providing access to road making materials. 'The said Commissioners shall set out and appropriate any other part or parts of the said Moors, Commons and Waste Grounds for the getting of sand, gravel and other materials, for making and repairing such public and private roads, as shall be set out,

[48] K.R.O., Westmorland Q.S. Petition Rolls, July 1823.
[49] C.R.O., RE/5/77, Dalston Enclosure Award, 1803.
[50] J. Stockdale, op. cit., p. 384.

appointed or continued within the said manor in pursuance of this Act.' Thus the Commissioners in these instances anticipated the work of McAdam in their actual road surface specifications and in their meticulous attention to details.

In addition to building new roads and improving existing ones, many of the enclosure authorities also concerned themselves with the future maintenance of these improved highways. They usually distinguished two kinds of roads: 'public' and 'private' carriageways, the former being subsequently the responsibility of the township through which they ran, whilst the latter were to be maintained by the landowner whose grounds adjoined them. In practice, however, the enclosure authorities were sometimes prepared to assist those responsible in their future maintenance work. For instance, the Cartmel Commissioners stated their intention of helping to repair highways other than those directly related to their own enclosures; 'if there shall be any overplus remaining of the money arising from the sale of such part of the Commons or waste grounds hereinbefore directed to be sold for the purpose aforesaid, the same shall be applied towards the repair of the public roads of the parish'.[51] They were also prepared to advance money on occasions to finance future parochial road repairs.

The work of the various enclosure authorities was a very important factor in the gradual improvement of parish roads. Dickinson, writing in 1853, acknowledged that 'roads both public and private are very much improved and probably require less improvement now than any other department concerned with agriculture'.[52]

However, not all new roads were built over common land and, although the Cumbrian enclosures almost certainly gave rise to less social dislocation than did their counterparts in the more intensively cultivated arable areas of central England, they did disrupt farming activities to some extent. Consequently, both the Enclosure Commissioners and the Turnpike Trusts frequently tried to ensure that their road building activities did not unduly antagonise local agricultural interests. For instance, where a diverted turnpike encroached upon enclosed land, some Trusts undertook to keep all appertaining walls and fences in repair for three years dating from their erection, or alternatively, to add an appropriate sum to the compensation which was paid to the owner of the land concerned.

Three different categories of land were usually recognised

51 J. Stockdale, op. cit., p. 382.
52 W. Dickinson, *Essay on the Farming of Cumberland* (1853), pp. 95–6.

when any such encroachment was envisaged. The first was 'Common Land', in which case neither permission nor compensation was necessary in the event of a road encroachment. The second category, 'Private Land', involved giving notice to the owner of the authority's intentions, depositing a plan of the proposed new road with the Clerk of the Peace, and also the payment of compensation to the affected landowner. The third category of land; orchards, gardens and immediate household property, was recognised to be immune from interference unless the owner agreed to accept the compensation offered. These rates of compensation varied according to the nature of the land encroached upon, and also, no doubt, according to the local importance of the landlord himself, A sum of £75 per acre seems to have been a fairly representative rate, but some landlords got considerably more than this. For instance, the Ambleside Trust paid Mr Easthead at the rate of £500 per acre when his land was encroached upon in the course of the Trust's widening of the Birthwaite road in 1855.[53] It was also common for a deprived landlord to be allowed the land of the stopped-up road as an alternative to a money compensation. Some landowners wanted the best of both worlds. James Cleminson only agreed to the encroachment of the new highway upon his land in the township of Thwaite 'in consideration of the old Highway being given to and vested in me and also in consideration of the sum or at the rate of £150 per acre for so much of the land as shall be used for the purpose of the intended new highway'.[54]

Many landlords no doubt struck a hard bargain where possible, but it must be remembered that the disruption to their farming pattern was often quite considerable and cannot always be measured simply in terms of the land annexed for the building of the new road. The road might split a field and leave two sections of an inconvenient size for cultivation, or alternatively cut a section of their land off from a good water supply. Thus, William Thompson demanded an 'adequate recompense' from the Carlisle–Eamont Trust for the loss of 'the most valuable part of my field situated near Milestone Course'. He went on to say that this land contained 'a valuable spring of water'.[55] Similarly, Mary Simpson claimed that the same Penrith road improvements reduced the value of her land by one third on account of 'the

[53] K.R.O., Ambleside Trust Minutes, 15 December 1855.
[54] C.R.O., Cumberland Q.S. Petition Rolls, Midsummer 1825.
[55] C.R.O., Carlisle–Eamont Trust, Misc. Papers, Letter William Thompson to Trust, 10 July 1830.

new line of road passing through the field in such an oblique direction and cutting off two small parcels on each side of an open ditch and rendering it very difficult to plough and manage on account of its mangled form'. She claimed £200 per acre compensation for the loss of this land.[56]

However, to prevent unduly prolonged delays in the construction of new stretches of Trust road, it was agreed that, in the event of a landowner continuing to refuse the Trust's offer of compensation, the question would be examined by a Jury of 'twelve indifferent men' who had power to authorise his acceptance of the Trust's offer. At the same time, it was understood that the Trust should not begin any road deviation until the appropriate compensation had been paid. Similarly, the timing of the deviation might be further delayed on occasions so as not to disrupt unduly the landlord's farming activities. Thus the Ambleside Trust agreed on 28 March 1849, 'that the deviation on the south side of the Turnpike Road at Crookshaws be postponed until October next in consequence of the damage that would be done to the farmer's crop on the ground'.[57] There were also careful legalities to be complied with when any highway was 'stopped-up' in order to ensure that the community concerned should receive adequate notice of any impending action. A notice of the proposed stoppage was affixed to the roadside at each end of the highway in question and also to the door of the nearest parish church. The same notice also appeared in the local newspaper for four successive weeks. Similarly, two Justices were to view the highway and they could authorise its continuance if they felt it still to be necessary to the community concerned.

Thus, although the Turnpike Trustees, the Enclosure Commissioners and other local authorities had considerable powers in building new stretches of road, they still had to respect the rights of the local agricultural interests. It is also worth bearing in mind that not all landowners were concerned to promote or even encourage road improvements. 'Improving' road authorities were looked upon by many with disfavour as a source of high tolls and heavy rates generally. Houseman, writing in 1800, laments the lack of interest shown by many of the landed classes in road improvements.

---

[56] C.R.O. Carlisle-Eamont Trust, Misc. Papers, Letter Mary Simpson to Trust (n.d. but probably 1829 or 1830): The promoters of railway lines often had similar disagreements with neighbouring landlords over the severance of estates into allegedly uneconomic units (cf. Jackman, p. 498).

[57] K.R.O., Ambleside Trust Minutes, 28 March 1849.

'We find few places where they (roads) are judiciously made or kept in good repair. This neglect seems chiefly occasioned by the non-residence of the principal noblemen and gentlemen of landed property in the county, who, both for their own advantage and the benefit of the public, ought to be particularly careful that the surveyors of the highways punctually perform their duty.'[58] Jollie reiterated this complaint in 1811 although he also observed that 'In some places, however, the neighbouring gentlemen have exerted themselves in procuring good roads'.[59] McAdam also encountered 'considerable delay' in 1826 in completing the road from Ephill into the Hexham road near Haydon Bridge 'by a difficulty in obtaining consent for passing through the lands at Threapwood'.[60] Even the affluent Ambleside Trust was obliged, as a result of local opposition, to alter the alignment of a section of its road between Windermere Railway Station and Dunmail Raise in 1872.[61] However, the resistance of individual landlords to road diversions, whilst often retarding a particular improvement and perhaps altering the ultimate alignment of a section of road, was not of any great long-term significance in view of the considerable compulsory purchasing powers of the Turnpike Trusts, and the scope which extensive waste land afforded the Enclosure Commissioners for road building.

The agricultural interests did not by any means completely dominate the Cumbrian economy, and the proprietors of the region's mineral resources also had much to gain by promoting better road conditions. Mineral production increased considerably in West Cumberland during the first half of the nineteenth century. The tonnage of coal exported rose from 256,036 tons in 1819 to 530,650 tons by 1849.[62] Coal production increased particularly rapidly in the Whitehaven region at the beginning of the century: exports from the port amounted to 90,628 tons in 1802 but had risen to 153,728 tons by the end of the following year.[63] Many new pits were sunk during the war period, the most important of which, the 'William' Pit near Bransty, was completed in 1812.[64] This was considered to be one of the best

[58] J. Houseman, op. cit., p. 42.

[59] Jollie, *Cumberland Guide and Directory* (1811), p. 48.

[60] P.R.O., ADM/66/92, Greenwich Hospital (Northern Estates) Out Letters (1825–8), Letter from J. L. McAdam to Commission in London, 12 October 1826.   [61] K.R.O., Ambleside Trust Minutes, 3 October 1872.

[62] Oliver Wood, 'Development of the Coal, Iron and Shipbuilding Industries of West Cumberland, 1750–1914' (Unpublished Thesis for Degree of Ph.D. University of London, 1952), pp. 97–123.   [63] Ibid.

[64] Ibid.

equipped collieries in the kingdom. A fine pumping engine was introduced at the pit in 1810 and a high-pressure winding engine replaced the original machine in 1850.[65]

The Napoleonic Wars also stimulated iron mining: the Crowgarth mine at Cleator having an annual output of 20,000 tons of ore between 1800 and 1810.[66] Production declined at the end of the war, but the output increased again during the late 1840s when many old mines, including that at Crowgarth, were re-opened to supply the embryonic iron-smelting industry.[67] By 1849 the total production of haematite ore in Cumberland amounted to 100,000 tons, a fifth of the total United Kingdom output.[68] Ore shipments from Whitehaven rose particularly steeply during this period: from 84,960 tons in 1852 to 145,526 tons by 1854.[69]

In order to accommodate the increased shipping necessary to handle this mounting export trade, there were considerable harbour improvements at Whitehaven between 1824 and 1830. As a result of these developments, the number of vessels registered at the port increased from 181 with a tonnage of 22,220 in 1822, to 267 ships with an aggregate tonnage of 42,000 by 1846.[70] There were similar harbour improvements at Maryport in the years after 1833, when the Senhouse monopoly of the port's management was broken and a more progressive policy was adopted.[71] Developments in Furness were equally notable at this time, and in 1839 H. W. Schneider embarked upon a costly research programme into methods of haematite raising in the Dalton area.[72] Elsewhere in Cumbria, however, mining was, on the whole, a declining activity. Lead was still the most important deposit after coal and iron ore, but the productivity of the Alston mines was decreasing in the early nineteenth century.[73]

[65] Isaac Fletcher, 'The Archaeology of the West Cumberland Coal Trade', C.W.T. (O.S.), III, (1876–7), p. 293.

[66] Oliver Wood, 'Development of the Coal, Iron and Shipbuilding Industries of West Cumberland, 1750–1914' (unpublished Ph.D. thesis, Univ. London, 1952), p. 163.   [67] Ibid., pp. 163–95.

[68] Ibid., p. 169.   [69] Whellan, op. cit., p. 442.

[70] Ibid., p. 443.

[71] Oliver Wood 'Development of the Coal, Iron and Shipbuilding Industries of West Cumberland, 1750–1914' (unpublished Ph.D. thesis, Univ. London, 1952), pp. 178–95.

[72] J. D. Marshall, *Furness and the Industrial Revolution* (1958), pp. 173 et seq.

[73] Annual production only amounted to 11,496 bings in 1814 as compared to 20,000 bings in 1780 (Whellan, *History of Cumberland and Westmorland*, 1860), p. 511.

As a result, Alston was gradually losing its population which dropped from 5,244 in 1831 to 3,409 by 1851.

Although the population of the Alston area and the output of its mines was declining during this period, the local mine owners began, rather paradoxically, to show increasing concern with the state of their road communications. This had not always been the case. Thomas Sopwith, writing in 1833, recollected that 'The want of good or even of tolerable roads was for a long period the principal cause of the mining districts being so little known. About fifty years ago, scarcely a regularly formed road was to be found in them; goods were chiefly conveyed on horses or galloways, which followed the soundest tracks over the moors.'[74] Transport of food and equipment by pack-horse from Newcastle and the Vale of Eden up to the mines proved to be very slow and expensive, and the paternalistic London Lead Company, despite having a well organised carrying system, made heavy losses when selling grain to the miners at cost prices.

After the sale of their Derbyshire and Welsh leases in 1790, the London Lead Company was able to concentrate more effectively upon its northern estates and to 'embark on a period of active road building to link up their estates in Alston Moor, Weardale, Teesdale, Swaledale and Westmorland' on the instigation of the mining agents Robert and Joseph Stagg.[75] As a result of the surveys and reports of these two men, the Company was responsible for building several roads in this region between 1820 and 1830, notably those between Brough and Middleton in Teesdale and between Alston and Garrigill. Furthermoie, by 1823 they had expended over £1,500 in repairs to smaller roads and an almost equivalent sum in constructing new crossroads.[76] In fact, between 1815 and 1865 the Company spent an estimated £12,500 in direct grants to road schemes and a similar sum on their own labour on crossroads.[77]

The Company also collaborated in the unprecedently extensive road building operations of the Greenwich Hospital Commission. The Hospital had succeeded to the forfeited estates of the Earl of Derwentwater after the latter's attainder following the Jacobite Rebellion of 1715. In the early 1820s they began to build roads under the supervision of J. L. McAdam and by 1827 they had

---

[74] T. Sopwith, *An Account of the Mining Districts of Alston Moors, Weardale and Teesdale* (1833), p. 8.

[75] Arthur Raistrick, *Two Centuries of Industrial Welfare—The London (Quaker) Lead Company 1692-1905* (1938), p. 88.

[76] Ibid., p. 90.   [77] Ibid.

expended a total of £30,000 on the extension of the Alston Turnpike Trust.[78] The newly built roads extended from Hexham to Penrith and from Brampton to Alston. Despite this expense, McAdam still considered that a further sum of £6,492 would be necessary to complete the road repairs in which the Hospital was particularly interested.[79]

The London Lead Company and the Greenwich Hospital Commission were quite unequivocally concerned with the commercial and speculative advantages of their road building activities, and had little interest in improving roads which did not benefit their lead mines. Joseph Stagg had seen the commercial necessity for good roads as early as 1808.

'Though the Company must never expect to see any direct return on the money they advanced towards making and repairing roads and bridges, yet they would derive an ample return for the outlay in the reduction of the rates of carriage of lead, stores, etc.—in keeping down the rate of wages by facilitating the ample supply of provisions and necessities for the workpeople and by economizing the time of the agents, etc., in their journeys from mine to mine and from district to district.'[80]

In 1826, complaining of J. L. McAdam's expenditure on the Alston roads, the Hospital's Newcastle agents noted that 'we considered it our duty to draw Mr McAdam's attention to the road from Alston to the smelting mills and thence to Hexham and we have since constantly urged him to confine his expenditure as much as possible to that line'.[81] In a previous letter of 15 July 1826, the Greenwich agents, Wailes and Brandling, had made similar complaints against McAdam's over-expenditure and warned him that further subsidies from the Hospital would only be forthcoming 'if the operations are *strictly confined* to those parts in which the Hospital are *particularly interested*'.[82]

The Alston roads also offered a favourable field for speculation at a time when the lead industry was in recession owing to the competition of Spanish ores. Robert Brandling suggested the speculative potential of the area in 1830. 'The roads also, public

[78] P.R.O., ADM 66/138, Greenwich Hospital (Northern Estates), Out Letters (1825–7).

[79] P.R.O., ADM 66/92, Greenwich Hospital (Northern Estates), Out Letters (1825–8), Letter from J. L. McAdam to Commission in London, 23 May 1827.   [80] Arthur Raistrick, op. cit., p. 88.

[81] P.R.O., ADM 66/92, Greenwich Hospital (Northern Estates), Out Letters (1825–8), Wailes and Brandling to Commission in London, 21 October 1826.   [82] Ibid., 15 July 1826.

as well as private, notwithstanding the large sums that have been expended upon the former, afford the best field for the employment of capital by those owners of property within the district who wish to combine a certain public benefit with a reasonable prospect of advantage to themselves.'[83] McAdam, on the other hand, had broader objectives than his employers and wanted his roads to benefit the northern counties as a whole and not just the needs of a particular area. In 1827, when urging the expenditure of a further £3,000 by the Hospital on the road between Alston and the Hartley Bank coal mines, he pointed out that he considered its completion to be 'of extreme importance to the county at large but not of immediate consequences to the Hospital whose ores are smelted with their own fuel at Langley Mill'.[84]

None the less, despite their limited motives, the activities of the Greenwich Hospital were immensely beneficial to the Pennine region. Great care was taken by McAdam and his subordinates over the construction of the roads they built, and their efforts were of permanent importance in reducing the isolation of the area. 'The first fruits of the greatly improved state of the roads was the establishment of a post coach which commenced running between Hexham and Penrith by way of Alston.' In the following spring the proprietors introduced a new and elegant four horse coach from Newcastle to Penrith.[85] Thomas Sopwith was very appreciative of the Hospital's efforts. 'In the course of the last six years a vast improvement has been made by the formation of new lines and all the most interesting portions of the district are now traversed by roads which for gradual ascent and smoothness of surface are equal to any in the Kingdom.'[86] The Lead Companies continued to express satisfaction in the 1850s with the road system which they had created. 'Throughout the whole period of railway discussions the Company emphasised time after time their entire satisfaction with the efficiency of their road system. Their roads were maintained in good enough condition and surface to allow the use of carts between all their mining centres and the railheads, and even to allow cartage of timber to the remotest mines.'[87] In fact, as late as 1879, at a time when

[83] P.R.O., ADM 65/79, Greenwich Hospital (Northern Estates), In Letters (1808–31), Robert Brandling to William Hooper, 4 December 1830.
[84] P.R.O., ADM 66/92 Greenwich Hospital (Northern Estates), Out Letters (1825–8), J. L. McAdam to Commission in London, 23 May 1827.
[85] William Wallace, *Alston Moor—Its Pastoral People, Its Mines and Miners* (1890), p. 37.   [86] T. Sopwith, op. cit., pp. 8–9.
[87] Arthur Raistrick, op. cit., p. 93.

many turnpike roads had been allowed to fall into disrepair, the County Road Surveyor was still able to commend the Alston roads as 'the best managed roads I ever had the pleasure of looking over'.[88]

Improved road conditions in the northern Pennines, cannot, however, be attributed solely to the Greenwich Hospital Commission. The inauguration of the Brampton–Longtown, Sedbergh and Kirkby Stephen–Hawes Trusts all helped to facilitate travel within this region by linking the various north Pennine towns with the main 'through' routes over Stainmore and Shap. Similarly, older established Trusts were becoming increasingly aware of the need to improve their roads. For instance, the Brough–Bowes Trustees spent nearly £1,000 upon road deviations in the neighbourhood of Maiden Castle following their Report of 1835 upon the condition of these sections of road.[89]

The activities of the lead mining companies in the Alston area provide the clearest links between road building and mineral exploitation in Cumbria. Mining in West Cumberland, on the other hand, was still greatly dependent upon sea transport, but roads continued to play a valuable contributory role in the exploitation of the area's mineral wealth. Hence, the great landlords in this region found it worth their while to invest in the construction of roads and waggonways in order to facilitate communications between mine and coast for coal and iron ore.

The Lowther family, as we have noted, had every incentive as agriculturalists to invest in road improvements. However, their main source of revenue was derived from the rents of mining land and this was no doubt the greatest single factor in persuading them to subsidise Trust development in this region. Whitehaven continued to be the main exporting centre for the iron ore and coal mined on their estates, and in consequence the family retained a special interest in the roads administered by the Whitehaven Trust. In 1805, Sir William Lowther encouraged schemes to link Carlisle and Whitehaven more effectively either by an improved road or by canal.[90] One can also discern the influence of the Lowthers in the 1830s, 1840s and 1850s, during which time the Whitehaven Trust was devoting a high proportion of its

88 C.R.O., CCH 3/1, Cumberland Highway Papers (1879–84).

89 Heelis' Solicitors Office, Appleby, 'Report on the proposed deviation from the Brough and Bowes Turnpike Road at Maiden Castle' (May 1835).

90 C.R.O., Lowther MSS, Minutes of the Whitehaven Harbour Trustees (1782–1812), Letter from Sir William Lowther to the Mayor of Carlisle, 1 December 1805.

increasing toll receipts to road maintenance. The achievements of the Trust in this field were recognised by the *Cumberland Pacquet* in an editorial of December 1837. 'We question whether there is a road in the Kingdom on which such great improvements have latterly been made as on that under the Whitehaven Trust, or on which the revenue is more judiciously expended.'[91] It was also important for the Lowthers to have easy access to their more isolated mines in areas such as Ennerdale. Thus in 1866 they protested strongly against the stopping up of a road in this valley by the Ennerdale Enclosure Commission, on the grounds that 'if the road be stopped up as proposed, the facilities for beneficially working and carrying away such ore, stone, slate and minerals will be materially lessened'.[92]

In return for this assistance from agriculturalists and mining magnates, Trust law recognised that certain varieties of produce should be exempt from toll, or at least pay a reduced charge, for passage along the various turnpikes. Since the General Turnpike Act of 1822, fuel for domestic consumption and all articles of husbandary had been completely exempted from the payment of tolls on condition that such articles should be used by the carrier upon his own land.[93] Before this time, commodities such as lime and coal had been allowed to pay a reduced toll. The carriage of grain to local mills was also exempted from toll payment by the Act on condition that it be used for private consumption. Certain local industries might also receive preferential treatment on occasions if they were sufficiently influential. For instance, the Heron Syke Trust Act of 1815 exempted from payment of toll 'Any cattle or carriage employed in conveying cloth or other manufactured goods, or raw materials of wool to or from any mill already erected in any of the parishes or places in which any of the said roads lie'.[94] This provision was presumably designed to encourage the development of the woollen industry in favourable areas such as Burneside near the line of the Turnpike. At a later period, in 1850, the same Trust was to grant a partial toll exemption to Low Mills.[95]

Turnpike authorities were also scrupulous in protecting the waggonways of individual mining magnates. The Cockermouth–Maryport Trust Act of 1843, for example, was careful to specify that 'Nothing herein contained shall extend or be construed to

---

[91] *Cumberland Pacquet*, 5 December 1837.
[92] C.R.O., Cumberland Q.S. Petition Rolls, Mich. 1866.
[93] 3 Geo. 4, cap. 126.
[94] L.P.A. 55G3, cap. XXXVII. [95] L.P.A. 13–14V, cap. LXIV.

D

extend to authorise the said Trustees to affect, alter, remove, obstruct or disturb any waggonway or railway now formed or used for the purpose of conveying coal or the produce of any stone quarries, lime works, brick or tile kilns within any manor'.[96] The waggonways of the Earl of Carlisle which connected his coal and lime kilns with the town of Brampton, were similarly protected by the Alston Trust.[97]

These developments in agriculture and mining, together with a parallel increase in the size of towns and their markets, resulted in a very considerable volume of short distance traffic using the Cumbrian roads during the first half of the nineteenth century. The Turnpike Trusts acknowledged the significance of this traffic and, in view of the short distances which these carts and waggons frequently travelled, it was usually stipulated that vehicles should pay only one toll a day at any particular gate irrespective of the number of times which the gate in question was crossed and re-crossed. This provision encouraged certain categories of traffic, whilst the aforementioned concessions to fuels and manures, led to a particularly heavy growth of cart traffic in these two important commodities. Hutchinson noticed this development in the 1790s on the Cockermouth–Penrith and Carlisle–Skillbeck Turnpikes. 'Both these roads, besides the usual resort of travellers, are generally crowded with coal and lime carts from the inexhaustible stores on Warnell Fell.'[98]

As towns grew in size, fuel became an increasingly important requirement. Carlisle appears to have had particular difficulty in acquiring adequate supplies of fuel early in the century. In 1807 a meeting was called 'to consider of the best means of supplying the City of Carlisle with coals' and went on to explain that 'great difficulties have of late been found in obtaining the requisite supply of coals and that the retail price has been unusually high'. It was finally resolved at this meeting 'That the increased cost of coals appears to the Commission to have arisen from the high cost of cartage and occasional delays'. Consequently, the construction of a canal linking Carlisle with the Irish sea was strongly urged in order to free the city from its present complete dependence upon the local carrier service. This service was generally considered to be inadequate to meet the requirements of an expanding community.[99] A little later, in 1821, the inhabi-

---

[96] L.P.A. 6–7V, cap. XV.   [97] L.P.A. 5G4, cap. XXXIV.
[98] W. Hutchinson, *History and Antiquities of Cumberland*, II (1794), p. 422.
[99] C.R.O., Senhouse MSS, various reports on the proposed Newcastle–Maryport Canal (1794–1807).

tants of Whitehaven, Workington and Maryport, in petitioning Parliament for leave to ship stone and coal to Carlisle free of duty, were rather more sanguine of the economic utility of the carrier service around Carlisle.

'In estimating the value of Carlisle as a market for coal we should take into consideration the extensive and populous district of which it is the market town. This circumstance would enable the farmer to take coal as a back-carriage in the same carts in which he brings his produce to market, and thus coal might be distributed at a very light expense to a considerable distance around Carlisle.'[100]

The foundation of the Carlisle Gas Company in 1818 increased further the city's need for coal, and also opened up the prospect of a regular and lucrative traffic to favoured local carriers. William Lawson of Upperby, for instance, was soon able to come to an advantageous agreement with the Gas Company in which he contracted to supply them with eighteen cart loads of coal a week from Midgeholme.[101]

Many carts which distributed fuel also carried manures from the various towns to neighbouring farms. However, after a time cart traffic in fertilisers became increasingly concentrated upon the sea ports owing to the large scale importation of Chilean guano, in the 1840s.[102] For instance, the carriers accounts of Walter Berry reveal a very considerable traffic in guano between Kendal and Arnside after 1844, when the first imports of guano were recorded. This trade appears to have been particularly extensive in the mid 1850s, and between October 1854 and February 1855 a total of 627 bags of guano were carried by Berry's firm from the Sandside ports to various locations in the Kendal area. In February alone, 423 such bags were taken by Berry from Sandside to Milnthorpe by order of George Whittaker and Son of Milnthorpe. Similarly, between February 1854 and July 1855, Stephen Brunskill of Kendal imported a total of 778 bags of guano, most of which was carted from Arnside.[103]

Lime was still used extensively as an alternative fertiliser to guano, and lime carts were very conspicuous upon the Cumbrian roads in this period. For instance, the Ambleside Trust noted that 'there was 24 lime carts which came on the Staveley road

---

[100] *Whitehaven Gazette*, 16 April 1821.

[101] C.R.O., Carlisle Gas Company Minutes, 21 September 1825.

[102] *Cumberland Pacquet*, 1844 issues—contain frequent references to early imports of guano. [103] K.R.O., Account Book of Walter Berry.

consequently passed through each gate to the kiln and the same on their return'. In fact, for a total of twelve selected days distributed throughout the year 1855–6, seventy-eight carts passed through the Plumgarths Gate,[104] this being also at a time when there was a competing railway as far as Windermere. This suggests that virtually all the traffic was short distance agricultural carriage to and from the various intermediate farms. This traffic in fuel and fertilisers was of little financial importance to the Trusts by virtue of these aforementioned toll exemptions, but it was of great value to the Cumbrian towns and farming communities. In this respect, therefore, the carrier system, despite its limitations and inadequacies, helped to fulfil a very great need.

The mining magnates of West Cumberland were also dependent upon an efficient carrier service to transport coal and iron ore for short distances from their mines to the appropriate ports for export. Alternatively, these carts provided a 'feeder' service to nearby waggonways and, later, to railway lines. A study of the pattern of toll incomes for the different West Cumberland Turnpike Trusts during the period from about 1820 to 1840, reveals the increasing volume of traffic using these roads. In view of the expansion of mining operations in this region, it is fair to asume that a considerable proportion of this large toll revenue comprised cart traffic in minerals. Thus the tolls at Maryport gate, through which coal would pass on its way from the Ellenborough collieries to Maryport Harbour, were let for £271 11s 5d in the year 1826–7;[105] by 1843 this gate, together with its recently erected sidegate at Risehow, was worth £465 15s 3d.[106] Similarly, the Cockermouth–Workington Trust was receiving a total toll revenue of £868 at its various gates by 1839,[107] as compared to £333 18s 0d for the year 1823–4.[108] The Whitehaven Trust recorded the most spectacular toll increases during this period, and its receipts provide evidence not only of the increased mineral traffic entering Whitehaven at this time but also a corresponding increase in market and general passenger traffic into the town. The toll income of the Trust increased from £1,168 in 1806[109] to a sum of £4,232 10s 11d by 1855.[110]

A particularly high proportion of this traffic passed through the Scragill gate on the road from the Hensingham iron ore mines

---

104 K.R.O., Ambleside Trust Minutes, 1 October 1855.
105 C.R.O., Cumberland Q.S. Petition Rolls, Easter 1828.
106 Ibid., 1844.   107 Ibid., 1840.   108 Ibid., 1825.
109 *Carlisle Journal*, 14 March 1807.
110 C.R.O., Cumberland Q.S. Petition Rolls, Easter 1854.

into Whitehaven. In the year 1823–4 the Scragill Tolls were let for £488 7s 1d;[111] in 1829–30 they amounted to £747 18s 1d,[112] and by 1833 they had reached £814. Subsequently, they continued to rise steadily and in 1854–5 they were let for the unprecedented sum of £3,109.[113] The bulk of these tolls 'arose from the traffic coming from the iron ore districts'. The *Cumberland Pacquet* acknowledged the importance of the Scragill gate and commented that, in 1845,

'there are seven Turnpike Gates within the Whitehaven Trust and a toll being paid at any one of the number, the remaining six are free. Scragill it may be said is checked by four gates all within a distance of five miles and yet it lets for the large sum of £1,200! The Whitehaven Trust is decidedly the least expensive to travellers of any in this part of the country, and yet more money is realised upon it than all the Toll Gates in West Cumberland put together. These are facts which speak largely for the enormous traffic in and out of Whitehaven, as all the Toll Gates are within six miles of the town.'[114]

The *Pacquet* again drew attention to subsequent further increases in the Scragill tolls: from £1,600 in 1849 to £1,955 in 1850. 'The increase upon the Scragill Gate is a heavy one, and at its present rental upwards of six hundred carts at 2d each must pass through it daily before the farmer (toll) realises the money he stipulates to give.'[115]

The increased volume of carrier traffic during this period, whilst being in part the result of a greater demand for such services, also owed much to technical improvements in the vehicles themselves and to the improved organisation of the carrier service as a whole. Most carrying was originally done by pack horses and many such carriers survived into the nineteenth century. Even in the economically advanced region around Whitehaven it was recorded that 'a string of seven or eight pack horses might be seen laden in the streets of Whitehaven so late as 1830 conducted by one woman of nearly eighty years of age. These were too near the era of railways to be longer encouraged and are the last of the class remembered by the writer.'[116] Similarly, Daniel Scott recalls that pack horses were still fre-

---

111 C.R.O., Cumberland Q.S. Petition Rolls, 1844.
112 Ibid., 1831.   113 *Cumberland Pacquet*, 14 August 1838
114 Ibid., 4 October 1845.   115 Ibid., 10 September 1850.
116 William Dickinson, op. cit., p. 39.

quently used for the carriage of manufactures in the Kendal area in the early nineteenth century.[117]

Towards the end of the previous century, carts had begun to supersede pack horses, but they were usually badly built; the wheels consisting of two circular boards fixed without spokes and immovably attached to the end of a cylindrical axle. The gradual replacement of these 'clog carts' by spoke-wheeled carts at the beginning of the nineteenth century 'effected an entire revolution in the carrying department of the farm, and substituted the present light and easy drawn vehicle as the confirmed cart for general purposes'.[118] The single horsed cart was found to be particularly useful by the farmers of uneven countryside where waggons and two-horse carts would be too cumbersome and in danger of overturning on the hillsides.

During the first four decades of the nineteenth century the number of carriers in Cumbria grew steadily and served an increasing number of places with greater speed and regularity. As early as 1812 there was a total of twenty-two carriers registered at Whitehaven, performing an estimated ninety journeys a week.[119] Consequently, a greater degree of organisation was becoming necessary in order to co-ordinate the activities and timetables of these multifarious carriers. By 1800, some of the Cumbrian carriers had built up quite extensive businesses, using their own warehouses and employing clerks. For instance, the Carlisle firm of Holmes was sending waggons to London, York, Liverpool, Manchester and Leeds in this period. Holmes also had another warehouse at Penrith from which his agents traded with north-eastern England.[120] The London Lead Company were particularly dependent upon their carrying traffic before the Alston Trust was extended, and consequently Robert Stagg took great pains to improve the organisation of the local carrying services. As a result of Stagg's reforms, it was recorded in August 1815 that 'The saving in the carriage of lead ore, etc., is estimated at £1,543 this year'. In the following March a further saving of £1,431 was recorded.[121]

Sometimes a particular district would be dominated by one powerful, well-organised firm of carriers such as the Bennetts of

---

[117] Daniel Scott, *Bygone Cumberland and Westmorland* (1899), pp. 217–18.
[118] William Dickinson, op. cit., p. 39.
[119] *Westmorland Gazette*, 31 August 1812.
[120] D. Berry, 'The Social and Economic Development and Organisation of the Lake District, 1750–1814' (unpublished M.A. thesis, Univ. Manchester), p. 202.   [121] Arthur Raistrick, op. cit., pp. 90–1.

Ambleside who had forty men and horses covering the whole of Cumbria.[122] The Berrys (father and son) were also dominant figures in the Westmorland carrying trade, particularly between Kendal and the ports of Glasson, Milnthorpe and Arnside. Most of the Glasson trade had probably disappeared by about 1820 with the opening of the Preston to Kendal Canal, but during subsequent decades a brisk trade between Liverpool and the Sandside ports of the Kent estuary necessitated a stable of some twenty-five horses to cope with the delivery. The coasting vessels brought mainly flour and salt and returned with agricultural produce, rolls of hempen cloth and sacking, rope and twine.[123] The surviving Account Books of the family of Walter Berry give some indication of the extent and range of their business. For instance, the firm's trade for a single day, 19 December 1844, comprised the following articles, all of which were taken off the ship, the *Dee*, at one of the Sandside ports and from there carted to Kendal:

'10 Sacks of Oil Cake.
  1 Hogshead of Sugar and 1 Punchion of Treacle.
  1 But of Oil.
  1 Cask of Tallow and 2 bags of Shumac.
96 Salted Hides.
  1 Punchion Oil.
  1 Punchion of Syrup.
77 Hides.
  4 Boxes of Soap.
     do.
  1 Bag of Rice.
  3 Casks of Sugar and Cask of Currants.
  2 Bags of Rice and 1 Bag of Raisins and 1 Box
    of Sundries and 1 Caddy of Tea.
  1 Bag of Seeds.
  1 Jar of Brandy.
     do.
  1 Cask and 2 Jars of Spirits.
  2 Jars of Spirits and 1 Hogshead of Gin.
  1 Hogshead of Gin.
  1 Jar of Brandy.
  1 Barrel of Currants.
  2 Bags of Soap and 1 Box of Sundries.
  8 Barrels and 2½ Barrels of Cement.

122 William T. Palmer, *The Verge of Lakeland* (1938), p. 126.
123 J. F. Curwen, *History of Heversham with Milnthorpe* (Titus Wilson & Son, 1930), p. 77.

> 10 Sacks of Linseed and Meal.
> 100 Fire Bricks.
> 12 Common Bricks.
> ½ a Pack of Bran and 2 Quarts of Oil.'[124]

Other items which the Berry firm carried on different occasions included gunpowder for the Low Wood mills in addition to the aforementioned consignments of guano. The above load is larger than average, but there are some comparable deliveries referred to elsewhere in Berry's Account Books and a few were even greater in volume, if not in range of commodity carried. It reflects considerable credit upon the organisation of Berry's carrying business that the family could deal with such a diverse and heavy volume of trade over quite a long period of time. None the less, despite the improved organisation of the carrying trade as a whole during these years, it was still slow and relatively costly. These limitations were clearly exposed with the onset of railway competition.

Carts were useful for short distance travel but waggons were more frequently used for the long distance carriage of freight. Their principal function locally was to carry wool across the Pennines to and from the Kendal area; thus replacing pack horse traffic along these routes. They also served a very useful function in providing a cheaper form of passenger travel. By the 1790s there were a good many advertisements in the local newspapers giving the timetables of 'Expeditious Stage Waggons'; these being lighter and faster than their cumbersome 'wool-pack' counterparts. Messrs Handleys of Carlisle appear to have operated a quite extensive waggon trade during this period and on 24 November 1790 they issued a notice to the effect that their 'Expeditious Waggons' would run

'In ten days from Carlisle to London, and the same in return by way of York every week. Messrs Handleys respectfully inform their friends and the public in general that they have erected stage waggons which leave Carlisle early on Thursday morning and arrive at York on Thursday night, and Leeds on Saturday morning (where goods for all part of the south are regularly forwarded by the respective carriers), arrive at the White Bear, Bassinghall Street on Friday night, and set out every Monday morning and arrive and leave York on Tuesday morning for Richmond, Barnard Castle, Burgh, Appleby, Penrith and arrive

124 K.R.O., Account Book of Walter Berry (1842–7).

at Carlisle on Friday evening, where goods are immediately forwarded to Wigton, Cockermouth, Workington, Whitehaven and any other part of Cumberland.'[125]

This notice implies the existence of a considerable degree of organisation in the long distance carrying trade by the early nineteenth century. It appears that the large firms at least were able to issue a fairly precise and detailed timetable and were co-ordinating their services with those of other carriers, both long distance and local. A Kendal handbill of 12 May 1794 reveals the presence of a similarly well-organised passenger service by stage waggons, and gives notice of 'Flying Stage Waggons' between London and Preston every Tuesday and Friday; the whole journey taking about four days.[126]

The most spectacular developments, however, took place in passenger travel by stage coach. Coach services became more frequent, quicker and more reliable, and the various timetables were more co-ordinated to allow for a variety of connecting passenger services. This pattern was repeated nationally, as Jackman's extensive researches have shown. For instance, between 1760 and 1820 the number of stage coaches passing through Leicester had increased from 3 to 50. Likewise, between 1810 and 1830 the number of coaches leaving Preston for various destinations rose from 12 to 67.[127]

Local newspapers and Guides provide the main source for a study of these services within Cumbria; the Directories for 1811 and 1829 being particularly useful in this respect. The former Directory, by Jollie, reveals the considerable expansion which the coaching business had undergone since the 1760s. Carlisle, Kendal and West Cumberland all had regular coach services by 1810; seven coaches leaving Carlisle daily whilst a further seven left the town twice a week. Similarly, by 1812 an estimated thirty coaches were leaving Whitehaven in any single week.[128] The editor of the *Westmorland Gazette* drew attention to this heavy Whitehaven coach traffic, commenting that 'This is the more extraordinary as Whitehaven is no thoroughfare'.[129] These coaches from Whitehaven included three a week to Penrith by the *Volunteer* coach, a daily service to Carlisle by the *Royal Sailor*, leaving at 5 a.m. via Wigton and returning at 5 p.m., also, a

[125] Daniel Scott, op. cit., p. 216.
[126] J. F. Curwen, *Kirkbie Kendal* (1900), p. 277.
[127] Jackman, p. 311.
[128] *Westmorland Gazette*, 31 August 1812.   [129] Ibid.

service to Kendal three times a week by the *Good Intent* coach. These coaches also stopped at Workington, and the *Royal Sailor* included Maryport in its route. There was also a connecting service between Whitehaven and Furness by this time; Jollie giving notice of 'A postchaise to Ulverston from the Wheat Sheaf Inn, every Saturday, Monday, Wednesday and Friday, according as the tides answered'.[130] Thus, the West Cumberland towns had by now direct access to the daily post coach service between Kendal and London which had begun to operate in 1793, and also, to the thrice weekly Glasgow and Edinburgh services. Other coaches to run from Kendal by 1810 included the *Union* coach which ran a daily service to Leeds via Kirkby Lonsdale, Settle, Skipton, and Bradford; at Leeds there were connections for York, Hull, Sheffield and London.[131] Thus Cumbria was also in regular contact with eastern England by this period.

Contemporary demands for further improvements to the mail and stage coach services inevitably led to an increased attention being paid to road repairs on the main 'through' routes of north-west England: notably, between Lancaster and Glasgow and between Carlisle and Portpatrick. The former route posed a particularly difficult problem in view of the steep gradients between Kendal and Penrith. At first, improvements on this route were mainly confined to the area further south, around Milnthorpe, where a new Trust was inaugurated in 1817 to facilitate communications between North Lancashire and South Westmorland. This road was built in the face of protests from the neighbouring Heron Syke Trustees who feared that the introduction of a parallel Trust road would reduce the revenues of their Burton Gate.[132] Similarly, a newly built turnpike, leading from the Milnthorpe road at Levens Bridge to Ulverston, was of great value in linking Furness more effectively with the main north-south line of communications, thus reducing this region's isolation.

The newly constituted Milnthorpe Trust lost little time in promoting further road improvements, and the *Westmorland Gazette* had 'much pleasure in informing our readers that the Trustees are immediately going to make a very considerable improvement in the Milnthorpe Turnpike by deviating from the old road and thereby avoiding the hill at Sizergh Fell which is a

---

130 Jollie, *Cumberland Guide And Directory* (1811), p. 96.
131 Ibid., p. 113
132 J. F. Curwen, *Records relating to the Barony of Kendal*, III (1923), p. 2.

deviation of 180 roods. .... The deviation will be shorter than the old road—upon a dead level and will probably cost about £1,000'.[133] By 1824 the proposed deviation was virtually complete, and on 27 March the *Westmorland Gazette* was able to announce that 'The workmen have at last cut through the hill between Heversham and Milnthorpe, and the new road is expected to be open to the public before Whitsunday'.[134]

Further to the north, the Heron Syke Trustees were just as eager to improve their section of turnpike, and in 1815 they announced their intention of completing a series of widescale road repairs during the next few years. In order to subsidise these 'various improvements and deviations in the line of the road' the Trust borrowed a total of £17,000 during these years.[135] By November 1821, considerable progress had been made in improving this line of road, and the *Westmorland Advertiser*, in appreciation of the Trust's work, noted that 'The alterations upon the road betwixt Kendal and Penrith are of such a magnitude and extent as will soon avoid the steepest and worst parts.[136] Similarly, J. Briggs, writing in about 1824, considered that 'The improvements recently effected between Selside and Shap are truly astonishing'.[137]

The section of road over Shap represented the greatest challenge to the Trust engineers, and it explains the unusually heavy maintenance expenses of the Heron Syke Trustees. The Eamont Bridge Trustees were equally conscientious in attending to the road between Carlisle and Penrith during this period. Thus, between 1805 and 1808 the Penrith Trustees reduced the gradient of Kempley Bank Brow at the southern entrance to Penrith, and their road maintenance activities during this period were considered to be 'of great magnitude'.[138] In 1830, following the passage of their Renewal Act of that year, the Eamont Trustees began another spate of road improvements. The Northern Division borrowed £900 to help finance deviations at Harraby and Gallows Hill,[139] whilst the Southern Division indulged in a

---

[133] *Westmorland Gazette*, 31 December, 1819.

[134] Ibid., 27 March 1824.

[135] *Parl. Papers*, 1850, **XLIX**, 336.

[136] *Westmorland Advertiser*, 10 November 1821.

[137] J. Briggs, *Westmorland as it was—Notes and Observations* (1824), p. 251 (Arthur Foster of Kirkby Lonsdale).

[138] C.R.O., Carlisle—Eamont Bridge Trust, Miscellaneous Correspondence relating to Road Bill of 1808, Letter to Thomas Bleaymire (n.d.).

[139] C.R.O., TT/1/4, Carlisle–Eamont Trust, Miscellaneous Papers relating to Harraby Dispute of 1858–9.

series of more extensive repairs upon the Penrith approach roads and borrowed £5,000 for this purpose.[140] Similarly, the improvements wrought by the Brougham Bridge Trustees around Carleton in 1833 at a cost of £500, also contributed to the improvement of the Penrith approaches and helped to provide a more integrated road network within this region by linking up the Brough–Eamont and Carlisle–Eamont Trust roads.[141]

As a result of these and other improvements, stage coach traffic underwent further expansion, and the years immediately after 1817 appear to have been particularly notable for the growth of coach facilities in Cumbria. In the following year, the *Lord Exmouth* coach provided the first direct service between Kendal and Newcastle, via Sedbergh and Kirkby Stephen.[142] A year later, the *Westmorland Gazette* reported, with respect to Kendal, that, in the year ending April 1819, 'We have not less than sixty arrivals and departures of coaches to and from this town. The *Good Intent* has long possessed the Whitehaven road without a rival, but it has now found a competitor in the *Royal Liverpool* from the Commercial Inn'.[143] In the same year, following the opening of the Ulverston–Carnforth Turnpike road, a regular coach service was established between Kendal and Ulverston for the first time; the *Royal Exmouth* coach being advertised to travel this route thrice weekly.[144] By 1825, the *Royal Exmouth* was running daily and a second daily service was now provided to Ulverston by the *Telegraph* coach.[145] Similarly, the coaches from Kendal to Glasgow were also operating a daily service by this time.[146] A further service was introduced in 1828 when *The Balloon* stage coach began to run between Penrith and Hexham via Alston as a direct result of the Alston road improvements,[147] and in the following year a new four horse coach began to run between Newcastle and Penrith.[148]

Parsons and White, in their Directory of 1829, provide the most

[140] C.R.O., TT/1/5, Carlisle and Eamont Trust, 1859 Road Bill, Minutes of Evidence of Select Committee of H. of C., 29 March 1859.

[141] C.R.O., Brougham Bridge Trust, Miscellaneous Papers, Letter from Edward Bleaymire to James Brougham, 12 February 1833.

[142] Diary of a Kendal Man, 1806–55 (documents in possession of Mr R. G. Plint of 'Townview', Kendal).

[143] *Westmorland Gazette*, 17 April 1819.

[144] Ibid., 13 November 1819.

[145] J. Melville and J. L. Hobbs, 'Furness Travelling and Postal Arrangements in the Eighteenth Century and Nineteenth century', C.W.T., **XLVI** (1946), p. 88.   [146] Ibid.

[147] T. Sopwith, op. cit., p. 9.   [148] Ibid.

comprehensive survey of the Cumbrian coach services. By this time, there was a daily coach service between Kendal, Carlisle and Glasgow; two coaches ran thrice weekly to Edinburgh; and a service also operated three times a week from Carlisle to London via Penrith, Appleby, Greta Bridge and York. There was also a daily service to Manchester and Liverpool from Carlisle and Kendal, whilst a second daily coach ran to Manchester with appropriate connections for London. The *True Briton* coach provided a similar daily facility between Carlisle and Newcastle. West Cumberland was also well served by stage coach; there being a daily coach from Whitehaven to Carlisle via Workington, Maryport, Allonby and Wigton; and a thrice weekly service between Whitehaven and Penrith through Workington, Cockermouth and Keswick. The *Defiance* coach which operated on this last named route was met at Keswick by a branch coach which provided a regular connecting service with Kendal via Ambleside. South-West Cumberland was also becoming somewhat more accessible by this time; there being a thrice weekly 'Car' from Ulverston to Whitehaven, via Broughton, Bootle, Ravenglass and Egremont, whilst at Ulverston there were daily connections for Lancaster by the 'Oversands' route.[150]

Another notable development during these years was the institution of a mail delivery service. The first records of posting in Cumbria date back to the late seventeenth century when Sir Daniel Fleming, in describing the Stainmore Road, refers to 'the post passing twice every week betwixt Brough and Bowes'.[151] Horse and foot posts became more regular during the course of the eighteenth century, and in 1735 Ralph Allen of Bath[152] established a regular postal service running thrice weekly between Lancaster and Carlisle.[153] The service had increased to six times weekly by 1764.[154] The development of the mail service here, as elsewhere, no doubt owed a great deal to the initiative of John Palmer who had urged in 1783 the establishment of mail coaches protected by well-armed guards, to replace the slow and unsafe

150 Parsons & White, p. 723.

151 J. Nicholson and R. Burn, *The History of Westmorland* (1777), pp. 577–8.

152 Ralph Allen improved the mail service in 1720 by introducing Post Boys to carry mail along cross-routes between centres of population. He was granted the farm of cross-posts by the government between 1720–61 (Jackman, pp. 323–4).

153 R. C. Woodall, 'Postal History of Carlisle and Carlisle Mails—Early Transmission of Letters', *The Philatelist*, August and September, 1950.

154 Ibid.

system of horse posts. His reforms 'gave rise to a new era in both postal and travelling facilities'.[155]

The impact of Palmer's reforms was soon felt in Cumbria. In 1786 the first mail coach began to run between Manchester and Glasgow,[156] and ten years later a second such coach was travelling between Kendal and Carlisle.[157] By 1809 a mail coach was running between London and Edinburgh over Stainmore,[158] and in 1811 a further three mail coaches were passing daily through Carlisle: one from Liverpool, one from Edinburgh and a third from Newcastle.[159] Westmorland was also increasingly well served by the mail during this period, and the *Gazette* of 23 November 1816 recorded that 'The Postmaster General has given orders that the post to and from Kendal, Bowness, Ambleside and Hawkshead shall be sent every day of the Week, Tuesdays excepted'.[160] By 1829, improvements in the mail service had, broadly speaking, kept pace with stage coach facilities generally, and there were daily mail services from Carlisle to London, Manchester, Liverpool, Glasgow, Edinburgh, Portpatrick and Newcastle. The first named coach travelled to London by the Stainmore route thus giving a daily postal delivery to Appleby, Brough and Bowes, whilst the Manchester and Liverpool mail coaches served all places on the North Road down through Cumberland and Westmorland.

There was an equally significant extension of cross-posts to less accessible areas, notably: those parts of Eastern Cumberland and Westmorland which were not served by Stainmore, Furness, Cartmel and West Cumberland.[161] In 1820, letters between Penrith and Alston were still carried by mule and an inhabitant of the Alston area recalls that 'Instead of the promptitude and cheapness of this railway world, there was something of incident and adventure attending the delivery of a letter'.[162] By 1829, however, it was recorded that 'Letters from all parts are brought to Alston from Penrith on Monday, Tuesday and Saturday'.[163] Not all areas were so fortunate as Alston, and the Sedbergh region was still dependent entirely upon horse post at this date.[164]

Furness and Cartmel relied mainly upon the 'Oversands' coaching traffic until the construction of the Ulverston–Carnforth

155 Jackman, p. 327.   156 Ibid.   157 Ibid.

158 Ibid.   159 R. C. Woodall, op. cit.

160 *Westmorland Gazette*, 23 November 1816.

161 See Parsons & White for further details of these posts.

162 Miss Powley, 'Past and Present amongst the Northern Fells', C.W.T., III (1875), p. 174.

163 Parsons & White, p. 461.   164 Ibid., p. 657.

Turnpike in 1819. There was an irregular postal service oversands between Lancaster and Ulverston in 1760[165] and by 1793 a mail coach left the *Globe Inn*, Ulverston, for Whitehaven on Mondays, Wednesdays and Saturdays 'according as the tide suits at Esk',[166] returning to Furness the following day. Cartmel, on the other hand, had no regular post at this time; letters for this region were carried to Flookburgh where the messenger met the Ulverston–Lancaster post 'which goes and comes every day, or may be conveyed every Tuesday and Friday by the carrier who goes between Lancaster and Hawkshead'.[167]

By 1825, as a result of the road improvements following the inauguration of the Ulverston–Carnforth Turnpike Trust, a 'Post-Mail Gig' provided a connecting service at Milnthorpe and Burton to link the Furness mail with the main north-south running coaches. There was also a branch coach and a number of foot posts which ran into Cartmel in conjunction with this main mail service, and there were corresponding horse posts to Coniston and Hawkshead by this time.[168] By the 1830s, therefore, there is evidence of a much faster and better co-ordinated mail service to Furness and Cartmel than had been conceivable at the beginning of the century. Thus, in 1836 the mail left London at 8 p.m., passing through Burton in time to allow the connecting local Gig to reach Ulverston by 6 a.m. on the second day. This, in turn, enabled the Whitehaven Gig, which was now operating daily, to start at 6.25 a.m.; it being due back at Ulverston at 6 o'clock that evening.

Despite these improving mail facilities, however, it appears that the West Cumberland commercial interests regarded their own mail service with rather mixed feelings during the early decades of the nineteenth century. In 1822, the first regular mail coach link out of Whitehaven was provided by means of a Kendal coach travelling over Dunmail Raise. In the following year a connecting mail service from Whitehaven to Penrith was also established with a Gig for Workington meeting the mail coach at Bridgefoot.[169] These two services continued to function subsequently, although the Kendal mail was discontinued for a short period in 1830.[170]

None the less, the merchants of Whitehaven were still not

---

[165] J. Melville and J. L. Hobbs, 'Furness Travelling and Postal Arrangements in the Eighteenth and Nineteenth Centuries', C.W.T., **XLVI** (1946), p. 92.   [166] Ibid., pp. 93–4.
[167] Ibid., p. 94.   [168] Ibid., p. 95.   [169] Ibid., 5 April 1823.
[170] Diary of a Kendal Man, op. cit.

satisfied with their mail service, and a Liverpool merchant, writing in the *Cumberland Pacquet* of 1837, complained bitterly about the inadequacy of the current mail connections out of Whitehaven as a result of the uneven acceleration of the mail delivery service.

'The whole of West Cumberland should take some steps towards getting the mail despatched from these places earlier than at present. It appears to me that by the improvement of the North mail, it passes through Penrith, the place at which the Gig from your town meets it, two hours earlier than it used to do and consequently that your letters are just too late for it by these two hours. If they were despatched from you two hours earlier they would arrive in the old course which, as regards Liverpool, would be of great consequence, as the letters might then be answered the same day. At present they have to remain twelve hours for the North Mail, and twenty-three hours elapse here before they can be answered.'[171]

This correspondent appears to have ignored the alternative Liverpool mail service via Ulverston, but, nevertheless, his general comments concerning the insufficient co-ordination of the mail service to West Cumberland seems to have reflected contemporary commercial opinion in the Whitehaven area.

A committee met at Whitehaven in November 1837 to consider this problem, and the introduction of two new mail coach services between Penrith and West Cumberland was proposed in order to eliminate the current delays in forwarding the mail from Penrith. One coach was to leave Penrith immediately after the arrival of the Manchester mail from the south at 9.45 p.m., and the second mail coach was to be despatched as soon as possible after the arrival of the London mail from the north at 4 a.m. It was questioned at the meeting whether this system would allow sufficient time at Whitehaven for letters to be answered before the return of the post, but the Committee gave assurance that

'A four horse mail despatched from Penrith at 3.15 a.m. would be in Whitehaven before 9; and if it left again at 1 p.m. it would reach Penrith in time for the old Manchester mail from the north a few minutes before 7 p.m. We should in that case have three full hours to answer letters, a time too limited we admit if it could

[171] *Cumberland Pacquet*, 12 August 1837.

be avoided, but under existing circumstances we look upon it as decidely the best arrangement that can be effected.'

The Committee also pointed out that they were 'extremely dissatisfied with the inefficient and unprotected means provided for the conveyance of mails' between Penrith and Whitehaven. It was recommended, therefore, that a regular guard should be provided along with the proposed new mail coaches.[172]

It appears that the Committee's resolutions were speedily acted upon by the Postmaster General, since by December 1837, the editor of the *Cumberland Pacquet* was able to point out certain alterations in the timing of the West Cumberland mail-coach service, and concludes that 'Every person we believe is perfectly satisfied'. There were now three mail coaches entering Whitehaven daily: one from Penrith delivering London and Yorkshire letters, which arrived at 9 a.m. and despatched the mail at 3 p.m. A second mail coach brought letters from Scotland, Northumberland and Northern Ireland and despatched them so as to reach Glasgow and Edinburgh the following morning and Belfast the following evening. At the same time, a third mail service, branching off from Burton through Ulverston and Egremont, provided connections with South Wales, Cheshire, Lancashire, Furness and South-West Cumberland, 'By this mail, letters are delivered the succeeding morning at Liverpool and Manchester and at Birmingham in the evening following'.[173] However, the latter service was not altogether satisfactory, and the editorials in the *Pacquet* continued to be critical of the Lancashire mail delivery by this route, which was alleged to be 'nearly an hour or more behind the time specified. This is an inconvenience, inasmuch as its late arrival renders it almost impossible to answer a letter by return'.[174] There was a corresponding need for a mail service between Whitehaven and Carlisle, and the Whitehaven Committee tempered their acclamation of the 1838 improvements, with a reminder of the continued need for 'the establishment of a two horse mail to Ulverston and another to Carlisle, both of which are needed before Whitehaven can boast of her post office arrangements being complete'.[175]

As a result of improvements in vehicular construction: the development of lighter frames and narrower wheels, the latter being encouraged by the removal of fiscal discrimination against them, the speed of coach travel increased considerably. The

---

[172] *Cumberland Pacquet*, 27 February 1838.   [173] Ibid., 26 December 1837.
[174] Ibid., 13 March 1838.   [175] Ibid., 27 February 1838.

mail coaches, unhampered by toll charges, set high standards in this respect and, with the increased competition of stage coaches along many important routes, stage coach proprietors had every incentive to emulate the mail coaches by providing a faster and more efficient service. The increase which took place in the speed of road travel between 1750 and 1830 was remarkable and unprecedented. The time taken by the journey from Kendal to London had been reduced from nine days to three days between 1734 and 1773.[176] Subsequently, with the development of mail coach services, travelling times, particularly on the main routes, were further reduced. By 1788, the Royal Mail took $51\frac{1}{2}$ hours to travel from London to Carlisle[177] and by 1821 the time taken for this distance had been reduced to 41 hours 40 minutes;[178] by 1825 it took 34 hours 7 minutes[179] and, finally, in 1837 a time of 32 hours 17 minutes was recorded between Carlisle and London.[180] However, this last time marked a special effort on the part of the coach proprietors concerned and was not a regular time for this route. There were proportional reductions along other main stage coach routes during this period.

Competition amongst the growing number of stage coach proprietors was intense, particularly on the main routes to Scotland over Stainmoor and Shap Fell. This often led to dangerously fast speeds being attempted by competing coaching concerns, who indulged in unofficial races on occasions to the considerable alarm of their passengers. One contemporary mail coach, nicknamed the *Calico*, was particularly lightly constructed and was timed to perform the 96 mile journey between Carlisle and Glasgow in 8 hours 32 minutes at an average speed of 11 miles an hour. This coach was involved in several accidents and lost much of its custom through being notoriously unsafe.[181] Nevertheless, there does not appear to have been any major stage coach accidents involving serious loss of life on the Cumbrian roads during this period.

Some coach proprietors eventually began to realise that an emphasis upon safety might provide better publicity than concentrating upon the speed of their vehicles. Thus T. Gregson and Co. let it be known in 1816 that 'the disgraceful and dangerous practice of RUNNING RACES AGAINST OTHER COACHES OR AGAINST TIME shall not under any circumstances be attempted by their

176 Ibid., 3 October 1776.
177 C. G. Harper, *The Manchester and Glasgow Road*, I (1907), p. 9.
178 Ibid., p. 2.   179 Ibid.   180 Ibid., p. 10.
181 R. C. Woodall, op. cit.

drivers, and this pledge they are better enabled to perform from the circumstances of their coaches being principally driven by the proprietors themselves'.[182] Similarly, in 1823 the proprietors of the *Robert Burns* coach, travelling between Carlisle and Liverpool, gave notice that they were 'determined not to race against other coaches and as far as possible they will unite their exertions to prevent furious driving'.[183]

This increased pace of travel also necessitated frequent adjustments to coach timetables, since the acceleration on different connecting routes was not necessarily uniform. The history of the Whitehaven mail service illustrates the problems which could arise as a result of speed changes along different connecting routes. Similarly, the acceleration of the London–Glasgow mail coach, in addition to its repercussions for the Whitehaven connections, led to a certain amount of confusion on other branch routes as well. For instance, in 1825 a resident of Dumfries with business interests in the south, complained about the great inconvenience he experienced because his correspondence, which was written in Dumfries on the Wednesday, did not reach Norwich until the Sunday morning, the day after the market. This delay was because the mail coach from Portpatrick, which went through Dumfries, did not arrive at Carlisle until after the departure of the London mail. However, as at Whitehaven and Penrith, arrangements were eventually made to remove this inconvenience. In the year following this complaint, the Portpatrick mail, instead of remaining four hours in Carlisle, was sent by the Glasgow service as far as Lockerbie where a riding post met the coach to take the mail on to Dumfries which thus received its letters three hours earlier than in the past.[184]

Thus the greater speed of travel, despite these attendant difficulties, did on the whole result in a more organised and co-ordinated coach service. The times of arrival of the various stage coaches were becoming increasingly predictable and it was now possible to arrange more precise timetables. Similarly, many coach proprietors began to realise that they could achieve more by combination than by rivalry, and thus began to incorporate details relating to the facility of change-overs in their advertisements. For instance, the proprietors of the *Royal Sailor* post coach, running between Whitehaven and Carlisle, assured the public in 1823 that they 'have made arrangements for the conveyance of passengers wishing to go forward by any of the other

---

[182] *Cumberland Pacquet*, 16 November 1816.
[183] *Kendal Chronicle*, 4 January 1823.   [184] R. C. Woodall, op. cit.

coaches out of Carlisle and they may be certain of having their seats secured by giving timely notice at any of the coach offices of the Royal Sailor'.[185]

Stage and mail coaches were dependent upon improved road conditions for their existence in the first place, but the increasing social and economic usefulness of these services provided a stimulus and an incentive for further road developments during this period. The Carlisle–Portpatrick road improvements, for example, were a direct result of the growing demands of the mail service, whilst the extensive improvements to the Eamont Bridge Heron Syke and Ambleside Trust roads during the 1820s and 1830s, reflected the requirements of an increasing volume of coach traffic along these roads at this time. A considerable proportion of these travellers, particularly upon the Ambleside Trust road, had come to visit the Lake District which was becoming increasingly well known during this period as a region of exceptional natural beauty.

The scenery of the Lake District was relatively unknown and unappreciated until the middle of the eighteenth century. Camden, however, writing in the seventeenth century, was not unimpressed by it. 'Though the northern situation renders the country cold, and the mountains are rugged and uneven, yet it has a variety which affords a very agreeable prospect; for after swelling rocks and crowding mountains, big as it were with metals, you come to rich hills clothed with flocks of sheep; and below these are spread out pleasant large plains, tolerably fruitful.'[186] A writer in the *Gentleman's Magazine* of 1748 had no reservations when describing the beauty of Lake Windermere. 'It presented one of the most glorious appearances that ever struck the eye of a traveller with transport.'[187] In 1758, Dr Dalton published a poem on the Lake District in which he points out that the savage grandeur of the area which frightened some contemporary visitors contained a transcendent beauty.

> Human life these at first alarm
> But soon with savage grandeur charm
> And raise to noblest thoughts the mind.[188]

Thus the concept gradually became established that beautiful scenery had an ennobling influence upon the human personality

185 *Whitehaven Gazette*, 11 February 1823.
186 Camden, *Brittania*, II (1753), p. 1002.
187 *Gentleman's Magazine* (1748), p. 563.
188 Thomas West, *A Guide to the Lakes* (1796), p. 199.

in so far as it awakened men's sensibilities and deepened and stimulated their poetic insight.

This approach to nature was one of the most dominant aspects of the romantic movement which gained momentum in the artistic world of western Europe towards the end of the eighteenth century, and which stimulated a very considerable interest in the Lake District amongst the leisured classes. In 1767, Thomas Gray, the poet, made the first of his two visits to the Lake District. He had little time to spend there but determined 'to go again the first opportunity'.[189] In 1769 he undertook his second visit and in a famous letter to Dr Wharton he spoke with rapture of what he saw. His description of Grasmere has become particularly well known. 'Not a single red tile, no gentleman's flaring house, or garden walls break in upon the repose of this little unsuspected paradise; but all is peace, rusticity and happy poverty in its neatest, most becoming attire.'[190] Gray's visits to the Lake District were of particular importance since he was the first truly national figure to eulogise the beauty of the region.[191] It is difficult to measure the extent to which Gray's writings enhanced the region's popularity in the first instance, but it is certain that during the next three decades a growing number of people followed his example. The writings of Dr Brown, who visited the Lake District at the same time as Gray, were also, apparently, quite influential, since Hutchinson, writing in 1794, talks of the interest aroused by Brown's comparison of the Lake District with Derbyshire, and of how his writings on the former area 'excited a general curiosity and drew many visitors to the Lakes'.[192] Other writers soon followed Gray and Brown; in 1772 Gilpin toured the Lakes and he was followed by Hutchinson in 1774. In 1778, West wrote the first of his Lake District Guides. These soon became classics of their kind and were frequently reprinted during the nineteenth century.[193]

By this time, with the onset of war on the Continent, opportunities of travel abroad for upper and upper-middle class Englishmen were becoming increasingly limited. Thus the Lake

[189] D. C. Tovey (Ed.), *Letters of Thomas Gray*, II (1909), p. 152.

[190] Ibid., p. 251.

[191] Gray's views reached a wide audience as they were incorporated into the Appendix of the second edition of West's *Guide to the Lakes*, published in 1780.　　[192] W. Hutchinson, op. cit., p. 161.

[193] By 1821 they had been published in eleven editions. For a survey of these early visitors to the Lake District see: W. G. Collingwood, *Lake District History* (1925), Chapter IX; and Norman Nicholson, *The Lakers* (1955).

District, in view of its favourable publicity and growing accessibility, became a viable alternative to Alpine resorts for a growing number of people. West had already made this point when advising people to see the Lake District before journeying to the Alps, 'as it will give in miniature, an idea of what they are to meet with there. The mountains here are all accessible to the summit and furnish prospects no less surprising and with more variety than the Alps themselves'.[194]

During the first half of the nineteenth century, a great many eminent contemporaries found solace and inspiration whilst living in the Lake District. Apart from the Wordsworth family, visitors and residents included Dr Arnold, Ruskin, Crabb-Robinson and De Quincey. It is of course with Wordsworth in particular that the area has become associated, and for him the natural features of the Lake District had a transcendent beauty and significance. 'I do not indeed know any tract of country in which within so narrow a compass may be found an equal variety in the influence of light and shadows upon the sublime and beautiful features of the landscape.'[195]

This growing interest in Lake District travel, reflected and stimulated improvements to the main roads running through the area: between Kendal, Ambleside, Keswick and Cockermouth. At the beginning of the nineteenth century, despite the favourable publicity which the area had of late received, some tourists were still deterred from visiting the Lake District, owing to the reputedly poor condition of certain sections of its turnpike roads, notably between Ambleside and Keswick. Thus, the Rev. John Barwis, writing in 1818, considered the section of road to the south of Keswick to be 'very rough and unpleasantly downhill'.[196] It appears that little was done in the following few years to repair the road, since Jonathan Otley of Keswick, writing in 1825, considered that 'At a time like the present, when road making is the order of the day, I cannot but wonder that so little attention is paid to the road between Keswick and Grasmere'.[197] However, by this time the Trust was beginning to appreciate the need for major improvements along this stretch of road, and the Trustees emphasised, in 1824, that 'certain parts of the roads hereby

---

194 Thomas West, *A Guide to the Lakes* (1796), p. 5.

195 W. Wordsworth, *Guide to the Lake District* (1835), p. 26.

196 F. B. Swift, 'The Reverend John Barwis and his Journals', C.W.T., XLV (1945), p. 79 (the author presumably means 'dangerously steep' when saying 'unpleasantly downhill').

197 *Cumberland Pacquet*, 24 October, 1825.

intended to be widened, improved and kept in repair situated in the Township of Grasmere and Rydal in the Parish of Kirkby Kendal, are very dangerous and incommodious to Travellers and Passengers by reason of the steepness and narrowness thereof and it would be of great advantage and convenience to the public if the Lines of courses thereof were altered or diverted'.[198] Permission for these improvements was incorporated into the 1824 Renewal Act, and in the following year the Trust borrowed a total of £500, 'for carrying into effect the White Moss Deviation'.[199] Later in the same year, they borrowed a further £600 for the same purpose.[200]

Subsequently, as their toll revenues increased, the Ambleside Trustees, despite occasional bouts of caution, were prepared to embark upon further improvements along the line of their road. In July 1828 they authorised the Trust surveyor to expend up to £400 upon the repair of the section of turnpike between Ambleside and Bowness,[201] whilst in 1839 ambitious schemes to widen the southern approaches to Ambleside were under consideration.[202] Subsequent improvements also included the reduction of the hill at Troutbeck Bridge in 1848[203] and of Hallhead Brow in 1857.[204]

Also, in order to absorb the growing numbers of tourists and to stimulate further traffic, it was necessary that these visitors should be adequately accommodated. The early stage coach inns grew up on the old pack-horse routes; Kendal being particularly well served in this respect. The principal Keswick hotel, the *Royal Oak*, also flourished as a centre for the local pack-horse trade during the eighteenth century, and became an important social and economic centre in the town.[205] The *Queen's Hotel* in Keswick was held in equally high repute during this period, and even Gray, who was a fastidious man, appears to have been quite content with his reception there in 1767.[206] Gray was less complimentary, however, in his description of the *Salutation Hotel* in Ambleside which he found 'dark and damp as a cellar'. West noted, a few years later, that this same hotel 'has been considerably

[198] L.P.A. 5G4, cap. XIV.
[199] K.R.O., Ambleside Trust Minutes, 5 February 1825.
[200] Ibid., 11 October 1825.
[201] Ibid., 8 July 1828.   [202] Ibid., 5 June 1839.
[203] Ibid., 12 July 1849.
[204] Ibid., 7 March 1857.
[205] W. T. McIntire, *Lakeland and Borders of Long Ago* (1948), pp. 161.
[206] Tovey (Ed.), *Letters of Thomas Gray*, III (1909), p. 152.

improved since Mr Gray's visit and is now as commodious as any in the country'.[207]

It appears from the scattered evidence available that several of the Lake District inns were making substantial attempts to improve their catering facilities during this period. The *Red Lion Hotel* at Grasmere was evidently determined to impress when Captain Budworth dined there, since he recalls having the following meal: roast pike and anchovy sauce, boiled fowl, veal cutlets and ham, beans and bacon, parsley and butter, cabbage, peas and potatoes, wheat-bread and oat-bread, butter and cheese, preserved gooseberries and cream. The whole meal cost 10d.[208] *The Globe* Inn must also have been able to cater on a large scale during this period since it accommodated 206 people at a pre-election dinner in 1796.[209] Apart from this expansion in the amenities of the various inns, other diversions such as organised wrestling and regattas were being provided by the 1780s as an added attraction for the growing numbers of tourists.[210]

It is difficult to assess accurately the volume of this traffic; few of the contemporary diaries, guide books and directories are very specific about actual numbers. None the less, it is possible to build up some sort of selective picture of the pattern of traffic by referring to the available Turnpike Trust records, and by placing a perhaps excessive reliance upon a few other isolated written sources. Thus, the *Cumberland Pacquet* records that in 1791, 379 coaches passed through Ambleside on tours of the lakes,[211] whilst in 1793, Keswick is reported to have had 1,540 visitors.[212] In 1819, the *Westmorland Gazette* noted a considerable volume of traffic passing through Kendal during the spring months. 'In the course of a week we have not less than 160 arrivals and departures of coaches to and from this town.'[213]

Rather more substantial evidence of this increased tourist traffic is provided by the toll receipts of the Cockermouth–Penrith and Ambleside Trusts during this period; these being the two Turnpikes most used by tourists.

The Ambleside Trust receipts only totalled £274 in 1803, but they increased rapidly during the next two decades. In 1807 they

207 Thomas West, op. cit., p. 214.
208 W. G. Collingwood, *The Lake Counties* (1902), p. 158.
209 C. R. O., Lowther MSS, Election Vouchers, 1796.
210 W. G. Collingwood, *Lake District History*, op. cit., pp. 167–8.
211 *Cumberland Pacquet*, 6 September 1791.
212 G. A. Cooke, *Description of the County of Cumberland* (1814), p. 3.
213 *Westmorland Gazette*, 17 April 1819.

had reached £344; in 1816—£401 10s 0d; and by 1825 the Trust gates were let for a combined rent of £895, which was in turn further increased to £1,042 by 1827.[214] These spectacular increases in total revenues between 1822 and 1825 were, no doubt, partly a result of the increasing toll rates sanctioned by the Renewal Act of 1824, but the figures as a whole for this period demonstrate beyond all question the steady increase in the volume of traffic using the road. It is also fair to assume that quite a high proportion of this traffic was represented by coaches carrying tourists from Kendal to Windermere, Ambleside, Grasmere and Keswick. A report on the nature of the passenger traffic passing through the Plumgarths toll bar between Kendal and Windermere for the year November 1843 to November 1844, provides the following significant figures in support of this argument:

> '728 pairs ave. 4 persons each—2912
> 572 Carts ave. 3   ,,   ,, —1726
> 468 Gigs ave. 2   ,,   ,, — 936
> 150 Carriages ave. 4½ persons each—675
> 300 phaetons ave. 3   ,,   ,, —900
> 450 Gigs ave.   2   ,,   ,, —900
> Passengers by Whitehaven mail   —365 days
> Ave. 7 persons per day   —2555
> Passengers by *Mazeppa* Coach for 20 weeks in
> Summer, 6 days a week—ave. 10 a day—1200.'

This amounts to a total passenger traffic of 11,804 for this stretch of road during a single year.[215] Traffic on the Turnpike between Cockermouth and Penrith was also very substantial during this period, and notably so during the 1840s. In 1841 the Trust's toll revenues amounted to £1,456 3s 1d; by 1849 they had risen to a total of £2,109 0s 10d, mainly as a result of the building of a new toll bar at Wythburn just south of Keswick on the Grasmere road.[216]

However, the principal attraction of the Lake District for the Romantics had been its solitude, and increasing concern began to find expression in these circles regarding the implications of any further expansion of tourism. It was feared that the increasing commercial exploitation of the area would do irreparable harm to its natural beauty. As early as 1791, a visitor foresaw the possible social and moral disruption which could follow a tourist

[214] K.R.O., Westmorland Q.S. Petition Rolls, Easter, 1828.
[215] K.R.O., Ambleside Trust, Minutes 28 December 1844.
[216] *Cumberland Pacquet*, 12 February 1850.

incursion on a large scale; speaking of a journey along the road between Penrith and Keswick, he noted that 'solitude and peace reign here undisturbed, except by the rattling tourist who excites envy and false ideas of happiness among the peaceful inhabitants'.[217] Wordsworth was the principal spokesman of these conserving interests during the nineteenth century and he constantly emphasised that the solitude of the area, the natural beauty of its scenery and the natural simplicity of its inhabitants were the region's paramount assets and must not be 'defaced by the intrusion of tourists'.[218]

A considerable amount of retrospective romance has been attached to stage coach travel. The writings of Dickens, De Quincey and others have evoked a mood of nostalgia for the coaching era amongst people living in a later age when travel, although quicker, was considered to lack the more intangible virtues of atmosphere and flavour. There is little doubt, however, that the early stage coach journeys were very long and uncomfortable. Charles Kirkpatrick Sharpe, writing in November 1800, eloquently describes the miseries of a journey between Carlisle and London. 'After passing a sleepless night at Carlisle, I was hurried away next morning without a morsel of breakfast and grew so very sick and ill in a little while that I had almost fainted twice, when we stopt at Penrith and took up an old gentleman. I then got a large dram of gin which did me much service; and we proceeded through ice and snow far and far and further that I can tell.'[219]

However, the 'golden age' of coaching came later than this, and lasted for at the most twenty years between about 1820 and the late 1830s. This is the period to which the Romantics refer, and there is no doubt that by this time, as a result of better roads and lighter carriages, travel was quicker and more convenient. It was almost certainly more comfortable also for some. Competing coach proprietors vied with each other to provide added comforts to their vehicles. Thus T. Croall & Co., when advertising their coach service between Lancaster and Edinburgh, pointed out that 'The coaches are splendidly fitted up with reclining cushions for the head; lined leather aprons for outside passengers and Croall's Safety Drag attached to each'.[220] By 1830, a Cumbrian magistrate

[217] A. Walker, *Observations made in a Tour from London to the Lakes in the Summer of 1791* (1792), p. 82.
[218] W. Wordsworth, op. cit., p. 70.   [219] C. G. Harper, op. cit., p. 16.
[220] Taken from a poster on the wall of the *Castle Boutique* shop in Castle Street, Carlisle.

appears to have had no doubt about the superior comfort of contemporary stage coaches. 'We travelled in great state in those days. We gave up going to town in our private carriages for the pleasure afforded by the speedy and safe conduct we had.'[221] J. F. Curwen, in his description of the *Kings Arms Inn*, Kendal, attempts to recapture the essence of the coaching age and concludes that much has now been lost.

'As a posting house there is none of the stir now, in these days of railway and electronic transmission of news, as was created by the dashing up of the "Royal Mail" with a fine team of greys, its smart guards and bluff weather beaten whip, to say nothing of the fluttering of dripping waterproofs, the pulling asunder of soaked plaids and the drying of gleaming cheeks that were red with rain. And within there is none of the bustle such as used to be, when a thousand servants seemed to be scampering about to assist and prepare a steaming and fragrant banquet by the time that warmer and dryer clothes could be put on. Oh it was a commotion and a welcome indeed to arrive in those days at this big, warm, comfortable, old fashioned Inn, and a succulent supper worth remembering, with that appetite whetted by a long ride in moorland air and flavoured with the agreeable recollection of past perils safely surmounted.'[222]

Another writer had rather more reservations. 'To have passed nearly 42 hours continuously on the roof of a coach in severe weather, with every hair standing up like a porcupine's quills, and with rain, dew and hoar frost one's dreary portion, forbade all the glamour with which the old era is regarded at this convenient distance of time.'[223]

There is probably some truth in both pictures. No doubt some coaching Inns did conform to the Dickensian prototype, and no doubt at times there was a pervasive jollity in travel which has since been lost. Railway stations never provided Punch and Judy entertainment like Dickens's Toll Gate,[224] and it is doubtful if future chroniclers will take much trouble to record their charms. On the other hand, the weather was not always fine and warm and not everybody travelled inside the coach. Travelling, despite many undoubted improvements, must have been very uncom-

---

[221] J. Fisher Crosthwaite, 'Recollections of the Keswick Post Office, Past and Present', C.W.S.L.S., XIV (1888–9), pp. 24–5.
[222] J. F. Curwen, op. cit., p. 275.
[223] C. G. Harper, op. cit., p. 15.
[224] Charles Dickens, *The Old Curiosity Shop* (1964 Panther ed.), p. 118.

fortable for many for a considerable part of the year at least, and quite divested of romance. A recent writer also points out that

'coaching was stimulated to its fullest extent in the growing industrial areas with their important population and commerce. Sentimentally attached though coaching may be with the open road and the rural scene, the services on the Leeds and Manchester and Sheffield roads greatly surpassed even those of important national routes such as the Great North Road on the London–York route, and industrial Leeds saw far more coaches in a week than York despite the latter's traditional importance'.[225]

Perhaps this generalisation is not altogether true for Cumbria, in view of its tourist connections, although there was also a good deal of road traffic associated with the West Cumberland mining region.

Improvements in the conditions of road travel in Cumbria played an important role in promoting a greater exploitation of the region's resources during the first half of the nineteenth century. Agriculture was becoming more intensive during this period and road improvements by the Turnpike Trusts and Enclosure Commissioners enabled farms to be linked up more effectively with local and regional market centres. Likewise, the expansion of mining in West Cumberland and around Alston necessitated improvements both in the condition of local roads and in the organisation of the carrier service. Apart from this specialised local traffic, there was a corresponding increase in the volume of longer distance traffic using the main through roads over Shap and Stainmore and between Kendal and Keswick. This in turn stimulated and reflected improved road conditions along these particular routes.

On the other hand, pressure for road improvements appears to have been less successful in South-West Cumberland, Furness and Cartmel, and these areas continued to be relatively isolated from the main Cumbrian through routes during the first half of the nineteenth century. South-West Cumberland was a particularly neglected area in every sense and it is significant that none of its roads were at any time turnpiked. The Whitehaven Trust ended at Egremont, and to the south the roads were administered entirely by the various townships, despite continued applications by the local inhabitants for the formation of a Turnpike Trust to remove their road maintenance burdens. Thus, in 1806 the

225 G. C. Dickinson, 'Stage Coach Services in the West Riding of Yorkshire', *Journal of Transport History*, IV (May 1959), p. 10.

parishioners of South-West Cumberland gave notice in the *Carlisle Journal* that 'Application is intended to be made to Parliament the next session, for a Bill for repairing, widening and improving the roads leading from Calder Bridge in the County of Cumberland through the market towns of Ravenglass and Bootle in the said county to Duddon Bridge'.[226] This application was unsuccessful, and in 1824, pressure for statutory help to promote road improvements was renewed, a parishioner informing the Editor of the *Whitehaven Gazette* that 'I believe the generality of your readers are aware to what a heavy expense these parishes situate to the south of Whitehaven beyond the limits of the Turnpike road are subject to in repairing their road: It would be a great relief to the inhabitants of this district if the Turnpike Road could be extended from Calder Bridge to Ravenglass'.[227] The petition concludes by conceding that the amount of traffic using these roads is 'comparatively trifling, but nevertheless improved conditions of travel in this area and the reduction of the present parochial burdens would effect a very valuable social service'.[228]

There was no satisfactory response to this further petition, however, and complaints about the poor condition of the South-West Cumberland roads were endemic throughout the nineteenth century. Thus the inhabitants of the Ravenglass area, in the course of complaining about high shipping duties upon coal, added that 'we have a long way to fetch it and the roads are so bad that it is a hard day's work besides wear and tear, so that we seldom get any coals'.[229] The mail service was also retarded by poor road conditions south of Egremont, and in 1835 the parishes concerned received a severe reprimand from the Whitehaven postal authority 'in consequence of repeated complaints from the Post Office that the mail gigs which run between Ulverston and Ravenglass and between Ravenglass and Whitehaven do not perform their respective journeys in the allotted time'.[230] The bad state of the roads was assigned as the principal reason for this delay.

There is no evidence that anything was done to improve the roads in South-West Cumberland in answer to these complaints. They appear, in fact, to have been equally unsatisfactory in the late 1870s when the newly appointed county road surveyor,

[226] *Carlisle Journal*, 30 August 1806.
[227] *Whitehaven Gazette*, 16 August 1824.
[228] Ibid.   [229] Ibid., 30 April 1821.
[230] *Cumberland Pacquet*, 3 February 1835.

George Bell, made his first inspection of the roads in this region. He considered the Millom and Bootle roads to be 'the worst kept and of least importance of any I have yet examined. The traffic is of the very lightest agricultural kind and the free use of the road is interrupted by the tide at Ravenglass and Eskmeals.'[231]

The explanation for the almost total neglect of this region is to be found in its physical isolation and its apparent lack of mineral wealth prior to the opening up of the Millom iron ore deposits. Consequently, none of the major Cumbrian land-owners appear to have considered it worth their while to press for road improvements on a large scale.

Furness was better served by road as a result of the construction of the Ulverston–Carnforth Turnpike, but the North Lonsdale Hundred devoted little money to the area's bridges, and the Cartmel roads were administered entirely by the various townships whose difficulties in engineering road improvements were illustrated by the Lower Holker litigation. Thus, Cartmel was still relatively isolated and the best southern approach to it was across Morecambe Bay. The 'Oversands' route also provided the best approach to Furness from the south, since the Ulverston Turnpike proved a somewhat circuitous route for travellers from Lancashire; it being 20 miles from Lancaster to Ulverston across the sands as distinct from 34 miles by road via Milnthorpe.

The oversands coach traffic was very considerable during the early decades of the nineteenth century, and a visitor to the area in 1820 gave a vivid description of this traffic crossing the Leven estuary.

'A more picturesque, grotesque, touresque, or whatever other esque scene you may think for it I think I never saw. There could not be fewer than 40 carts, gigs, horses, chaises, etc., with men, women, children, dogs and I can hardly tell what besides all in the river at once . . . The waves dashing through the wheels, the horses up to the breast in water—the vehicles, some driving one way, some another in all imaginable confusion—the carriers swearing, the drivers cracking their whips—the women and children screaming—and the apparent impossibility of any of them escaping formed a coup d'oeil as I never had seen nor ever expected to see.'[232]

231 C.R.O., CCH 3/1, Cumberland Highway Committee Papers (1879–84), County Surveyors Report, 21 May 1879.
232 Leonard Atkins, *Letters from the Lakes* (1820), pp. 26–7.

Even allowing for a good deal of artistic licence in this account, it could hardly have been a comfortable journey and this is further borne out by surviving accounts of losses of life along the oversands routes. For instance, in 1821 a post chaise was lost off Hest Bank, both the occupant of the chaise and the post boy being drowned.[233] In 1846, an even more tragic accident occurred when nine people were drowned in crossing the Leven sands.[234] Nevertheless, in spite of these hazards, many people continued to cross the sands on account of the relative shortness of the journey. Parsons and White advertised 'Daily Oversands Coaches from the Sun Inn and Bradyll Arms' in their directory of 1829,[235] and as late as 1851, the oversands journey was considered, 'the nearest and cheapest route from Ulverston to Lancaster'.[236]

The long continuance of this service would not have been possible, had George Stephenson's suggestion for building a main railway line up the West Cumberland coast been adopted. Stephenson recommended the construction of a viaduct to carry the line over the Morecambe Bay sands, and countered arguments as to the expense of this undertaking by remarking that, on balance, the cost of building this West Cumberland line would be relatively cheap as compared to the alternative route over Shap Fell. 'The crossing of the sands would be the most expensive portion of the line but the quantity of land reclaimed from the sea would more than compensate for the expense incurred in crossing them.'[237] Stephenson estimated that the construction of the Morecambe Bay viaduct would reclaim at least 20,000 acres of land. His recommendations were not carried out, and it was not until the 1850s that railways dealt a death blow to the 'Cross Sands' traffic. The Whitehaven and Furness Junction railway line, linking Whitehaven with Broughton in Furness, was opened in 1850, and then finally, in 1856, the Ulverston–Lancaster railway was completed and the oversands coach traffic ceased.

Thus the railways had solved a problem which the road authorities had only partly dealt with. South-West Cumberland, Furness and Cartmel were now more effectively linked with the main central 'through' routes as a result of the construction of these

[233] John Fell 'The Guides over the Kent and Leven Sands, Morecambe Bay', C.W.T., VII (1883), p. 12.

[234] Ibid., p. 13.

[235] Parsons & White, p. 729.

[236] L.R.O., Q.S.P. Q.S. Petition Rolls, July 1851.

[237] C.R.O., Senhouse MSS, 'Reports on the Formation of a Railway between Lancaster and Carlisle—with Observations on the Mode of Crossing Morecambe Bay', George Stephenson, 16 August 1837.

connecting railroads.[238] This enabled the iron ore deposits in these areas to be exploited more efficiently than hitherto, and this in turn provided the basis for the growth of iron manufacturing at Barrow, Millom, and also further north around Whitehaven and Workington. The failure to promote an iron industry within this region at an earlier date illustrates the continued limitations of road transport during the first half of the nineteenth century. There was no suitable coking coal in close proximity to the extensive iron ore deposits of West Cumberland and Furness. Hence, if iron smelting was to develop on any appreciable scale, coal would have to be imported from Durham and this was beyond the resources of the contemporary carrier services. They were able to cope increasingly well, as we have seen, with the demands of shorter-distance agricultural and mining traffic, but the carriage of heavy commodities over longer distances was a different matter. Railways, on the other hand, were well equipped for work of this nature, and had the additional advantage of being cheaper, both for freight and passenger transport.

[238] See Appendix B for details of opening of these railroads.

Chapter 4

COMPETITION FOR TRAFFIC

Travel by road was expensive in the eighteenth and early nineteenth centuries. Only the rich could afford to journey regularly by stage coach or to take advantage of the new mail delivery service. Stage and mail coach proprietors were obliged to pay considerable sums in taxation and were thus compelled to demand high fares of their passengers in order to run a profitable business. The principal tax to which stage coach proprietors were subjected in the early nineteenth century was a 'mileage duty'. This was assessed on the number of passengers which the stage coach in question was licensed to carry,[1] and had to be paid in full, irrespective of whether or not the coach was carrying a capacity load. Thus, for an average coach capacity of say nine to twelve passengers, the appropriate duty in the 1830s would be 2½d for each mile travelled. Other taxes to which the coach proprietors were liable included: a duty of £5 5s on all four-wheeled carriages let for hire and a corresponding levy of £3 5s on all two-wheeled carriages; also an 'assessed tax' on coachmen, guards and draught horses and an additional post horse duty. Turnpike tolls were also a heavy item in coach expenses, and it has been estimated that some of the largest coach proprietors averaged 11s 6d per mile per month in toll payments.[2]

It is difficult to generalise about the cost of passenger travel by road during the period from about 1760 to about 1830. Coach fares often fluctuated quite violently from year to year and from route to route. If a stage coach firm had a monopoly along a particular route, their fares would naturally tend to be high. If, on the other hand, several firms were competing for passengers along a line of road, fares would be forced down, sometimes to a level which was barely economic for the competing proprietors. Once this had happened, the various coaching firms might agree

---

[1] With the exception of the period 1822–32, when the duty varied according to the number of horses which pulled the stage coach in question.

[2] Jackman, p. 316.

E

upon a minimum scale of charges, in an attempt to restore fares to a reasonably high level. In the long run, there does not appear to have been any major alteration in stage coach fares for England and Wales as a whole during this period. However, by about 1820 there was a general tendency for fares to be lower on some of the more popular routes, particularly if the coach proprietors on such routes were facing competition from canals or coastal shipping.

The fare per mile tended to be higher over short distances,[3] but long-distance travellers, despite paying proportionately less, incurred additional expenses. They had to find accommodation, buy the necessary food and drink during their journey and also give substantial tips to the different coachmen and guards. Even travellers over shorter distances were not exempt from these supplementary charges, and 'A Commercial Traveller' complained bitterly to the Editor of the *Westmorland Gazette* about the costs which he had incurred whilst travelling between Whitehaven and Kendal; in addition to his fare of 18s he had to tip five different coachmen and the guard during the course of his relatively short journey.[4]

Although mail coaches did not have to pay tolls, the cost of sending letters was equally prohibitive for most people on account of these heavy mileage and carriage duties. The Post Office did not itself set up mail coaches and preferred 'to offer the contract to various coach proprietors'. Contracts for the supplying of horses were usually in the hands of the various innkeepers along the roads, a good many of whom also provided the necessary post coaches on branch routes and thus monopolised the mailing business in their particular area. There is little evidence relating to the cost of postage in Cumbria, but one writer on the subject concludes that it continued to rise throughout the early nineteenth century, and that by 1840 the cost of sending a single sheet from Carlisle to London was 1s 1d; whilst corresponding rates from Carlisle to Glasgow, Edinburgh, Manchester and York amounted to 9d per sheet.[5] In order to avoid these high postage rates many people resorted to the 'Common Carrier' to deliver their mail, and there was a great deal of illicit letter carrying by these men during the early nineteenth century. 'It was estimated that not one in six of the

---

[3] *Parl. Papers*, 1844, XI, p. 11.

[4] *Westmorland Gazette*, 21 April 1827.

[5] R. C. Woodall, 'Postal History of Carlisle and Carlisle Mails—Early Transmission of Letters', *The Philatelist*, August and September 1950.

letters sent from Manchester went by post, while from Glasgow it was said that the proportion was one in ten.'[6]

The general rates of land carriage were more uniform, however, and, in accordance with the Act of 1692, a fixed scale of charges was drawn up by the Justices. These rates were applicable in the various counties to which the goods were being carried, and varied according to the weight and distance involved.[7] Until the repeal of this Act in 1827, these carriage rates were subject, in theory at least, to regular reassessments by the various Justices. However, it has been argued that the majority of JPs were content to reaffirm previous carriage rates irrespective of any changes in the cost of living during the intervening period.[8] If Willan's argument applies to Cumbria, then the inflexibility of such charges would tend to reduce the relative cost of land carriage by the beginning of the nineteenth century in view of the current level of price inflation. However, the only local evidence I have found which throws any light on this point is a single list of carriage charges published in the *Carlisle Journal* of 3 May 1806 by order of the Clerk of the Peace. The list is prefaced by a warning of the £5 penalty to which any carrier would be liable in the event of his not obeying the Justices' injunctions. A detailed list of charges is then inserted in the notice:[9]

'PARCELS ABOVE 7 LBS

London	to anywhere in Cumberland	33s		per pack
Newcastle	to Carlisle	6s	1½d	do
do	to Whitehaven	10s	7½d	do
do	to Cockermouth	9s	2½d	do
do	to Penrith	8s	1¼d	do
do	to Brampton	5s	1¾d	do
Carlisle	to Whitehaven	3s	5¾d	do
do	to Cockermouth	3s	0¾d	do
do	to Penrith	1s	11½d	do
do	to Hesket	1s	5d	do
do	to Longtown	1s	1d	do
do	to Wigton	1s	2½d	do
Whitehaven	to Cockermouth	1s	5d	do
do	to Penrith	4s	8½d	do
Cockermouth	to Penrith	3s	3¼d	do

[6] R. C. Woodfall, 'Postal History of Carlisle and Carlisle Mails—Early Transmission of Letters', *The Philatelist*, August and September 1950.

[7] T. S. Willan, 'The Justices of the Peace and the Rates of Land Carriage, 1692–1827', *Journal of Transport History*, V (1962–3), pp. 197–8.

[8] Ibid., p. 198.   [9] *Carlisle Journal*, 3 May 1806.

Lancaster	to Whitehaven	5s 11d	per pack
do	to Penrith	5s 3d	do
do	to Carlisle	7s 2¾d	do
Kendal	to Whitehaven via Ambleside	6s 0¼d	do
do	to Penrith	2s 10¼d	do
do	to Cockermouth	4s 9½d	do
do	to Carlisle	4s 9½d	do.'

These high mileage and carriage duties were widely resented, and criticism of governmental fiscal policy was intensified during the early nineteenth century, when the stage and mail coach proprietors began to face serious competition, first from canals and then, later, from railways and, to a lesser extent, from steamships. It was argued by the coaching interests that these other forms of transportation had an unfair advantage in that they were comparatively lightly taxed and could thus afford to charge lower rates and undercut the stage coaches and carriages. The mileage duties upon rail travel amounted to only ½d per mile for every four passengers carried, whilst steam shipment, both by river and by sea, was totally exempt from taxation.[10] The road interests particularly resented the inequitable basis of the mileage duty; the railway companies, unlike coach proprietors, were only taxed according to the number of passengers actually carried by rail at any one time. Finally in 1837, in response to these reiterated complaints, a Select Committee of the H. of C. met to consider the whole question of taxation as applied to the various forms of transportation. In giving evidence before this committee, the coachmasters complained of their 'utter inability' to compete with the railways owing to the extremely heavy and discriminatory taxation to which they were subjected. It was estimated that for every passenger carried, the railway proprietors paid ⅛d per mile of duty, the stage coach proprietors ¼d and the postmasters ¾d; whilst carriage by water was duty free.[11]

The committee, after hearing the evidence of the various interests, confirmed that 'a great inequality exists between the rates of taxation imposed on the different modes of internal communication', and 'earnestly recommended the abolition of all taxes of public conveyances'.[12] The committee's recommendations were not acted upon, but road carriage duties were reduced substantially during the early 1840s. In 1842, the mileage duty was established at a uniform rate of 1½d per mile rather than at a

10 *Parl. Papers*, 1837, **XX**, pp. 293.
11 Ibid., p. 294.   12 Ibid., p. 295.

variable rate of between 1d and 4d[13] and in the following year, the £5 Licence Duty was abolished.[14] However, by this time the stage coach proprietors could never hope to regain the ground they had lost.

Sea transport, both of passengers and freight, was particularly cheap. In view of this factor, and also because of their greater carrying capacity, ships engaged in coastal trade were able to compete very effectively with a good many of the main 'through' roads of England and Wales during the eighteenth and early nineteenth centuries. Coastal shipping was particularly useful in areas such as South-West Cumberland where road communications were notoriously deficient and circuitous.[15] Heavy freight traffic went by sea whenever possible; the ships allowing greater bulk carriage at a cheaper rate than did the local carriers. In 1808, for instance, a waggon of coal was shipped from Whitehaven to Millom at a cost of £1 18s 6d; it was estimated that, had it been carried to Millom by road, a distance of 27 miles, it would have cost £3 3s.[16] Similarly, in 1821 the citizens of Whitehaven noted that 'At present though Liverpool is three times the distance of Whitehaven from Carlisle the merchants of Carlisle can have goods from Liverpool at half the expense of carriage which they cost from Whitehaven'.[17]

Passenger travel was also considerably cheaper by sea. The fare from Whitehaven to Liverpool was 15s by first cabin and 10s 6d by second cabin in the *Highland Chieftain* in 1821,[18] whilst the corresponding fare for the same journey by the *Independent* post coach in 1823 was 24s 'Inside' and 17s 'Outside'.[19] The introduction of steamships about this time appears to have given a further impetus to the coastal passenger service off the Cumberland and Lancashire coasts. In 1826, a Company was set up to establish steam navigation between Port Carlisle and Liverpool,[20] and in the following year the first steamships began to operate from Whitehaven.[21] Parsons and White acknowledged the importance and popularity of these early steam packets.

[13] *Parl. Papers*, 1870, XX, pp. 406–7.   [14] Ibid.

[15] See Chapter 7 for an extension of this theme.

[16] C.R.O., Bateman MSS, 6 June 1808.

[17] *Westmorland Gazette*, 16 April 1821.

[18] *Whitehaven Gazette*, 7 May 1821.

[19] Ibid., 20 January 1823.

[20] J. Bulmer, *Directory of East Cumberland* (1884), p. 54.

[21] Oliver Wood, 'Development of the Coal, Iron and Shipbuilding Industries of West Cumberland, 1750–1914' (unpublished Ph.D. thesis, Univ. London, 1952), p. 187.

'Few places have reaped greater advantage from the facilities offered by steam navigation than Whitehaven; until its introduction the man of business was occupied two entire days at a heavy expense in travelling by the Stage Coaches from Whitehaven to Liverpool; whereas by steam he now goes on board the packet in the evening where he can in moderate weather sleep as comfortably as in his own bed and be landed at Liverpool in the morning.[22]

Also, 'To Dumfries and the other towns on the Scottish coast the journey by land occupies from $1\frac{1}{2}$ to 2 days which by steam is performed in from 3 to 5 hours'.[23] Subsequently, the cost of travel by steamer appears to have been further reduced, and by 1854 it was possible to journey between Whitehaven and Liverpool for as little as 6s in the cabin and 3s on deck.[24] The steam packet services continued to be popular even after the railways had become established in the region, and Black recommends sea travel in his Lake District Guide of 1856. 'A packet sails several times a week to and from Liverpool, and as this mode of reaching Whitehaven is much more economical and expeditious than the inland one, many persons avail themselves of it for the purpose of arriving at the lake country.'[25]

Traffic between West Cumberland and Liverpool was particularly heavy during the middle decades of the nineteenth century. It was estimated in 1843 that 'upwards of 60,000 passengers annually pass by steam boats between Liverpool and Glasgow and the ports of south-west Scotland—also these boats convey large quantities of horses, carriages, cattle and parcels'.[26] A high proportion of these ships would stop at the more important West Cumberland ports.

Trade between Furness and Liverpool was also very considerable. During the eighteenth century, iron ore and salt had been the principal commodities exchanged; salt being imported from Cheshire through Liverpool and Milnthorpe,[27] whilst iron ore was exported by the Backbarrow Company from Ulverston to Liverpool and then along the Trent–Mersey Canal to the Shropshire ironworks.[28] The Liverpool trade increased considerably in range

[22] Parsons & White, p. 275.   [23] Ibid.

[24] *Cumberland Pacquet*, 25 July 1854.

[25] Black, *Black's Guide to the Lakes* (1841), p. 67.

[26] T.H.R., Prospectus of the Lancaster and Carlisle Railway, December 1843.

[27] W. T. McIntire, 'The Port of Milnthorpe', C.W.T., **XXXVI** (1936), p. 51.

[28] J. D. Marshall, *Furness and the Industrial Revolution* (1958), p. 36.

during the early nineteenth century and this is illustrated by the nature of the business conducted by the carrying firm of Walter Berry.[29] The Low Wood Gunpowder Company placed particular reliance upon coastal shipping facilities; they obtained their necessary raw materials of saltpetre and brimstone from Liverpool and then re-shipped their manufactured powder and its various waste products such as tar acid.[30] The Company rarely resorted to road carriage until after about 1815, and there is only one surviving record of their making use of local carriers before this date. This one exception occurred in 1805, when, by a misunderstanding, 200 bags of saltpetre which the Company had asked to be conveyed by Pickfords from London to Liverpool, were forwarded directly to Kendal, 'and as a result additional transport had to be paid for to Low Wood, and the Company lost the advantage of the cheaper sea transport to Liverpool'.[31] Other exports from Furness and South-Westmorland to Liverpool included finished marble from the Kendal factories,[32] and large quantities of slates from the Kirkby Ireleth quarries.[33] Also, after the construction of a railway link to Fleetwood, a regular steamer service was established between Fleetwood and Piel in Furness.[34]

The West Cumberland ports, together with Barrow in Furness, participated in a more specialised coastal freight service: the export of iron ore to the South Wales ironworks. By 1856, a total of 200,000 tons of ore were being shipped annually from Barrow to South Wales,[35] whilst a further 124,630 tons were exported from Whitehaven.[36] Exports declined during the next decade as an increasing proportion of ore was being utilised locally to feed the growing iron industries in Furness and West Cumberland.

There was also a significant quantity of short distance coal traffic between West Cumberland and Furness and Cartmel in the eighteenth and early nineteenth centuries. South Westmorland lacked coal and used to import a certain amount of fuel from Whitehaven, before the opening of the Lancaster canal enabled Kendal manufacturers to utilise the Lancashire coal reserves.

[29] K.R.O., Account Books of Walter Berry (1838–52).

[30] L.R.O., D.D.L.O., Low Wood Gunpowder Company: Cash Books 1798–1839, and Cartage Accounts 1815–38.

[31] L.R.O., D.D.L.O., Low Wood Gunpowder Company Cash Books 1802–5.

[32] Parsons & White, p. 639.　　　　　　　[33] Ibid., pp. 715–16.

[34] Melville and Hobbs, 'Furness Travelling and Postal Arrangements in the Eighteenth and Nineteenth Centuries, C.W.T., XLVI, p. 98.

[35] J. D. Marshall, op. cit., p. 206.

[36] V.C.H. *Cumberland*, II (1904), p. 386.

As early as 1729, it was estimated that 'there has been shipped at Whitehaven and discharged at Milnthorpe in five years past upwards of 368 chaldrons of coal'.[37] Iron ore was shipped for even shorter distances from Egremont to Whitehaven before being re-shipped to South Wales.[38] No doubt high land carriage costs discouraged cart traffic parallel to the coast; thus heavier commodities tended under these circumstances to be carried by sea irrespective of the distances involved.

However, one must not overestimate the importance of coastal shipping as a direct competitor to road transport. In the first place, by the 1820s, as a result of improvements in road engineering and vehicular construction, and the increasing co-ordination of the various coach timetables, land transport had at least the advantage of being, on the whole, substantially faster than coastal shipping. This advantage was particularly marked over longer distances. For instance, the average time taken by the trading vessels passing between Whitehaven and London in 1822 was 37 days;[39] and, despite the improved service wrought by the introduction of 'Langtry's smacks' on the route in the following year, the journey still invariably took at least six days.[40] Thus, the stage coaches had a preponderant share of long distance passenger traffic by virtue of their greatly superior speed of travel. Steam ships provided more formidable competition over shorter routes, but the stage coach business does not appear to have been affected unduly by these developments, and the coaching trade between Whitehaven and Liverpool was particularly prominent during the 1820s and 1830s. This is somewhat surprising in view of the fact that travel by the new steam packets, along this route at least, was cheaper and, on the whole, markedly faster. However, travel by road was probably somewhat more comfortable than by sea, particularly in winter; the passage between Ulverston and Fleetwood having a bad reputation at this time of year.[41] Thus the stage coach proprietors were assured of the custom of all who disliked the possibility of an uncomfortable sea voyage; and there was keen competition between the different stage coaches on the route between Whitehaven and Liverpool.

The competition of coach proprietors with each other and

[37] W. T. McIntire, 'The Port of Milnthorpe', C.W.T., XXXVI (1936), p. 51.   [38] Parsons & White, p. 206.
[39] Whitehaven Gazette, 7 July 1823.
[40] Ibid., 28 July 1823.
[41] H.L.R.O., Select Committee of H. of C. on the Ulverston and Lancaster Railway Bill, 13 May 1851.

with the steam packets gave rise to quite spectacular fare reductions on many routes in England and Wales during the early nineteenth century. One of the first recorded instances of this occurred on the Birmingham to Sheffield route. Here, the introduction of a new stage coach in 1808 compelled rival proprietors to reduce their fares from £1 10s to as little as 8s for 'inside' travel.[42] Another notable fare reduction took place a little later on the popular London to Brighton road. By 1828, 'inside' coach fares had been reduced from 21s to as little as 7s on journeys between the two towns.[43]

This pattern was repeated in Cumbria, particularly on routes which faced competition from coastal shipping. For instance, in 1819 the fare between Whitehaven and Liverpool was 36s 'Inside' and 24s 'Outside'.[44] By April 1822, the *Duke of Lancaster* steam packet was advertised as providing 'Cheap and Agreeable Travelling to and from Liverpool, Whitehaven, Workington, Maryport and Dumfries'.[45] The *Independent* post coach proprietors reacted promptly to this new competition and 'beg to submit to the public . . . very reduced fares'. These new rates included a reduction in the fare on the Liverpool–Whitehaven route to 24s 'Inside' and 17s 'Outside'.[46] The following month, a rival coach firm owning the *Royal Sailor* also cut their rates and advertised that they would carry passengers from West Cumberland to Manchester or Liverpool at a cost of only 19s 'Inside' and 13s 'Outside'.[47] A week later, the *Independent* coach firm answered the challenge by again cutting their fares for the second time within a month. They now contracted to carry passengers over the same route for 17s 'Inside' and 13s 'Outside'.[48] The coach's Preston fares, on the other hand, were only reduced to 22s and 14s 6d;[49] thus it was actually cheaper in this instance to travel a greater distance. There appear in fact to have been a good many fare cuts in north-west England during the 1820s, although there is some evidence to suggest that coach fares rose slightly again during the 1830s.

The road interests were unable to compete so readily for coastal freight traffic, but the development of coastal shipping and harbour facilities generally, gave an impetus to the local cart traffic in West Cumberland and Furness. Thus carriers were able

[42] Jackman, p. 313.
[44] *Cumberland Pacquet*, 11 May 1819.
[45] *Whitehaven Gazette*, 22 April 1822.
[46] Ibid., 20 January 1823.
[48] Ibid., 24 February 1823.

[43] Ibid.

[47] Ibid., 17 February 1823.
[49] Ibid.

to provide a feeder service in minerals, etc., to the various ports. There was also a certain amount of short distance freight traffic along the West Cumberland coast. For instance, coal shipments from Whitehaven and Workington to Carlisle were negligible on account of high coastal duties, and, in consequence, there was a considerable volume of cart traffic in coal and stone along this route.[50] Cart traffic was also of considerable importance in South-West Cumberland, and in 1844 it was estimated that 4,212 tons of general merchandise, 11,748 tons of agricultural produce and 5,000 tons of coal, lime and slate were carried from Whitehaven towards Ulverston.[51] There is also a certain amount of evidence that, on occasions, stage waggons were preferred to coastal shipping for freight transport to and from locations outside Western Cumbria. For instance, the Kendal Fell Trustees, a prominent improvement commission in the town, were prepared to entrust the fragile glass globes for their street lamps to a selected road carrier as early as 1779.[52] Even the Low Wood Gunpowder Company began to export some of their powder by road to Manchester after about 1815.[53]

Thus it can be said that Western Cumberland, Furness and parts of lowland South Westmorland relied to a large extent, but not exclusively, upon coastal shipping for long distance freight carriage. Long distance passenger transport, on the other hand, was dominated by the stage coach interests. There is not sufficient evidence to permit any firm conclusions about the mode of carriage of freight and passengers over shorter distances, but it is probable that lighter commodities tended to be transported by carriers cart whereas heavier fuel and ore traffic went by sea. With regard to passenger travel, it is certain that the new steam ships were able to provide keen competition for traffic in the region bounded by Liverpool and Dumfries, between about 1820 and 1850.

Before the building of railway lines, roads had carried most of the region's inland traffic. Inland water transport was not very important in Cumbria; none of its rivers were navigable for any great distance by the beginning of this period, and only three

50 *Whitehaven Gazette*, 16 April 1821.

51 H.L.R.O., Select Committee of H. of C. on the Whitehaven and Furness Railway Bill, 30 May 1845.

52 G. H. Martin, 'Street Lamps for Kendal', *Journal of Transport History*, VII (1965), pp. 37–43.

53 L.R.O., D.D.L.O., Low Wood Gunpowder Company: Cartage Accounts 1815–38.

peripheral canals were constructed.[54] None the less, these canals did for a time provide low cost competition to road transport in Furness, South Westmorland and North-West Cumberland. Canal transport was undoubtedly cheap, and Jackman concludes that 'the cost of canal carriage normally did not exceed half and in most cases was a quarter to a third of land carriage'.[55] It appears on the basis of an analysis of the Port Carlisle canal receipts, that a differential rating system was adopted by the canal proprietors according to the nature of the article transported, and, in consequence, freight charges ranged from ½d to 3½d per ton mile as compared to the land carriage rates of slightly over 1d per mile for each pack carried.[56] The average weight of these packs must have been considerably less than one ton, in view of the limited carrying capacity of the carts and the considerable variety of commodities carried at any one time. Therefore, it appears that canal carriage was probably considerably cheaper, although the evidence for this is too slight to allow any accurate assessment of the proportional difference in cost between land and canal carriage. The *Cumberland Pacquet*, however, had no doubts at all about the benefits of lower cost freight carriage which followed the opening of the Carlisle to Port Carlisle canal. 'Coals of good quality, full measure, are now selling at 3½d per Carlisle peck at the Basin. When the Canal was commenced three years ago, the same quantity of a similar article sold for 6½d.'[57]

It is possible to make a more direct comparison of passenger charges on canal barges as opposed to stage coaches. The *Westmorland Gazette* frequently exhorted its readers in the early 1820s to take advantage of the Lancaster canal when journeying between Kendal and Preston. 'The Coach fares between Preston and Kendal . . . are outside 8s, inside 12s. By the Packet they are: After Cabin—4s, fore Cabin—6s.'[58] Passenger travel along the Lancaster canal appears to have been particularly well organised. A daily passenger service between Kendal and Preston began to operate in 1820; the boats covering the 57 mile journey in 14 hours, and tea, coffee and refreshments being served on board during this time. It was recorded that in the first six months after this service was introduced, a total of 14,000 passengers were

[54] (a) Ulverston canal in 1796; (b) Lancaster canal in 1819; (c) Port Carlisle canal in 1823. [55] Jackman, p. 449.
[56] L.P.A., 59G3, XIII, Carlisle Canal Act.
[57] *Cumberland Pacquet*, 17 March 1823.
[58] *Westmorland Gazette*, 8 May 1824.

carried along the canal between the two towns.[59] By the early 1830s the proprietors of the barges on the Lancaster canal were also able to compete with the stage coaches with respect to speed of passenger travel. In 1833 a new express boat, the *Waterwitch*, began to run between Kendal and Preston at an average speed of 10 miles an hour; the whole journey taking 7 hours and a return trip being made the same day.[60] Under these circumstances, travel along the Preston–Kendal canal became increasingly popular; between September 1833 and March 1834 'no fewer than 16,000 passengers have been taken by the Waterwitch canal boat which runs between Kendal and Preston'.[61] After the railway had reached Lancaster a good many people still travelled by canal as far as Lancaster, continuing their journey southwards by rail. Passenger services along the Lancaster canal were discontinued finally in 1849.[62]

Canal barges were more important, however, as carriers of freight. The principal reason for the building of the Lancaster canal was to supply Kendal with coal from South Lancashire, whilst providing an exchange traffic in limestone from the Warton area for the Lancashire industries.[63] Other commodities shipped down the Lancaster canal included slates from the Coniston area; by 1812 it was estimated that 3,000 tons of slate could be carried annually down the canal from Kendal at an estimated saving of at least 14s per ton on the cost of land carriage.[64] Similarly, iron ore and slate traffic from Furness often travelled down the Ulverston canal in the period before the opening of the Furness railway.[65]

The Lancaster canal barges were also quite important carriers of agricultural products, and the traffic of grain to Kendal along the canal was considered by Parsons and White to be of particular importance.[66] This expanding grain traffic also, no doubt, owed a good deal to the improving road conditions in the Kendal area during the early nineteenth century. The tonnage of freight carried along the canal increased steadily during these years before the opening of the Lancaster to Preston railway line in 1840. In 1825, 459,000 tons of produce were shipped along the canal, and this total had risen to 617,000 tons by 1840.[67]

59 Charles Hadfield, *British Canals* (1950), p. 170.
60 J. F. Curwen, 'The Lancaster Canal', C.W.T., **XVII** (1916–17), p. 45.
61 *Westmorland Gazette*, 1 March 1834.
62 C. Hadfield, op. cit., p. 170.
63 J. F. Curwen, 'The Lancaster Canal', op. cit., p. 45.   64 Ibid.
65 J. D. Marshall, op. cit., pp. 89–93.
66 Parsons & White, p. 640.   67 C. Hadfield, op, cit., p. 204.

The development of a reliable freight service along the Lancaster canal undoubtedly handicapped some of the South Westmorland carriers; the Berry's trade with Glasson, for instance, being almost completely destroyed after 1819.[68] However, they were not seriously inconvenienced by this competition, and avoided further trade reductions by concentrating their carrying business upon the Sandside ports.[69] Similarly, the Heron Syke Turnpike Trustees foresaw the consequences of the opening of the Lancaster canal and were able to make an equally judicious adjustment of their resources to offset the expected loss of traffic on the section of Trust road south of Kendal. Thus, in 1817 they decided that 'in view of the loss of traffic which the Southern section of the Trust must shortly sustain, a new Toll Bar should be erected at Shap in order to reap the maximum possible advantage from the increasing traffic to the north of Kendal'.[70] As a result of these precautions, the overall Trust revenues were not reduced. The rents of the Burton and Netherbridge gates fell from £601 and £725, respectively, in 1816[71] to £491 and £626 by 1822,[72] but the newly erected Shap gate was already worth £422 by this latter date,[73] and the Clifton gate to the south of Penrith had increased its value from £395 to £481 during this same period.[74]

Canal transport was similar to coastal shipping in that, whilst it provided substantial competition to the local carriers along parallel routes, it also tended to stimulate feeder traffic to its termini. For instance, carts travelled considerable distances to collect the supplies of guano which were being shipped up the Carlisle canal in increasing quantities during the 1840s. It was observed that by 1845 there were regular carrying services established between Carlisle and the agricultural areas of East Westmorland, in order to provide the various farms with this new fertiliser.[75] There was also a considerable mineral feeder service to the Carlisle canal basin, notably in lead from the Greenside mines in Patterdale. Two carriers, Mrs Cowper and Richard Midcalf, were particularly conspicuous in this trade. The former being entirely concerned with the carriage of lead to the canal basin and coal by return cargo; whilst Midcalf would also carry

[68] K.R.O., Account Books of Walter Berry (1838–52).   [69] Ibid.
[70] J. F. Curwen, *The Later Records of North Westmorland* (1932), p. 4.
[71] *Westmorland Gazette*, 21 March 1817.
[72] Ibid., 15 March 1823.   [73] Ibid.   [74] Ibid.
[75] C.R.O., Carlisle–Eamont Trust, Misc. Papers., Dispute between Trust and Proprietors of Greenside Lead Mines over Toll Charges, 1844.

various parcels from the canal and railway depots before returning to Penrith. Both carriers usually made three return journeys to Carlisle each week. Their trade was regular and specialised.[76]

The canal proprietors appreciated the need for road improvements in the vicinity of their canal in order to encourage this feeder traffic. For instance, the Ulverston Canal Company pressed for the improvement of the branch road from the Kirkby Moor quarries in order to facilitate the passage of lead traffic to the canal basin. In 1802, they donated £21 15s towards the cost of repairing this road, and they also made arrangements with the local highway authority to collect tolls from the slate merchants using the road in order to subsidise its maintenance.[77] Similarly, the Lancaster Canal Company financed a number of diversions along the Turnpike between Milnthorpe and Crooklands.[78]

A survey of this history of the three Cumbrian canals has some interesting features but their importance was limited. None penetrated far into the region and they were soon eclipsed by the newly built railways.

The railways had a threefold advantage over road transport. They were faster, cheaper and had a greater carrying capacity than had the stage coach, stage waggon and carrier cart services which they displaced. Jackman concludes that the average stage coach fare was from 3½d to 4d per mile for 'Inside' travel on most main routes. The equivalent 'Outside' coach rate was about 2d per mile on average.[79] The fares adopted by the leading railway companies, on the other hand, were about 3d per mile for first class carriage, 2d per mile for second class, and 1d to 1½d for third class.[80] If one equates 'Inside' coach travel with first class rail accommodation and 'Outside' coach travel with third class railway rates, it appears that rail fares were, on average, slightly cheaper than stage coach charges for first class travel and substantially cheaper for third class travelling. A comparison of Cumbrian coach and rail rates appears, on the whole, to support Jackman's national generalisation.

By the mid 1830s, the cost of coach travel was still relatively high, despite the price cutting of the 1820s, and there is little doubt that the introduction of railways into this area effected a substantial reduction in the cost of passenger travel. For instance,

[76] C.R.O., Carlisle-Eamont Trust, Misc. Papers., Dispute between Trust and Proprietors of Greenside Lead Mines over Toll Charges, 1844.
[77] J. L. Hobbs, 'The Turnpike Roads of North Lonsdale', C.W.T., LVX (1955), p. 290.   [78] K.R.O., Kendal Canal Minute Book (1818–35).
[79] Jackman, p. 605.   [80] Ibid.

in 1838 the stage coach fare between Whitehaven and Kendal amounted to 20s 'Inside' and 15s 'Outside'.[81] By 1850, it was possible to travel from Whitehaven to Liverpool by rail for as little as 10s 11d.[82] The cost per mile of travelling to Newcastle by rail was particularly low at this time and there were regular excursions from Carlisle at a fare of 5s; a mileage rate of slightly under 1d.[83] The stage coach proprietors were also undercut on the longer routes. Before the introduction of rail travel it cost £4 4s to travel by coach from London to Liverpool;[84] subsequently, the same journey could be made by rail for 37s first class and 27s second class.[85] In fact, the difference between the average cost of travel by road and rail was in all probability rather more pronounced than these figures suggest, in view of the fact that rail travel usually obviated tipping, overnight accommodation, and an accumulation of food and drink bills.

Railways also provided cheaper freight carriage. Thus, the cost of carrying general merchandise between London and Manchester, which had been as high as 80s a ton during the pre-railway period, dropped to about 30s a ton when carried by rail.[86] The only available Cumbrian record of actual, as distinct from anticipated railway freight charges, is for the Eskdale narrow gauge railway, linking Boot with Ravenglass. This line was opened in 1875. Before this, the Eskdale iron ore had to be carted nine miles to the nearest railway station at Drigg, at a cost of 10s per ton, but after the railway had been built the cost of transporting the ore was reduced to 2s 2d per ton.[87] These reduced freight charges also benefited the ordinary consumer as well as the various mining magnates and industrialists. For instance, the shareholders of the Newcastle–Carlisle railway estimated that the completion of their line would reduce the cost of Brampton coal for the Carlisle householder from 8s to 1s 6d per ton.[88]

Railway engines were also capable of speeds greatly in excess of those attained by the fastest stage coaches and steam ships. The average rate of rail travel by 1844 was about 24 miles per hour,[89] whereas no contemporary stage coach could hope to exceed 12 miles an hour. Thus, a journey from London to Glasgow which had taken 45½ hours by the fastest stage coaches

[81] *Cumberland Pacquet*, 19 June 1838.
[82] Ibid., 5 November 1850. [83] Ibid., 7 April 1846.
[84] See Jackman: Appendix. [85] Jackman, p. 607.
[86] Ibid., p. 608. [87] *Whitehaven Guardian*, 11 May 1876.
[88] John S. Maclean, *The Newcastle and Carlisle Railway, 1825–62* (1948), p. 12. [89] *Parl. Papers*, 1844, XI, p. 17.

in the mid 1830s[90] could be performed within 12 hours by rail
in 1850.[91] Shorter rail journeys within Cumbria were equally
expeditious by this time; it was possible to get from Whitehaven
to Ulverston in slightly over $2\frac{1}{2}$ hours[92] whereas it had taken
$6\frac{1}{4}$ hours to cover the same distance by stage coach.[93] Similarly,
the journey from Whitehaven to Carlisle took only 2 hours
10 min in 1850[94] as compared to 6 hours by stage coach in 1838.[95]

Railways also had the advantage of a vastly superior carrying
capacity both for freight and passenger traffic. In 1845, it was
recorded that by the time the train from Newcastle had reached
Manchester it was carrying upwards of 1,000 passengers in
thirty-five carriages.[96] This was admittedly quite exceptional, but
it does serve to illustrate the potential carrying capacity of the
railway. The stage coaches, by comparison, could rarely carry
more than about fifteen people at any one time. Even on a route
where there was a particularly high density of coach services, as
for instance between Liverpool and Manchester, the various
coaches seldom carried more than 500 passengers a day between
them.[97] After the construction of the Manchester–Liverpool
railway line, however, over 1,200 passengers were carried regularly
each day by train between the two towns.[98] Similarly, the railways
were able to accommodate far more freight than the local carriers'
carts. The latter were also frequently idle during the winter in
areas such as Furness, on account of difficult road conditions,
and, as a result, ore dumps accumulated at the various loading
points. After the Furness railway had been opened these dumps
were no longer necessary, and 600 to 700 tons of ore could be
transported daily by rail to the coast throughout the year. Soon
'the highway between Dalton and Barrow was becoming grass
grown for lack of use'.[99] The northern section of the West
Cumberland coalfield, in the hinterland of Maryport, also benefited markedly from the cheaper carriage rates and greater carrying
capacities of rail transport. Previous to the opening of the
Maryport to Aspatria railway in 1840, the costs and delays of
road carriage had discouraged the exploitation of the more inland
collieries around Aspatria. The building of this railway and its
subsequent extension to Whitehaven by the Whitehaven Junction

90 Jackman, Appendix, p. 701.
91 *Cumberland Pacquet*, 1 January 1850.
92 Ibid.   93 Ibid., 19 June 1838.
94 Ibid., 1 January 1850.   95 Ibid., 19 June 1838.
96 Ibid., 26 August 1845.   97 Jackman, 606–7.
98 Ibid.
99 *Ulverston Advertiser*, 5 April 1849.

line in 1847, laid the foundations for a very marked increase in the volume of coal traffic entering Maryport during the 1840s and 1850s. As a result, coal exports from Maryport rose from about 110,000 tons in 1839 to 333,871 tons by 1857.[100]

Thus, the railways began to take an increasing amount of traffic off the various roads in England and Wales, and a growing number of turnpike trusts became affected as parallel railway lines deprived them of their former income. Parliament was made increasingly aware of the financial difficulties of a good many trusts during the 1830s, and in 1839 a Select Committee met 'To ascertain how far the Formation of Railroads may affect the interests of Turnpike Trusts and the Creditors of such Trusts'.[101] The evidence given before the Committee by the various trust officials clearly revealed their incapacity to compete effectively with parallel railway lines. The great coach proprietor, Edward Sherman, was especially pessimistic and asserted that only 'timid people' now travelled by road.[102]

By 1840, several Cumbrian trusts were sharing in this general decline. The Newcastle to Carlisle railway had been open along its whole length since 1838, and the Maryport to Carlisle Railway Company had completed the section of their line between Maryport and Aspatria. It appears from the evidence incorporated into the Appendix of the 1840 Parliamentary Report, that 7 out of the 14 Cumberland trusts[103] and 3 out of 10 Westmorland trusts[104] considered that they had been adversely affected by the recent railway developments.[105] The turnpikes along the route between Newcastle and Carlisle suffered particularly from railway competition at this period. The Carlisle–Temon Trust sustained the most spectacular loss of traffic. The toll revenue of this trust was reduced from £877 18s 6d in 1835[106] to £594 5s 10d in 1836.[107] In 1837 it underwent a further reduction and its gates were only worth £295 15s 0d by the end of the year.[108] Other parallel turnpikes in East Cumberland were also affected by the opening of the Newcastle–Carlisle railway: the Carlisle–Brampton Trust

[100] W. Whellan, *History of Cumberland and Westmorland* (1860), pp. 319–20.
[101] *Parl. Papers*, 1839, **IX**, p. 371.   [102] Ibid., p. 386.
[103] Alston, Brampton–Longtown, Cockermouth–Maryport, Cockermouth–Workington, Cockermouth–Carlisle, Carlisle–Temon, and Carlisle–Brampton.
[104] Kirkby Lonsdale–Kendal–Milnthorpe, Brough–Bowes and Brough–Eamont.
[105] *Parl. Papers*,1840, **XXVII**, pp. 75–82, 482–7.
[106] C.R.O., Cumberland Q.S. Petition Rolls, Easter 1836.
[107] Ibid., Easter 1837.   [108] Ibid., Easter 1838.

receipts were reduced from £544 13s 1d in 1835[109] to £316 2s 5d by 1837,[110] and the neighbouring Brampton–Longtown Trust also suffered a considerable reduction in tolls, from £477 13s 4d in 1836[111] to £324 16s 6½d by 1838.[112] Similarly, the Brough–Eamont Trust reduced its rents from £1,205 12s 6d in 1835 to £926 in the following year.[113] The same Trust also claimed that a further toll reduction from £926 in 1838 to £850 in 1839 was a direct result of the opening of the railway line from the south to Preston; thus decreasing the amount of 'through' traffic using the Great North Road.[114]

The Newcastle–Carlisle railway did not only absorb a large part of the existing traffic between the two towns; it also encouraged the growth of a great deal of new traffic which had never previously made use of the various turnpikes. The *Cumberland Pacquet* noted this fact in 1844.

'Previous to the opening of that line all the traffic between those two towns was carried on by means of a few Carriers Carts, and all the passengers were conveyed to and fro by means of two coaches daily. During the past week the receipts on the Carlisle and Newcastle railway amounted to the extraordinary sum of upwards of £1,900—a sum which at no very remote period prior to the opening up of that Railroad would have conveyed all the passengers and parcels between those two towns for more than a twelvemonth.'[115]

Likewise, the opening of the railway line between Maryport and Carlisle was said to have nearly trebled the coal traffic coming into Maryport by 1844.[116]

During the early 1840s, the Eamont, Heron Syke and Milnthorpe Trusts along the main route between Lancaster and Carlisle, whilst admitting to being unaffected as yet by railroads, were not at all sanguine of their future prospects.[117] They feared the consequences of the inevitable extension of the railway from Preston to Carlisle. In 1846 this line was opened and the Trust receipts fell dramatically.

[109] C.R.O., Carlisle–Brampton Trust Minute Book (1828–63).
[110] Ibid.
[111] C.R.O., Brampton–Longtown Trust, Misc. papers.
[112] Ibid.   [113] *Parl. Papers*, 1856, **LVIII**, p. 179.
[114] *Parl. Papers*, 1840, **XXVII**, p. 483.
[115] *Cumberland Pacquet*, 9 July 1844.
[116] *Carlisle Patriot*, 23 March 1844.
[117] *Parl. Papers*, 1840, **XXVII**, pp. 484, 486.

Table 1.   The effect of the opening of the Lancaster to Carlisle railway
upon the parallel Trust roads.*

	Year	Receipts		
Carlisle–Eamont (Northern Division)	1846	£1275	13	0
	1847	£593	0	6
	1848	£397	1	0
Carlisle–Eamont (Southern Division)	1846	£872	14	7
	1847	£457	17	4
	1848	£399	5	9
Heron Syke–Eamont Bridge	1846	£2048	13	5
	1847	£838	3	1
	1848	£751	15	7
	1849	£672	19	5
Milnthorpe Levens	1846	£494	0	0
	1847	£400	0	0
	1848	£308	10	4½
	1849	£305	0	10

* See Appendix C for further details of where Trust Receipts obtained.

The West Cumberland Trusts also began to be affected by
railway competition at about this period; the Cockermouth–
Workington Trust receipts were reduced by half as a result of the
opening of the railway between the two towns in 1847.[118] The
revenues of the Cockermouth–Maryport and Cockermouth–
Carlisle Trusts, on the other hand, declined very slowly during the
1840s and 1850s. Their decline can be attributed to the gradual
erosion of road traffic by a developing railway network rather
than as a direct result of competition from any particular line.[119]
The Whitehaven Trust did not share in this decline in the late
1840s and it remained exceptionally prosperous until the Whitehaven–Cleator and Egremont railway was opened in 1856. This
line was immediately successful in capturing a large proportion
of the mineral traffic which had formerly used the turnpike, and
in the first six months after its opening, 50,000 tons of ore and
11,000 tons of coal were transported to Whitehaven by rail
from the various mines.[120] Consequently, the Whitehaven toll
receipts diminished rapidly: in 1855 the annual toll revenues of
the Trust amounted to £4,232 10s 11d; in 1856 they had dropped

[118] *Cumberland Pacquet*, 7 November 1849.
[119] See Appendix C.
[120] A. Wood 'Development of the Coal, Iron and Shipbuilding Industries
of West Cumberland, 1750–1914' (unpublished Ph.D. thesis, Univ. London,
1932), p. 241.

to £3,034 7s 10d; by 1857 to £2,707 8s 8d; and by 1858 the total revenues amounted to £1,797 12s 4d. Subsequently, the Trust's receipts remained fairly stable until its dissolution.[121]

The Whitehaven Trust was particularly reliant upon the mineral cart traffic using the roads into Whitehaven. A good many other Cumbrian Trusts, however, depended to a large extent upon coach traffic and suffered accordingly when the stage and mail coaches were withdrawn along many 'through' routes. Many of the most important stage coach routes fell into relative disuse during the 1830s and 1840s as parallel railway lines were constructed. Edward Sherman reported to the Select Committee of 1839 that he had seen 'a reduction on the North Road since the opening of the Railroad of 15 Coaches daily'.[122] Also the postmasters on the same road were said to have lost half their former business by this date, whilst their counterparts on the London–Birmingham road had lost three-quarters of their trade.[123] The loss of stage and mail coach traffic had been particularly dramatic on the Liverpool to Manchester road. Before the opening of the connecting railway in 1830 there had been a daily service of 22 regular and 5 occasional coaches on the road. Within five months of the railroad's opening, all but 4 of the coach services had been abandoned, and by 1832 there was only 1 coach operating between the two cities.[124]

By 1850, stage coach services had ceased on a good many Cumbrian roads. This was a very important loss for the Trusts concerned. The Heron Syke Trust, for instance, reported that in 1841 toll revenues derived from stage coach traffic using the road amounted to £952 12s 6d; this was a very substantial part of the Trust's total toll revenue and it had been completely lost by 1850.[125] It is reasonable to assume that the two divisions of the Eamont Trust, which formed a northerly extension of the Heron Syke road, suffered a corresponding loss through the withdrawal of stage coach services. Similarly, old coaching centres such as Brough lost most of their former trade if the railways by-passed them. One historian, when writing of Brough in 1860, noted that it was now 'little more than a village, the railway having destroyed the coaching trade which from its position on the North Mail Road it formerly possessed'.[126] The custom of the hostelries along these old coaching routes was correspondingly depleted. Some

121 See Appendix C for further details.
122 *Parl. Papers*, 1839, **IX**, p. 384.
123 Ibid., p. 377.   124 Jackman, p. 608.
125 *Parl. Papers*, 1850, **XLIX**, p. 336. 126 W. Whellan, op. cit., p. 730.

inns had, no doubt, lost some of their former custom before the railway period; trade being concentrated in a smaller number of hostelries as the accelerated coach services allowed for fewer stops than previously. Once a railway was opened, trade was concentrated on an even smaller number of favoured hostelries at the various rail termini. As Brian Harrison points out, 'Sobriety in the nineteenth century probably owed more to faster travel than to temperance agitation'.[127]

Parliament was particularly concerned about the prospects of those creditors who had lent money to the different Trusts for road improvements during the temporary boom in road transport in the first three decades of the nineteenth century. James McAdam reported that many Trusts all over the country were unable to repay these debts as a result of their losses in toll revenues through rail competition.[128] Therefore, a good many of the affected Trusts were compelled to surrender control of their toll gates to their creditors; thus preventing further road repairs by the Trusts concerned and placing the entire burden of road maintenance upon the various townships through which the road passed. Several of the Cumbrian Trusts had incurred heavy expenses during the early nineteenth century. A total of eleven new Trusts were inaugurated, whilst several old established bodies such as the Heron Syke, Carlisle–Eamont and Brough–Eamont Trusts indulged in a spate of extensive road building during this period. Thus additional debts were contracted. The Southern Division of the Carlisle–Eamont Trust borrowed £4,850 between 1830 and 1832,[129] whilst the Brough–Eamont Trust increased its debt by £1,000 in 1820.[130] Neither these Trusts nor their creditors could possibly have foreseen the unprecedented expansion of railway building which was to take place during the next two decades, and, in consequence, by the late 1840s a good many Trusts in Cumbria, in common with those in other regions, were confronted with the dilemma of financing increased principal and interest repayments to their creditors, on a greatly reduced budget.[131]

Despite the tremendous impact of rail competition, however, the road interests often displayed considerable resilience. At first,

127 Brian Harrison, *Drink and the Victorians*, p. 51.

128 *Parl. Papers*, 1839, IX, pp. 409–17.

129 C.R.O., Carlisle–Eamont Bridge Trust (Southern Division), Account Book (1823–75).   130 *Westmorland Advertiser*, 24 March 1821.

131 See Chapter 6 for an extended discussion of Trusts and their Creditors during this period.

the potential of rail transport was not widely appreciated and there was a good deal of local prejudice against the building of certain early lines.[132] For instance, when the Newcastle–Carlisle railway was originally projected, the *Carlisle Patriot* continued to favour the construction of a canal between the two towns. 'The Railway scheme ought to be and we have no doubt will be opposed by every man of sense and spirit in the district: it would blast the hopes of the living and chain down our posterity to move in almost the same confined limits in which circumstances have compelled us to move all our lives.'[133] Even after the early lines had been laid down and steam traction introduced, many doubts were entertained at first as to the safety of this new mode of travel. The *John Bull* magazine was very sceptical of this new phenomenon, and felt that 'No reasonable man would allow himself to be dragged through the air at the alarming rate of 20 miles per hour'.[134]

The stage coach and turnpike interests naturally opposed the early railways, but they did not always foresee the full implications of rail transport. A good many trustees considering that it was only a temporary setback, and that the reduction of tolls which succeeded the building of parallel railway lines, was a reflection of the over-pessimistic calculations of the toll lessees and thus did not truly indicate the nature of rail competition. It was therefore considered to be very important that the turnpike roads should be maintained in good condition so that they could later re-assume their former traffic. 'Otherwise your Railways will fail and you will have no good Turnpike roads to fall back on.'[135] The Brampton–Longtown Trust was notably sanguine as to its future recovery. 'When it is considered that, in process of time, many of the present Railways will be abandoned or the Companies become insolvent, the necessity for some power in the Trustees to maintain the passage along the road of which they are appointed Guardians is apparent.'[136] Even when it became manifest to all observers that the railway lines were becoming an established part of the country's transport system, a good many people still felt that in a growing economy both road and rail could share the fruits of increased productivity. This view was held by the

[132] This is an interesting minor theme in George Elliot's *Middlemarch*, (cf. 1959, Everyman ed.), pp. 107–16.
[133] *Carlisle Patriot*, 19 July 1824.
[134] M. Kirkpatrick, *The Story of Wetheral* (1956), p. 16.
[135] *Parl. Papers*, 1839, IX, p. 383.
[136] C.R.O., Brampton–Longtown Trust, Misc. Papers.

Greenwich Hospital Commission's agents who welcomed the construction of the Newcastle–Carlisle railway on the grounds that improved communications would engender a greater exploitation of the area's resources, the benefits of which would be shared by both road and rail transport.[137]

These prognostications appeared for a few years to have some substance, and a good many northern roads enjoyed an 'Indian Summer' during the late 1830s and early 1840s. For instance, cross-Pennine coach traffic between York and Manchester survived for a time in spite of railway competition, 'because of the circuitous early rail routes from Leeds to York and Manchester, which kept fares high and journeys relatively long'.[138] Most of the railways built through the Cumbrian counties had more direct routes than this, but some had not as yet been embarked upon, whilst others were only half completed. Consequently, the volume of traffic tended to increase on most roads which extended beyond existing railway termini or which provided a link between disconnected sections of line on half completed railways. In order to derive the maximum possible advantage from this temporary increase in traffic, it was important that the various stage coach proprietors and carrying organisations should provide a more flexible service on shorter routes. It was also necessary that they should link up where possible with rail, sea and canal services in order to share in an increasingly co-ordinated transport network. Thus the most important factor in reducing the volume of road traffic along 'through' routes, was not so much the opening of a section of parallel railway line as the completion of the whole length of line along the route in question.

By 1840 there was a railway from Newcastle to Carlisle, and the line from London had reached as far north as Preston. Thus railways were now carrying travellers to the fringe of Cumbria without as yet providing substantial competition for traffic in most parts of the region. Therefore, the connecting turnpikes between Carlisle and Preston probably benefited from the increased traffic to and from the two rail termini. For instance, the receipts of the Carlisle–Eamont Trust (Southern Division) increased from £720 9s 1d in 1839 to £827 8s 9d by 1840.[139] Like-

[137] P.R.O., ADM. 66/93, Greenwich Hospital Northern Estates MSS, Out Letters (1828–30), Wailes and Brandling to the Commissioners, 3 March 1829.

[138] G. C. Dickinson, 'Stage Coach Services in the West Riding of Yorkshire', *Journal of Transport History* (1959), p. 5.

[139] *Parl. Papers*, 1859, XIII, p. 717.

wise, the Heron Syke tolls rose from £1,901 10s in 1838 to £2,380 0s 6d by 1841.[140]

It is difficult to assess the extent to which these toll increases were the by-product of connecting 'through' traffic between Preston and Carlisle, but there is little doubt that the stage coach proprietors on these connecting routes made considerable efforts to co-ordinate their services with the new railway timetables. In 1839, the *Carlisle Patriot* advertised that

'The *North Britain* and *Invincible* Coaches leave the *Bush* and *Coffee House* Hotels Carlisle daily for Preston, Liverpool, Manchester, London, etc., at 8 p.m., immediately after the arrival of the train from Newcastle, and arrive at Preston in time for the first morning trains South—N.B. the same coaches return from Preston in time for the morning train to Newcastle.'[141]

By 1844, a further two stage coaches were operating regular connecting services along this route.[142]

There was an equally conspicuous demand for 'connecting' coach services in West Cumberland and Furness during this period, and in some cases the railway companies began to run their own coaches in order to link up half-completed lines. For instance, in 1844 the Maryport–Carlisle Railway Company advertised their intention 'To afford increased accommodation to the public' by running 'Two large and commodious coaches carrying 18 passengers each between Whitehaven and Maryport and between Aspatria and Wigton'. The Company were to operate twice daily services on both routes, and thus fill a temporary need by linking up the incompleted section of their own line whilst, at the same time, providing an extended service southwards from Maryport to Whitehaven.[143] A similar coach service was introduced in 1849 between Ravenglass and Broughton in Furness,[144] these coaches serving to supplement rail transport along the route of the Whitehaven and Furness Junction railway. At the same period, regular coach services were installed extending from the terminus of the Furness railway at Dalton, to Ulverston and Newby Bridge.[145] The Ulverston coach service underwent a further extension after the opening of the Lancaster to Carlisle railway, and it was announced in 1846 that 'A Coach is to be forthwith started between Ulverston and Milnthorpe in

140 *Parl. Papers*, 1850, **XLIX**, p. 338.
141 *Carlisle Patriot*, 9 February 1839.
142 *Cumberland Pacquet*, 25 June 1844.   143 Ibid., 5 March 1844.
144 Ibid., 16 April 1850.   145 Ibid.

order to meet the Railway trains as they severally pass through that place to both the north and south'.[146]

The various carriers also found adequate occupation whilst the new railways were being constructed. For instance, the carters in the Shap region were fully employed in moving the necessary stones during the building of the Lancaster–Carlisle railway.[147] Also, the construction of the Leven viaduct by the engineers of the Ulverston–Carnforth railway link, gave employment to certain of the Sandside carriers who were engaged in transporting the necessary girders.[148]

Short distance freight traffic was undoubtedly stimulated by the development of rail transport. In June 1846 it was recorded that,

'At the time arrangements were entered into by the Company for conveying Goods from Whitehaven to the station at Workington, two or three carts per week were found sufficient to remove all the Goods that offered, but within the present month as many as fourteen cart loads in a day have been sent from Whitehaven to the station to be despatched per train to Carlisle, Newcastle and various other places.'[149]

Although the volume of freight carried in areas more remote from the main routeways would be considerably smaller, there is little doubt that the carriers' cart continued to provide a valuable and profitable service in linking up such areas with the various towns and railway stations. The traffic in lead and coal from the Patterdale area to the Newcastle and Carlisle railway station and the Carlisle canal basin illustrates the continuing value of this cart traffic.[150] Similarly, the Mardale farmers exported 3,000 pounds of butter weekly by rail to Manchester, the carriers' waggons picking up their baskets from the isolated farms in the dale.[151] The traffic along the Cockermouth–Penrith Trust road in the neighbourhood of these two towns was also very considerable. They were both important market centres for the surrounding areas, and agricultural traffic along the Greystoke road into

[146] *Cumberland Pacquet*, 15 December 1846.

[147] C.R.O., Lowther MSS, Memoranda Book re Elections (1833–44).

[148] W. T. McIntire, 'The Port of Milnthorpe', C.W.T., **XXXVI** (1936), p. 54.

[149] *Cumberland Pacquet*, 16 June 1846.

[150] C.R.O., Carlisle–Eamont Trust, Misc. Papers, Dispute between Trust and proprietors of Greenside Lead Mines over Toll Charges, 1844.

[151] Harriet Martineau, *Complete Guide to the English Lakes* (1855), p. 175.

Penrith was particularly heavy.[152] Market traffic also approached Penrith from the south along the Eamont Trust road, and the collector at the Milehouse toll bar on this latter stretch of road recollected that he used to collect an extra 30 per cent in toll receipts on market days.[153]

Carlisle was a particularly important focal point for short distance traffic. The city expanded rapidly during the mid-nineteenth century, particularly along Botchergate and, to a lesser extent, along Warwick road. This in turn led to a growth in the volume of market and commuter traffic entering the city, notably from the Harraby area to the south.[154]

It is impossible to assess the cumulative volume of market and railway feeder traffic upon the various parish roads, but the increased receipts of a good many toll gates on the outskirts of the various Cumbrian towns during the middle decades of the century, testifies to the compensatory value of this short distance traffic for the Trusts concerned. The Carlisle–Brampton Trust benefited the most from this traffic. This Trust had lost most of its 'through' traffic during the 1830s as a result of the opening of the Newcastle to Carlisle railway, and the revenues of the Corby Hill gate declined from £230 in 1832[155] to £51 by 1839.[156] The Botcherby gate, on the other hand, maintained its former income; the gate was situated on the outskirts of Carlisle and was able to take advantage of the growing suburban traffic along Warwick road. In 1832 the gate was let for £280[157] and in 1839 its receipts amounted to £243;[158] it had declined only marginally in value during these years despite the opening of the railway. Subsequently, as Carlisle continued to expand, the toll revenues of the Botcherby gate increased and eventuallys urpassed all pre-railway figures until by 1873 the gate was worth £398.[159] Similarly, the Harraby gate on the south side of Carlisle managed to retain a good deal of its short distance traffic; it was let for £283 as late as 1858[160] whereas the Hesket gate, which relied for its receipts

152 See Chapter 5 for further details of this traffic.
153 C.R.O., Bleaymire and Shepherd Collection, Cockermouth–Penrith Trust, Misc. Papers re 1856 Road Bill.
154 See Chapter 5 for further details of the expansion of Carlisle.
155 C.R.O., Carlisle–Brampton Trust Minutes, 3 March 1832.
156 Ibid., 28 September 1839.
157 Ibid., 3 March 1832.   158 Ibid., 30 April 1839.
159 C.R.O., Carlisle–Brampton Trust Minutes, 26 July 1873.
160 C.R.O., TT/1/15, Carlisle–Eamont Bridge Trust (Southern Division), Minutes of Evidence before the Select Committee of the H. of C. on the 1859 Road Bill, 29 March 1859.

upon 'through' traffic passing between Carlisle and Penrith, was only worth £120 by this date.[161] Previous to the opening of the Lancaster to Carlisle railway, the Hesket bar had been the more prosperous gate of the two.[162]

The Heron Syke Trust was able to make equally effective use of local traffic to and from Kendal; the Netherbridge gate on the outskirts of the town retaining the greater part of its rental value throughout the railway period. None the less, this was not sufficient to compensate for the loss of 'through' traffic along the Trust road. By 1876, the Netherbridge gate was worth $1\frac{1}{2}$ times the combined rents of the other four Trust gates, and the total toll revenues of the Trust had, on balance, declined very substantially since the early 1840s.[163] Despite this, however, it is fair to say that this sustained local traffic in the vicinity of Kendal prevented far greater losses by the Heron Syke Trust during this period.

The Whitehaven Trust also maintained a proportion of its mineral and market traffic after the opening of the Whitehaven–Cleator and Egremont railway in 1856. It was estimated, for instance, that as late as 1864, 67,747 tons of iron ore were being sent annually to Whitehaven by carriers cart,[164] and the toll receipts of the Trust amounted to £1,973 16s 2d in 1867,[165] a comparable figure to its income during the 1830s. The Whitehaven Trust was therefore still relatively wealthy despite railway competition. It had simply lost the unprecedented volume of mineral traffic which had begun to make use of the road in the 1840s.

The railways also brought a growing number of tourists to the Lake District.

'The Lake District is entirely surrounded by railways and approachable on all sides. The London and North Western Company has access at Kendal, Windermere, Shap, Penrith (for Pooley Bridge), Troutbeck (for Ullswater) and Keswick, and the Furness Company (in connection with the Midland) at Grange, the foot of Windermere (Lakeside), Broughton, Coniston and Seascale (for Wastwater and Ennerdale). So far as the public is concerned what more could be wished? In the very heart of the

---

[161] C.R.O., TT/1/15, Carlisle–Eamont Bridge Trust (Southern Division), Minutes of Evidence before the Select Committee of the H. of C. on the 1859 Road Bill, 29 March 1859.   [162] Ibid.

[163] See Appendix B for details of sources of Trust receipts during this period.   [164] *Cumberland Pacquet*, 6 June 1865.

[165] C.R.O., Cumberland Q.S. Petition Rolls, Easter 1868.

district the traveller is within 3 or 4 hours drive of a railway station.'[166]

Thus, although railways brought travellers to the fringe of the Lake District, they did not, with the possible exception of the Cockermouth–Penrith Line, encroach upon the area.

A considerable number of travellers approached the Lake District through Furness, after the opening of the railway link between Preston and Fleetwood and the subsequent establishment of a connecting steamship service to Piel. In 1844, the *Cumberland Pacquet* noted that Ulverston

'was unusually gay and bustling in consequence of the great number of Tourists constantly arriving and departing by the steamer from Fleetwood and the *Windermere* from Liverpool, as well as by the various public vehicles which now ply the roads in all directions. Since the great facilities were given to travellers by steam, Ulverston may be ranked among the various points from which tourists set out on their excursion among the Lakes.[167]

This steamer service was soon supplemented by a rail approach route: from Preston to Kendal and then on to Windermere. The opening of this latter branch line from Kendal in 1846 was a particularly important factor in accelerating the development of a tourist industry. Windermere now became the principal starting point for a tour of the various lakes, and the coach services for Ambleside, Keswick, Cockermouth, Hawkshead and Coniston were timed so as to connect up with incoming trains. It was also important, both for the Turnpike Trusts and the Railway Companies, that the region's lakes should be exploited to the full. Consequently, steamboat services were introduced on Windermere, Coniston and Ullswater and there was provision for regular connections between rail, stage coach and lake steamer on the various advertised Lakeland tours. By 1846 there were two regular steamship services on Lake Windermere, Waterhead being the principal junction point for connecting stage coach services to Ambleside and Grasmere.[168] Similarly, passenger services down Coniston lake provided an extension of the excursion trips along the Coniston railway,[169] whilst the Ullswater steam boats in turn

---

[166] Robert Somervell, *A Protest Against the Extension of Railways in the Lake District* (1876), p. 54.

[167] *Cumberland Pacquet*, 30 July 1844.   [168] Ibid., 28 April 1846.

[169] Melville and Hobbs, 'Furness Travelling and Postal Arrangements in the Eighteenth and Nineteenth Centuries', C.W.T., **XLVI**, pp. 50–1.

connected up with the Keswick to Pooley Bridge coach services.[170]

The Ambleside Trust benefited greatly from the increased tourist traffic brought by the Windermere railway. This branch line only duplicated the first section of the Trust road between Kendal and Windermere and, overall, was much more important as a 'feeder' to this road than as a competitor. The receipts at Waterhead and Grasmere gates rose from £396 in 1846 to £570 by 1848; a direct result of the opening of the Kendal to Windermere railway.[171]

The more remote lakes of Western Cumberland were of little importance as routeways and attracted fewer visitors, but there is evidence that the opening of the Whitehaven and Furness Junction railway did stimulate connecting coach and chaise services up Ennerdale and Wasdale from the various stations along the railway line; carriages being installed at Seascale and Drigg stations specifically for this purpose.[172] In order to cater for these tourists, the *Scawfell* hotel was built at Seascale;[173] the whole undertaking being completed within a year. It was hoped that this hotel would prove a popular stopping place for tourists travelling to Wastwater.

However, the *Seascale* hotel did not prove to be quite so popular as its promoters had anticipated. It was felt that the area's remoteness from the main centres of Lake District tourism discouraged traffic. There were plans to remedy this by building a 'Coach road' over Styhead Pass, linking Seathwaite in Borrowdale with Wasdale Head, and in 1896 the Highway Committee of the Cumberland County Council issued a circular supporting this proposal.[174] The road was not built, but Seascale does appear to have been attracting more tourists by the turn of the century This was recognised by the 1905 Edition of *Black's Guide:* 'Seascale has risen much of late and is fast becoming the chief resort of pleasure seekers on this coast'.[175]

It was of crucial importance for the various coaching interests that railways should not penetrate into the Lake District. Such an encroachment would adversely affect the coaching trade and

[170] *Black's Picturesque Guide to the English Lakes* (A. & C. Black, 1844) p. 171.

[171] K.R.O., Ambleside Trust Minutes, 15 September 1846 and 12 September 1848.

[172] John Linton, *A Handbook of the Whitehaven and Furness Railways* (1852), pp. 64–5. [173] *Cumberland Pacquet*, 28 May 1850.

[174] CCH/1/4, Cumberland Highway Comm. Minutes, 13 July 1896.

[175] *Black's Picturesque Guide to the English Lakes*, op. cit., p. 197.

would also destroy the profits of the Cockermouth–Penrith and Ambleside Trusts. In an attempt to forestall projected rail developments on the former route, local coach proprietors resorted to a programme of concentrated fare cutting: by 1850, the coach fare between Cockermouth and Keswick had been reduced to 1s and the *Pacquet* noted that 'This in point of cheapness beats even 3rd Class Railway travelling'.[176] It was also proposed to extend the Windermere railway through Ambleside to Keswick but this line was never built and, in consequence, the Ambleside road remained the only Cumbrian Trust to be largely free from railway competition throughout its life.

The fight against the Windermere to Keswick railway was long and bitter and the campaign enlisted the support of a good many 'national' figures, notably Matthew Arnold and Ruskin. Wordsworth had originally written a couple of strongly-worded letters to the *Morning Post* condemning the projected Kendal to Windermere railway on the grounds that 'The staple of the district is, in fact, its beauty and its character of seclusion and retirement'.[177] It was undesirable in his opinion that large numbers of the poorer classes should be conveyed to the area by cheap railway excursions; such people had not the capacity to appreciate its beauty and must first be trained to admire less intense forms of scenery nearer home. 'The perception of what has acquired the name of picturesque and romantic scenery is so far from being intuitive that it can be produced only by a slow and gradual process of culture.'[178] Above all, Wordsworth feared that railways would lead to the commercial exploitation of the Lake District and the destruction of all that was simple and natural.

'Let us glance at the mischief which such facilities would produce. The directors of Railway Companies are always ready to devise or encourage entertainments for tempting the humbler classes to leave their homes. Accordingly, for the profits of the shareholders and that of the lower class of Innkeepers we should have wrestling matches, horse and boat races without number and pot houses and beer shops would keep pace with these excitements and retreats. . . . The injury which would thus be done to morals, both among this influx of strangers and the lower class of inhabitants is obvious.'[179]

176 *Cumberland Pacquet*, 20 August 1850.
177 W. Wordsworth, *Guide to the Lake District* (1835), p. 148.
178 Ibid., p. 157.
179 Ibid., p. 155.

Despite the patronising tone of much of his writing on this subject, Wordworth's attitude was not ostensibly one of 'aristocratic' exclusiveness. He was prepared to welcome any person, irrespective of station, 'who coming hither shall bring with him an eye to perceive and a heart to full and worthily enjoy'.[180]

Wordsworth was unsuccessful in his fight to prevent the opening of the Kendal–Windermere railway, but subsequent attempts to prevent a further extension of the railway, from Windermere to Keswick, were finally successful. The campaign against this 'Dunmail' railway reached its height in the 1870s and was headed by John Ruskin and Robert Somervell. Ruskin's philosophy on this subject was similar to that of Wordsworth, but his writings were rather more restrained and, unlike Wordsworth, he endeavoured to avoid charges of being selfish and patronising in his allusions to working men's excursions to the region. He recognised the value of railways in bringing tourists to the fringe of the area, but insisted that they should subsequently travel by road. Such travel would be slower and more restful and would allow a fuller and more sustained appreciation of the region's beauties, unsullied by incongruous and disfiguring railway lines. 'The Traveller can go by Train; rejoicing to Windermere, to Coniston Water, to Derwentwater and close to Ullswater. Surely he might walk or ride to Wastwater and Thirlmere and Grasmere. He will be all the better for it if he does, and if he cannot, he will lose little by losing all that he would see from the windows of a train.'[181] Despite some differences in emphasis, therefore, Ruskin agreed fundamentally with Wordsworth in fearing the extension of 'mechanical decrepitude' into the Lake District.

The 'Dunmail' railway project was defeated but the fight with the railway interests continued. The Cockermouth–Penrith line was opened in 1864 and there were schemes to build an extension line from Braithwaite to Buttermere in order to exploit the Honister slate quarries. This latter project was defeated in 1883 as was a parallel attempt by the Furness Railway Company to build a branch line up Ennerdale.[182] In the same year, at a meeting of the Wordsworth Society, presided over by Matthew Arnold, it was proposed that a Lake District Defence Society be set up 'To protect the Lake District from those injurious encroachments upon its scenery which are from time to time attempted from

[180] W. Wordsworth, *Guide to the Lake District* (1835), p. 165.

[181] R. Somervell, op. cit., p. 47.

[182] E. F. Rawnsley, *Canon Rawnsley: An Account of His Life* (1923), pp. 49–54.

purely commercial or speculative motives without regard to its claims as a National Recreation Ground'.[183]

This aesthetic opposition to railway incursion into the Lake District helped to give an unprecedented monopoly to road transport in the central parts of the region throughout this period. The Ambleside Trust, in particular, benefited from this monopoly; in 1855 a total of 21,480 carriages are recorded to have passed over Troutbeck bridge,[184] whilst a further 15,420 vehicles journeyed beyond Ambleside towards Grasmere and Keswick.[185] As a result, the rents of the Waterhead and Grasmere toll gates along this line of road increased steadily during the middle years of the century, and by 1865 were let for a total of £899; an increase of £329 since 1848.[186]

The various Lake District hotels inevitably profited from this increased tourist traffic, and they gave considerable publicity to their catering facilities. The *Royal Oak Hotel* at Keswick, for instance, was described in 1868 as having 'Hot Cold and Shower Baths'.[187] Other hostelries, such as the *Queens Hotel* at Ambleside, drew particular attention to the range of excursions which left their doors during the summer season to tour the various local beauty-spots.[188] Unfortunately, it is impossible to ascertain the numbers of visitors staying at the different Lake District hotels, although it appears, from the evidence of a single surviving 'Visitors Book', that the *Salutation Hotel* at Ambleside became increasingly popular during the middle years of the century. In 1858, between the months of May and December 351 visitors are recorded to have stayed at this particular hotel. In 1862, the hotel had 547 visitors during the whole of the year, and by 1868 this number had further increased to a total of 751 guests: including 21 from America, 2 from Hamburg and individual travellers from Frankfurt, Heidenheim, Rome, Paris and Amsterdam.[189]

No doubt the hotel management had a considerable interest in the promotion of the various coach excursions which left their premises during the summer season. It would also be interesting to speculate on the extent to which the Lancaster–Carlisle and

---

[183] E. F. Rawnsley, *Canon Rawnsley: An account of His Life* (1923), pp. 49–54.

[184] K.R.O., Ambleside Trust Misc. Papers, Details of Traffic using the Trust Road, 1 May 1855–30 April 1856.   [185] Ibid.

[186] K.R.O., Ambleside Trust Minutes, 14 September 1865.

[187] Frederick Wright, *Leaves from Our Diary or Tales of a Tour to the English Lakes 1868–9*, p. 22.   [188] Ibid.

[189] Armitt Library, Ambleside, Visitors Book of the *Salutation Hotel*, Ambleside (1858–74).

Coniston Railway Companies financed the extension of these stage coach and steamship excursion services. However, no information has as yet come to light on this subject. All one can say is that the stage coach services appear to have been successful in absorbing these increasing tourist demands, and in providing a wide range of excursions to all parts of the Lake District.

There was a corresponding expansion of one or two villages along the main tourist routes, Windermere and Bowness in particular undergoing rapid changes after the opening of the branch railway line from Kendal and the introduction of a ferry service across the lake. Harriet Martineau, writing in 1855, noted that 'A few years previously the area was so secluded that it was some distinction even for the most travelled man to have seen it. Now there is a Windermere railway station, and a Windermere post-office and hotel; a thriving village of Windermere and a prosperous locality'.[190] However, she did not consider these changes to be for the worse; on the contrary, unlike some of her literary contemporaries, she maintained that 'any infusion of the intelligence and varied interest of the townspeople must, it appears, be eminently beneficial; and the order of workpeople brought by the railways is of a desirable kind'.[191] Therefore she concludes that 'the best as well as the last and greatest change in the Lake District is that which is arising from the introduction of the railroad'.[192]

The growth of tourist centres such as Windermere and Bowness gave a stimulus to the local carrying trade. Thus the Plumgarths and Staveley gates on the turnpike between Kendal and Windermere were able to retain their value despite the opening of the railway; increased short distance market traffic into Windermere and Bowness compensating for the loss of 'through' traffic along the road.[193]

Therefore, although road traffic in Cumbria as a whole declined considerably owing to railway competition, there was undoubtedly an increase in the volume of short distance traffic in the neighbourhood of the growing towns. Also, one should bear in mind the importance of 'feeder' traffic to the various railway stations. The carrier's cart continued to perform a valuable social and economic role throughout the nineteenth century. Finally, it is important to note the significance of the tourist trade in

---

190 H. Martineau, op. cit., p. 1.   191 Ibid., p. 143.

192 Ibid., p. 146. Her attitude is, of course, hardly surprising if one takes into account her Utilitarian leanings.

193 K.R.O., Ambleside Trust Minute Book (1824–75).

F

attracting traffic to the region, whilst giving road transport a virtual monopoly in the Lake District area. As a result of these factors, the Carlisle–Brampton Trust increased its toll receipts during the railway period as did the Ambleside Trust. All the other Cumbrian Trusts were adversely affected to some degree by rail competition. However, the growth of short-distance traffic proved a partial compensation to some Trusts and, also, it is necessary to bear in mind that two of the most important Cumbrian roads, the Cockermouth–Penrith and Whitehaven Trusts, were not affected by rail competition until comparatively late in their history; the Whitehaven–Cleator–Egremont railway was not opened until 1856 and the Cockermouth–Penrith line did not begin to operate until as late as 1864.

On the other hand, road traffic did decline quite spectacularly on the main passenger route between Kendal and Carlisle. Rail transport was undoubtedly the most important factor in reducing the volume of road traffic; but it is also important to consider the resilience of certain road interests in the light of this sustained challenge. A good many roads still enjoyed considerable traffic after the railways were built. The volume of this traffic was, on the whole, considerably reduced in extent and vehicles usually travelled for shorter distances, but they still used the roads and they merit consideration here.

Table 2.   Cumbrian annual toll receipts (based upon receipts of twenty Turnpike Trusts calculated at five-yearly intervals, 1825–70).*

1825	£905	1850	£823
1830	£1,021	1855	£954
1835	£985	1860	£840
1840	£1,028	1865	£761
1845	£1,015	1870	£756

* These receipts do not include tolls taken upon stage coach traffic. Hence, the loss of revenues by the various Trusts in the post-railway period is a little greater than these figures indicate.

Chapter 5

SOME PROBLEMS OF
URBAN GROWTH

Between 1801 and 1861 the population of Cumberland rose from
117,230 to 205,276.[1] During this same period the population of
Westmorland increased from 40,805 to 60,817.[2] This expansion
in both counties and also in Furness was particulary marked
during the first thirty years of the nineteenth century: Cumberland
registering a 45·5 per cent growth, Westmorland expanding by 32
per cent, whilst Furness and Cartmel grew from 17,887 to 24,311[3].

A considerable proportion of this increased population
was concentrated in towns. Carlisle, in particular, expanded
with unprecedented vigour and doubled in size during the
first half of the nineteenth century. In addition, Appleby,
Keswick, Penrith, Brampton and Kendal all registered a
population growth of at least 50 per cent during this period.
There was a corresponding expansion of industry in these various
towns. The development of mining and ship-building operations
in the neighbourhood of the West Cumberland towns has been
dealt with elsewhere, but inland locations such as Carlisle,
Penrith and Kendal were equally active in expanding their
industries during this same period.

Table 3.   Population increase in Cumbria (1801-61).

	1801	*1831*	*1861*
Carlisle	10,221	20,006	29,417
Whitehaven	8,741	11,393	18,842
Workington	5,716	6,415	6,467
Maryport	471	3,877	6,037
Kendal	6,891	10,015	12,029
Penrith	3,801	6,059	7,189
Keswick	1,350	2,159	2,610
Appleby	711	1,459	1,569
Brampton	1,682	2,842	2,379
Cockermouth	1,545	4,536	7,057

[1] An increase of 75 per cent.   [2] An increase of 49 per cent.
[3] An increase of 36 per cent.

Carlisle's industries developed rapidly. By 1851, despite certain setbacks during the war years, the town had eleven spinning mills containing over 80,000 spindles. In 1847 a gas works was built and by 1860 Whellan noted that 'Power Looms have recently been introduced on a large scale. There are numerous cotton-mills; and one belonging to Messrs Dixon, by its extent, rivals some of the largest in Lancashire. The Woollen industry is again "looking up", two large factories having lately been established. Carlisle is likewise noted for its extensive biscuit manufactures'.[4]

Kendal also expanded considerably both as a market and as a manufacturing centre during the early decades of the nineteenth century, and these changes were emphasised by Parsons and White when composing their authoritative *Directory* of 1829. At one point the two authors compare contemporary Kendal with the town as they remembered it thirty years previously. 'At the former period, no wheat was exposed here for sale and 30 loads of oats was considered a full market . . . but a great change has taken place, and now it is not uncommon to see 200 loads of wheat and a much greater quantity of oats and other meal in the market.' There was a corresponding expansion of Kendal's textile industry during this same period, whilst the 1830s also saw the beginnings of a boot and shoe industry in the Netherfield district of the town, under the direction of the Somervell brothers.[5]

It is interesting to note that all these towns attained their highest rate of growth in the period before the introduction of rail transport into the region. They were thus almost entirely dependent upon road traffic and coastal shipping facilities to provide food and raw materials for their growing population and developing industries. The rapid growth of these towns also suggests that the available carrying services were able to provide an adequate supply of the necessary building materials.

Subsequently, the railways came to monopolise long distance carriage to the various towns, but at the same time the provision of short distance road 'feeder' traffic became increasingly important for the urban and railway authorities. It was equally necessary for the carriers and Turnpike Trusts, in view of their greatly reduced share of long distance traffic, to capitalize upon this new source of income and to adapt their organisation accordingly.

The carrier services contrived to do this with considerable

[4] W. Whellan, *History of Cumberland and Westmorland* (1860), p. 96.
[5] C. Nicholson, *The Annals of Kendal* (1835), p. 278.

success, as we have seen, but the turnpike authorities were frequently unable to realise the full potential of this suburban, market and railway feeder traffic on account of the hostility of the various towns to the siting of toll gates within their suburbs or within close proximity to their boundaries.

This had already been a problem in the eighteenth century, but relations between the Turnpike Trusts and certain urban authorities deteriorated further during the course of the nineteenth century, as towns grew in size and maintenance costs upon urban approach roads increased. Disputes were most frequent in those parts of the country which were more heavily urbanised. For instance, Middlesex was reported to be particularly hostile to toll gates near town boundaries,[6] and industrial Lancashire and Yorkshire witnessed similar disputes. The Leeds Borough Council was even prepared to go to the length of paying off the debts of the Leeds–Hunslet Trust in order to hasten its dissolution and thereby avoid the possibility of future toll charges on the outskirts of the city.[7]

This right to collect tolls upon short-distance urban traffic became an issue of increasing importance to a good many Cumbrian Trusts by the middle of the nineteenth century. Their receipts had declined as a result of railway competition whilst their debts had in the meantime increased and creditors were becoming impatient. Furthermore, several Trusts were having to face increasing road maintenance expenses during these years as a result of the development of abnormally heavy suburban traffic and its consequent wear and tear of short stretches of Trust road. It was essential therefore that Trusts in this position should be recouped for these added expenses by taxing short-distance traffic. On the other hand, urban councils, neighbouring agriculturalists, carrying and railway interests were equally determined to resist the Turnpike Trusts on this issue.

Dissension was particularly rife along the line of the main Cumbrian 'through' route between Lancaster and Carlisle. The Trusts along this road had suffered particularly heavy toll reductions as a result of railway competition, and were thus very greatly dependent upon regular toll payments by short distance

6 *Parl. Papers*, 1836, **XIX**, p. 351.
7 J. L. Hanson, 'Transport Developments in West Yorkshire From the Industrial Revolution to the Present Day' (Ph.D. thesis, London, 1949). On the other hand, one should note that John Copeland in his recent book on Road Transport—*Roads and Their Traffic, 1750–1850* (1968)—has cited instances of co-operation between certain urban Improvement Commissions and their respective neighbouring Trusts: at Yeovil in 1833 and at Exeter in 1840.

traffic in order to recoup some of their losses. Therefore, they were very eager to erect toll gates within town suburbs whenever possible and, in particular, to intercept railway feeder traffic whenever a particular station was situated outside the legal boundaries of a town. The Milnthorpe railway station was in this category, and in 1855 the Milnthorpe–Levens Trust built a toll bar to intercept the traffic which passed between the town and its station; a distance of about three-quarters of a mile.[8] The installation of the gate gave rise to much opposition, both from townsmen who travelled out to the station and also the surrounding farmers and tradesmen who came into Milnthorpe. It was argued that the gate should be removed one mile further back along the Crooklands road and that the tolls at this gate should be reduced by a half; 'whilst the remaining Bar on the Kirkby Lonsdale Road should also charge one half toll rather than being cleared as at present by payment at Milnthorpe. Thus the absurdity of taxing those who travel only two hundred yards to the Railway Station with the repair of ten miles of Turnpike Road for the good of Kirkby Lonsdale would no longer exist'.[9] Another complaint against the Kirkby Lonsdale interests on the Trust was couched in rather more colourful terms. 'The Cerberus who guards this gate says, "Oh, but the payment may clear you to Kirkby Lonsdale"—it may! but I don't want to go to Kirkby Lonsdale nor does one out of twenty of us, why should we be taxed to save the Kirkby Lonsdale people THEIR fair payment for repairs of THEIR Roads'.[10] Finally, after renewed agitation, the unpopular gate was taken down in 1875.

Carlisle was the most important town along this line of road north of Lancaster, and its Council was particularly insistent upon the need to resist the building of toll gates near to the city's boundaries. In 1818, for instance, the Act inaugurating the Carlisle–Glasgow Trust specified that only one toll should be levied between Carlisle and Allison Bank, and that no such gates should be erected within 2 miles of the city boundary.[11]

The Carlisle Corporation was equally careful to ensure that the newly formed Carlisle–Brampton Trust should not impinge upon the city's suburbs; the 1828 Act inaugurating this particular Trust body stipulated 'That nothing in this Act contained shall extend or be constructed to extend to alter, prejudice, impeach or lessen the rights, powers or privileges of the Mayor, Aldermen,

---

[8] J. F. Curwen, *The Ancient Parish of Heversham with Milnthorpe* (1930), p. 66.   [9] *Westmorland Gazette*, 23 March 1867.
[10] Ibid., 16 March 1867.   [11] L.P.A., 59G3, cap. XC.

Bailiffs and Citizens of the City of Carlisle in any wise howso-ever'.[12] Notwithstanding this precaution, however, the subse-quently increased receipts at the Botcherby gate on this road suggest that the Trust was eminently successful in utilising the short distance traffic along the Turnpike into Carlisle.[13]

The Carlisle–Eamont Trust was not so fortunate, and its dispute with the Carlisle City Council over the siting of a toll gate and the maintenance of a stretch of road on the south side of Carlisle, was long, bitter and costly. The road was heavily used early in the nineteenth century, and between 1806 and 1808 considerable improvements were being considered along its route. The Trust required extra revenues in order to subsidise these repairs without substantially adding to its principal debt, and the Trust officials hoped to finance these undertakings by taxing the short-distance market traffic which made regular use of the road in the vicinity of Carlisle and Penrith. Thus by 1807 the Trustees were campaigning for an alteration in the forthcoming Renewal Act allowing them to erect toll gates within a mile of both towns.[14] Sir James Graham supported the Trust's campaign on the grounds that there was a great need for these proposed road improvements and that the somewhat disproportionate taxation of short distance traffic was the only means by which the Trust could sufficiently supplement its toll receipts so as to finance these repairs

'I have only to say that unless sufficient Tolls are collected the road must always remain in a bad state and in every case they must bear harder upon some persons than the generality of Travellers. It certainly would be desirable to make everyone pay according to the length of road travelled, but if Gates are not allowed to be put within a mile of Carlisle or Penrith, I am afraid the Tolls will fall short and I really cannot see how any reasonable man can object to a small Toll to be taken at these Gates; or perhaps an exemption may be given to particular Farms near these intended Gates.'[15]

Eventually a compromise was reached, and the 1808 Trust Renewal Act allowed for the construction of three toll gates: one at the foot of Botchergate in Carlisle, a second gate at Penrith Townhead and a third at Kempley Bank, between Eamont

[12] L.P.A., 9G4, cap. XX.
[13] C.R.O., Carlisle–Brampton Trust Minute Book (1828–63).
[14] C.R.O., Carlisle–Eamont Bridge Trust, misc. Papers re 1808 Renewal Act.   [15] Ibid., Letter Sir James Graham to Trustees, 9 June 1807.

Bridge and the village of Carleton. At the same time, the Act stipulated that 'all person and persons who shall pass or repass through the said Turnpike or Toll Gate to be erected at the foot of Botchergate on Carlisle market days, on horseback or with a Cart or Carts, and carrying provisions only to Carlisle market and who shall not travel more than one mile upon the Turnpike Road—shall not be charged with or liable to pay any of the duties aforesaid'.[16] A similar stipulation was made concerning the payment of tolls at Penrith Townhead.

Thus the Carlisle–Eamont Trust was unable to capitalize upon the shorter distance market traffic but, despite this limitation, all three gates became increasingly profitable to the Trust as the towns of Carlisle and Penrith continued to expand during the years following the 1808 Act. The Southern Division of the Trust was particularly concerned to retain control of the Kempley Bank gate. This gate had been erected temporarily in 1808 in order to reimburse the Trust for its extensive road improvements on Kempley Brow during the preceding three years. It was understood at the time that, since the gate was situated little more than half a mile from the southern end of Penrith, it could not justifiably be made a fixture in view of its proximity to the town centre. Consequently, it was generally understood by both town and Trust that the gate was to be dismantled as soon as its receipts had paid off the Kempley improvements. The gate proved to be exceptionally profitable in view of its strategic location and it had repaid the improvement expenditure long before the expiration of the Trust Act in 1830. None the less, the gate was not removed; the Trustees were determined to continue to tax traffic entering Penrith in order to subsidise further road improvements in the vicinity of the town. However, although Penrith was obliged to suffer the inconvenience of two toll gates near its boundaries during this period, it at least enjoyed the compensation of improved approach roads.

There is no evidence of any correspondingly extensive road improvements in the vicinity of Carlisle during this period, and the City Council in consequence began to remonstrate increasingly against surrounding toll gates on the basis that the revenues of these gates were not being used in the interests of the town. The toll gate at the foot of Botchergate gave rise to particular dissension, and opposition to it was intensified when in 1829 the site of the proposed Newcastle–Carlisle Railway Station was pro-

---

[16] L.P.A. 48G3, cap. XXVIII.

visionally fixed at a point 360 yards to the south of the Botchergate toll bar.[17] Thus the Carlisle Corporation and the Newcastle–Carlisle Railway Company had a common interest in opposing the continuance of the Botchergate toll bar in its present position. 'As it would catch all this new and extended traffic and be a great grievance to the inhabitants of Carlisle.'[18]

The Carlisle Trustees were hopeful that the Trust Renewal Act of the following year would recognise the justice of their claims and authorise the removal of the disputed Gate southwards as far as Harraby. The 1830 Act satisfied them in this respect, but it also stipulated that 'none of the tolls shall be laid out in the repair or improvement of any street within the city of Carlisle or the suburbs thereof, or within the town of Penrith, nor shall any tolls be collected therein by virtue of this Act'.[19] Hence, it was made clear to the Carlisle ratepayers that, although suburban road traffic would no longer have to pay tolls, the Trust for its part would no longer be required to maintain suburban roads.

In practice, however, the Trustees were able to ignore this latter section of the Act, since it was not made at all clear precisely what constituted the 'surburbs' of either Penrith or Carlisle. As a result, the Carlisle and Penrith interest groups amongst the Trustees continued to use toll revenues for the repair of suburban roads. This allocation of Trust funds was, of course, less satisfactory to the villages along the line of road between Carlisle and Penrith, but they were not so strongly represented on the Trust body. However, it soon became apparent that the costs of repairing the Carlisle suburban roads would amount to far more than the equivalent sum for Penrith. Carlisle was expanding rapidly in this period and the opening of the Newcastle–Carlisle Railway station in 1836 increased further the volume of short-distance traffic using Botchergate. Hence, the Penrith section of the Trust now had good reason to feel that it was subsidising repairs at the Carlisle end of the road and, in view of this, the Carlisle authorities ought either to contribute to their own suburban road improvements or else permit the re-instalment of the Harraby Toll bar at its former site on Botchergate.

In 1846 the Trust's revenues declined dramatically following the opening of the Lancaster–Carlisle railway. This did not influence the growth of short-distance traffic within the suburbs

[17] C.R.O., Carlisle–Eamont Bridge Trust, misc. Papers re to 1859 Renewal Bill, Brief for Opposition.
[18] Ibid.   [19] L.P.A., 11G4, cap CX.

of Carlisle but it did affect the Trust's capacity to pay for the increased wear and tear which this heavy traffic was inflicting upon such roads.

These new developments occasioned a special meeting of the Trust in May 1849 at which the Penrith Trustees presented their case for the repair of Botchergate becoming a civic responsibility. In support of their argument they estimated that the 1,400 yards of road between the City 'Bounder stone' and the Harraby Toll Gate were costing as much to repair as any other 8 miles of the same road.[20] The Trustees' next step was to approach the Newcastle–Carlisle Railway Company with a view to persuading them 'to contribute annually a reasonable sum towards the repair of the mile of road in question'.[21] The reply to this was not encouraging. Railway Companies in general had little incentive as a rule to repair approach roads to their respective stations. For the most part they were confident that people and freight would continue to travel by rail regardless of the condition of the feeder roads to the station. In the final analysis, the dependence of the road users on the railways would in itself be a sufficient guarantee against connecting roads deteriorating to any great extent.

Finally, the Penrith interests on the Trust took the law into their hands and on 8 November 1858 removed the Harraby Toll Bar back to its former position along Botchergate between the Newcastle–Carlisle railway station and the City 'bounder stone'.[22] This action was promptly contested by the Carlisle Trustees on the grounds that the gate's removal contravened the 1830 Act which forbade the collection of tolls within the suburbs of Carlisle. They also pointed out that no section of the Trust stood to gain from this action by reason of the illegality of the Gate's removal and the consequent difficulties of enforcing toll payments at Botchergate.

The gate lasted exactly a month at its new site before it was dismantled.[23] Whether this was done by disgruntled road users, or at the instigation of the Carlisle Trustees is not at all clear, although there is no doubt that the latter welcomed its removal. Both sets of Trustees now concentrated upon framing sets of proposals which they hoped would influence the shape of the Trust Renewal Act in the following year. Their recent experiences had convinced the Penrith Trustees that it was impractical to

[20] C.R.O., Carlisle–Eamont Trust, Misc. Papers re to 1859 Renewal Bill, Brief For Opposition.
[21] Ibid.   [22] Ibid.   [23] Ibid.

make any further attempts to establish a toll gate within the suburbs of Carlisle, and they were now ready to admit that a literal interpretation of the 1830 Act forbade such toll collections. However, they also pointed out that the Act was equally definite in forbidding the expenditure of toll revenues upon suburban roads. The Carlisle Trustees were reluctant to concede this point.

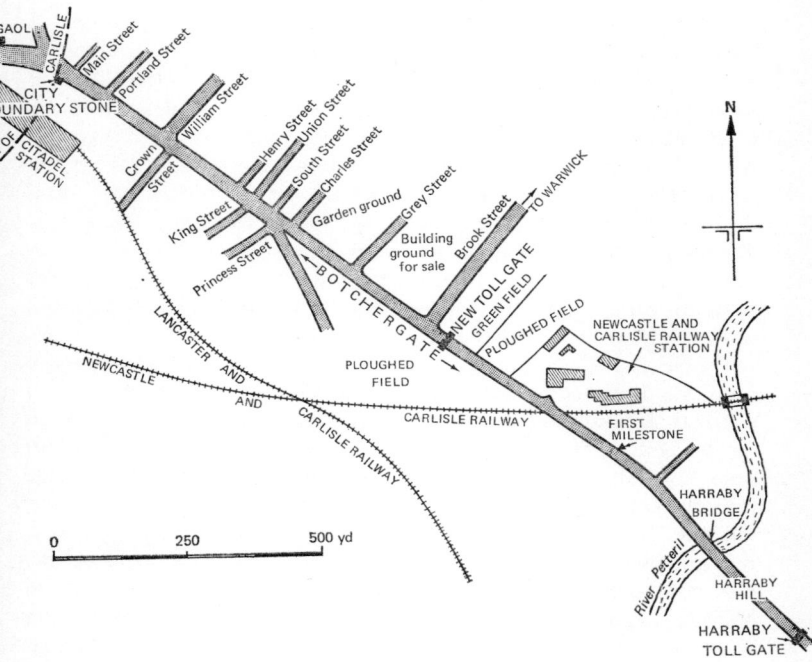

Fig. 1.   Map illustrating the Harraby dispute.

They admitted that there was a case to be made for the repair of Botchergate becoming a civic responsibility on the grounds that it carried a high proportion of city traffic. This did not apply, it was argued, to the remaining suburban roads in Carlisle which were used mainly by traffic from the surrounding rural areas. However, to make an exception of Botchergate would set a difficult precedent for the City and they would soon 'have every inch of road within the boundary of the city thrown upon the rates'.[24]

[24] C.R.O., Carlisle–Eamont Trust, Misc. Papers re to 1859 Renewal Bill, Brief for Opposition.

The Home Office was asked by both sides to arbitrate in this dispute, and it was finally resolved that the toll gate should remain at Harraby Bridge, but that the Trust should 'relinquish to the local Board, who now repair the footways, the portion of road lying within the present city boundary—namely from the city bounder stone to Harraby'.[25] This judgement at least had the virtue of being unambiguous. Unlike the 1830 Act, it no longer spoke of 'suburbs', and instead specified the precise section of road to be maintained in each case.

This proved to be the last word on the subject. After a dispute extending over at least half a century it was finally decided that the Carlisle Corporation should be responsible for the repair of Botchergate, whilst at the same time this road should be free from toll gates.

The town of Penrith also featured in a contemporaneous and equally lengthy dispute involving the Cockermouth–Penrith Trust. However, on this occasion, the Trustees presented an apparently united front and their main conflict was with the agricultural interests in the surrounding townships rather than with the Penrith Corporation.

When the Cockermouth–Penrith Trust was inaugurated in 1761, its Trustees were empowered to place a toll bar across the road at a point near to Penrith Castle, at the junction of the roads leading from the several villages of Blencow, Newbiggin and Stainton. Thus the gate was advantageously sited to capture the market traffic approaching Penrith from the surrounding villages. It was also stipulated in the Act that the Trust had a responsibility to contribute to the repair of these side roads, and was consequently required to lay out a quarter of the duties to be collected at the toll bar for this purpose.[26] It appears that the Trust was reluctant to spend money on these branch roads, notwithstanding its statutory obligations, and the Trustees had to be reminded of their maintenance responsibilities in the Renewal Act of 1824.

During the next two decades the receipts of the Castlegate bar increased considerably, particularly after the erection of a second toll gate at Skirsgill, about a mile distant from Penrith along the main Stainton road, in 1843.[27] Thus there were now two toll gates upon the Stainton road, but three years later the Castlegate bar was removed on to the Greystoke branch road,[28] this alteration

[25] C.R.O., Carlisle–Eamont Trust, Misc. Papers re to 1859 Renewal Bill, Brief for Opposition.
[26] C.R.O., Bleaymire and Shepherd Collection, Misc. Papers re Cockermouth–Penrith Trust Renewal Bill, 1856.   [27] Ibid.   [28] Ibid.

being the end product of a series of diversions and changes brought about by the construction of the Lancaster–Carlisle railway line in 1846. This gave rise to renewed controversy. The Trust was now charging tolls upon a branch road whilst at the same time refusing to spend money upon the upkeep of this road.

This taxing of market traffic was a distinct disincentive to progressive agriculturalists, and was unpopular in Penrith itself in addition to the surrounding townships, by virtue of its raising food prices within the town. The townsmen and agriculturalists had added cause for complaint when they contemplated that the Trustees' rapacity was brought about by the demands of 'outside' creditors who had no interest in the area and its problems and were simply concerned with the repayment of their debt. The Trustees were consequently accused of lack of sympathy with the economic needs of the region and of being virtually the pawns of distant creditors.

Fundamentally, the townships were no worse off than they had been twenty years previously. The only difference was that now

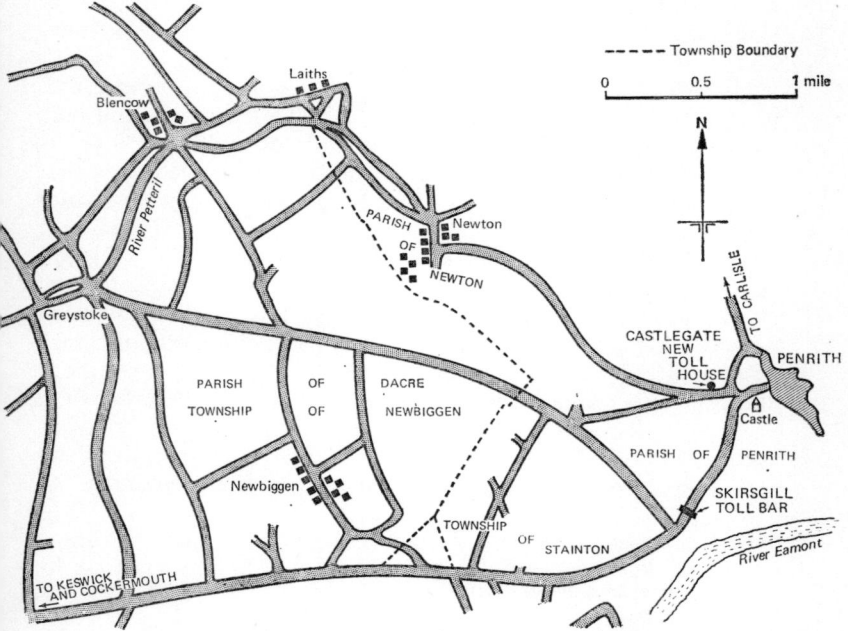

Fig. 2.   Map illustrating the Castlegate bar dispute.

they were being taxed before they had even reached the turnpike road, as distinct from being charged an equivalent sum for travelling a very short distance along the Turnpike into the town. None the less, the erection of a toll gate outside the legal boundaries of the Trust was of sufficiently doubtful legality to justify the townships' campaign. As a result of this opposition, the Trustees found it increasingly difficult to collect tolls at Castlegate and in September 1853 the lessee of the gate felt obliged to instruct his toll collector 'to cease demanding as being of no use'.[29] Once this decision had been taken, through traffic immediately began to use the Greystoke road. The attraction of travelling toll free was such that farmers and merchants were prepared to make very circuitous journeys in order to avoid the Skirsgill toll gate. A witness in the dispute reported that he had 'frequently seen Fleming, the Dalemain miller, making use of the Greystoke road, that the direct road from his mill to Penrith is not more than 2½ miles—that he used to go round by Stainton and then take one of the side roads and come upon the Greystoke road'.[30] The Eamont Trust also lost traffic in this way and the toll collector at the Milehouse bar reported, six weeks after the closure of the Castlegate toll bar, that his own receipts 'immediately fell by 20 per cent to 30 per cent on the market days'.[31]

However, the Cockermouth–Penrith Trust was, of course, the main sufferer and its losses were heavy. The Castlegate toll bar was worth at least £350 a year in actual rent; and in addition it was virtually certain that the removal of this gate would render the Skirsgill toll bar 'of very little value to the Trust as owing to the great number of Side Gates which communicate between the Greystoke Road and the main Turnpike Road—2 persons may easily get from the Greystoke Road on to the main Turnpike Road and so escape the Skirsgill Bar.'[32] In fact, it was estimated that it would be necessary to erect toll houses at eight of these side roads in order to prevent traffic avoiding toll payments by judicious evasion of the main route.[33] This was hardly a feasible alternative in view of the estimated £100 which would be necessary to build each toll house. It was therefore imperative that the Trust should maintain a toll gate near to the boundaries of

[29] C.R.O., Bleaymire and Shepherd Collection, Misc. Papers re Cockermouth–Penrith Trust Renewal Bill, 1856.   [30] Ibid.
[31] Ibid., Minute of Select Committee of H. of C. on Cockermouth–Penrith Road Bill, 6 May 1856.
[32] C.R.O., Bleaymire and Shepherd Collection, Misc. Papers re Cockermouth–Penrith Trust Renewal Bill, 1856.   [33] Ibid.

Penrith. It was impossible to prevent this discrimination against short-distance traffic, if long-distance traffic was not to escape toll.

The surrounding townships also wanted a solution to this question although for a different reason. Heavier traffic on the various side roads was increasing their own road maintenance expenses, and hence it became all the more important that the Greystoke road in particular should become a Trust responsibility.

Non-local users of the roads concerned, however, had no axe to grind in this respect and welcomed the Castlegate litigation which enabled them to avoid all toll payments when travelling to Penrith. Such travellers enjoyed a couple of toll-free years until an inevitable compromise was arrived at in September 1855 and incorporated into the Trust Renewal Act of the following year. The Act allowed for toll collections to be made on the Greystoke road, 'provided always that after the first day of October 1857, the Trustees shall not collect any toll on the Greystoke road unless and until they shall have laid out the sum of £400 in widening of such road'.[34]

On this occasion, the Trustees were prepared to honour their repair obligations. The events of the previous few years had convinced them that the potential profit to be derived from Greystoke traffic outweighed any future maintenance expenses which they were likely to incur along this particular line of road.

The agricultural interests in the area between Cockermouth and Maryport appear to have had similar cause for grievance against the disproportionately heavy tolls which were being levied by the local Trust upon market traffic. One farmer summarised their position in a letter to the *Cumberland Pacquet*:

'Sir, it appears to me that the Trustees of the Wigton, Maryport and Cockermouth Turnpike Trust are imposing upon the public by having removed the Toll Bar at Maryport to Ellen Grove, and erecting a new one a little further from the town at the end of the Workington Road near to the bridge, and exacting three full Tolls between Ellen Grove and Cockermouth, a distance of only eight miles . . . should the imposition be continued, the Trustees must not blame the farmers if they send to Wales for Rebecca to lead them in a campaign against the said Toll Bars.'[35]

[34] L.P.A., 19–20 V, cap LXIV.
[35] *Cumberland Pacquet*, 30 July 1844.

It appears from the surviving records of the Cockermouth–Maryport Trust, that the number and position of gates along the line of road in 1866 was identical to the siting of 1844. Therefore this suggests that the farmers' complaints were not met by the Trust, although there is no evidence as to how they reacted to this rebuff or whether they received any other form of compensation from the Trustees.[36]

This lengthy summary of the Harraby and Castlebar disputes in particular, throws a good deal of light upon a number of facets of social and economic change in the Cumbrian area. Town Councils, Turnpike Trusts, local landowners and Railway Companies were all concerned in these disputes, whilst the installation of new toll charges had a direct effect upon the cost of living in the towns concerned.

The Harraby dispute illustrates the problems which could arise when suburban expansion outstripped the official boundaries of a town. In these circumstances, neighbouring Trusts often had little option but to place their toll gates as close as possible to the town boundary in order to ensure that traffic entering the town did not escape toll payments. Once a suburb had expanded sufficiently to generate its own commuter traffic, such vehicles might also be charged tolls at a similar rate. There was also the likelihood that if the local Trust proved unable or unwilling to maintain suburban roads, they would become a charge upon the rates. Hence there was every incentive for local ratepayers to seek election to Turnpike Trust Boards in order to prevent these twin evils of suburban toll gates and increased rates. The presence of urban pressure groups upon Trust bodies encouraged other Trustees drawn from the various smaller towns and villages along the road to combine forces in opposing any attempt to modify Trust policy with regard to suburban roads. There is no doubt that the siting of toll gates within suburbs militated unfairly against local commuter traffic, but it was not always possible for Trusts to be more flexible in this respect. Trustees could reasonably argue in some cases that the withdrawal of suburban toll gates might enable outside traffic to avoid toll payments altogether. However, in other cases, this argument could be hypocritically used, and the Penrith Trustees fall rather more into this category. Harraby Bridge was quite a good site for a toll gate and was unlikely to be by-passed by very much traffic. The Penrith Trustees were not likely therefore to acquire very much additional

[36] See Appendix C for details of sources from which Trust Accounts obtained.

toll revenue from outside traffic by moving the Harraby toll gate near to the centre of Carlisle, but they would gain a great deal in toll revenues from commuter traffic, and this was undoubtedly their main concern.

Such policies were particularly likely to appeal to Trust creditors, although creditors living in Carlisle must have had divided loyalties in this respect. As ratepayers they were opposed to any attempts to make the repair of Botchergate a civic responsibility; yet at the same time they had a vested interest in the Eamont Trust remaining relatively prosperous, at least until their own personal investment had been recouped in full by the Trust.

The Cockermouth–Penrith Trust creditors had less cause for concern in this period, as there was no loss of 'through' traffic along this line of road until the mid 1860s. However, the Trustees here were equally keen to exploit short-distance traffic and, in the process, prevent longer-distance traffic avoiding toll payments. Hence, local travellers into Penrith felt the same sense of grievance about having to pay regular tolls for travelling short distances.

Both Trusts also found it difficult and perhaps inexpedient to reach clear-cut decisions as to the precise length of road they covered, although the areas of conflict were different in each case. The Cockermouth–Penrith Trustees were not so concerned about suburban encroachment, as the towns along this line of road were smaller and growing at a slower pace. Instead, difficulties arose as to whether or not certain branch roads could be reasonably regarded as constituting part of the Trust for purposes of either toll collection or road maintenance.

Chapter 6

TRUST DISSOLUTION AND
ITS AFTERMATH

The discussion in previous chapters has served to illustrate the increasing importance of short distance traffic for the various Turnpike Trusts, and also the extent to which the exploitation of this traffic had repercussions for both rural and urban interests. Nevertheless, local traffic was seldom sufficient to compensate fully for the loss of long distance transport along the Trust roads, and by the late 1830s, considerable concern was being felt in Government circles about the position of the turnpike authorities in the light of railway competition.

It was generally recognised by now that Turnpike Trusts should be dissolved. They were widely disliked by all road users and the frequent stoppages to traffic which toll gates necessitated, were an impediment to the more expeditious carriage of people and goods along the main roads. In fact, they were now considered to have outlived their usefulness, on the grounds that, in an increasingly complex economy, most of the population benefited directly or indirectly from improved travel conditions and therefore all should contribute to the cost of road repair, irrespective of whether or not they were regular users of the various roads. Nevertheless, the general consensus of official opinion expressed in these Reports determined that preparations for Trust dissolution must be long and gradual and that all due precautions must be taken. The principal reason for this caution was a recognition of the need for the creditors of the various Trusts to be repaid in full. Thus, in common with a good many other nineteenth century changes, as for instance in the Army and Civil Service recruitment, the dissolution of Turnpike Trusts was dominated by a consideration of the amount and nature of compensation to be given to any vested interests which might be affected by these changes.

In 1838, the total debts of the Turnpike Trusts in England and Wales amounted to £8,345,267, whilst unpaid interest arrears added a further £1,123,623 to this debt.[1] Only two Trusts in Cumberland and Westmorland, the Carlisle–Temon and the Kingstown–Westlinton roads, were free from debt by this time.[2] The debts of the remaining Trusts totalled £135,202 3s 9d for Cumberland[3] and £52,497 11s 0d for Westmorland.[4]

The Government was also reluctant to countenance the abolition of Turnpike Trusts until such time as the country's railway network had become well established as an alternative means of communication. Many well informed people quite seriously envisaged the possible collapse of the various Railway Companies in the early years of their history, and were consequently anxious that the main roads should not be allowed to fall into disrepair through any premature abolition of their governing bodies. For instance, the well known political economist, J. R. McCulloch, whilst conceding that, with the advent of the railways 'a new era has commenced in travelling', also had certain reservations about the future role of rail transport. He considered that 'the advantages likely to be derived from the extension of the system to other parts of the country have, we believe, been a good deal exaggerated'.[5] Even after the permanence of rail travel had become manifest to all observers, it was still considered important to maintain Trust roads in order to provide necessary competition for the railways, thus helping to keep down the cost of travel. Similarly, short distance traffic was making increased use of localised sections of turnpikes during this period, and it was important that these stretches of road should be kept in particularly good repair.

Another factor which served to delay the dissolution of certain closely related Trusts was that, in the event of an early closure of a solvent Trust, any parallel Trust road would lose the bulk of its traffic, which would now choose to travel toll free along the alternative route. An example of this is afforded by a comparison of the later histories of the Carlisle–Temon and Carlisle–Brampton Trust roads which served a similar area between Carlisle and

---

[1] *Parl. Papers*, 1840, **XXVII**, p. 9   [2] Ibid., pp. 78–80

[3] Ibid., pp. 75–82 These figures include a total sum of £76,184 owed by the Alston Trust, £20,850 by the Heron Syke Trust,
[4] Ibid., p. 487 £13,740 by the Cockermouth–Penrith Trust and £10,705 by the Whitehaven Trust.

[5] J. R. McCulloch, *A Descriptive and Statistical Account of the British Empire*, **II** (1847), p. 183.

Brampton. In the 1860s it was suggested that the former Trust, being clear of debt, should be dissolved, but it was argued by the local Trustees that, in view of the continuing debt of £1,150 upon the Carlisle–Brampton Trust, any such dissolution of the Temon Trust 'would be unfair inasmuch as the effect would be to increase the traffic on the "Free Road" and to reduce the revenue of the other and thus to increase unduly the charge of maintenance of the one by the parishes and to materially diminish the creditors' security for the monies chargeable on the other'.[6]

Despite the emphasis placed upon the delaying of Trust dissolution, it was widely recognised by 1840 or so that such dissolution was inevitable and that the Trusts must prepare for this event by making every possible economy, in order to accumulate a 'Sinking Fund' to repay their 'Principal Debt' and Interest arrears. Trust expenditure had undoubtedly risen very considerably during the 1820s and 1830s, but not all this money was spent judiciously, and there are reiterated complaints in the Select Committee Reports of this period concerning the 'wasteful expenditure of the funds of some Trusts'.[7]

In spite of these allegations, however, some Trusts, although disinclined to amalgamate to reduce administrative costs, were beginning to make provision for Sinking Funds to pay off their debts during this period. The Cockermouth–Workington Trust was taking active steps to repay its debt as early as 1823; a clause being inserted in its Renewal Act of that year to the effect that the equivalent of 1 per cent of the Trust's Principal Debt was to be apportioned to form a Sinking Fund for this purpose.[8] Finally, in 1849 it became compulsory for all Trusts to set aside 5 per cent annually on all newly contracted loans, towards the establishment of a Sinking Fund.[9]

Many Trusts also gave priority to interest repayments over road repairs when apportioning their expenditure, and the Appleby–Kendal Trust in 1824,[10] the Brough–Eamont Trust in 1856[11] and the Eamont Bridge Trust in 1859[12] all gave precedence to interest payments and took pains to ensure that, in the event of there being a considerable surplus in any one year, there would be a clearly understood restriction upon road maintenance expenditure. Similarly, the Ulverston–Carnforth Trust specified that after higher priorities had been satisfied, not more than £250 was to be

6 C.R.O., Carlisle–Temon Trust Minutes, 31 October 1868.
7 *Parl. Papers*, 1836, XIX, p. 338.   8 L.P.A., 4G4, cap. XXIII.
9 12–13 Vic., cap. 87.   10 Ibid., 5G4, cap. XV.
11 Ibid., 19–20 Vic., cap. LXXII.   12 Ibid., 22–23 Vic., cap. XXV.

expended annually upon road maintenance.[13] Some Trusts were even more stringent with regard to road improvements. For instance, both the Appleby–Kendal and Heron Syke Trusts had relegated road repairs to the bottom of their expenditure priorities by 1851.[14] Therefore, by the 1850s it had become apparent to the Cumbrian Turnpike authorities that the various Trusts would inevitably be dissolved in the not too distant future. Consequently, they recognised this fact when allocating their expenditure.

Some Trusts ceased to spend money on their roads altogether; notably when creditors took over control of their toll gates. Thus between 1846 and 1850 three of the Cumbrian Trusts, namely the Ulverston–Carnforth,[15] Heron Syke[16] and Appleby–Kendal bodies,[17] were required to devote their entire toll revenues to the repayment of their 'mortgage debts'. This extreme situation was relieved as soon as the Trusts in question had repaid their interest arrears, but nevertheless, road maintenance expenditure continued to be severely restricted in most parts of Cumbria and, in consequence, an increasing number of parishes and 'Highway Districts' were compelled to subsidise the maintenance of Turnpike roads. Such maintenance costs might, as we have noted, be very heavy if the parish concerned was situated near to the boundary of a growing town.

Parochial complaints against Trust parsimony were brought to a head by the impending dissolution of the various Trusts and the consequent implication that, in future years, parishioners would be solely responsible for maintaining all roads; thus entailing the levying of very high rates to finance these increased commitments. By the late 1860s, Turnpike Trusts in different parts of the country were apparently planning organised resistance to any wide scale Trust dissolution. For instance, the clerk of the Worcester Turnpike roads communicated with his Carlisle–Eamont Bridge counterpart, expressing his hope that the Penrith Trustees would join forces with the Worcester agitators and 'take immediate steps by Petitions and all other means in their power to oppose the Bill'.[18] A petition to Whitehall was drawn up by a

---

13 L.P.A., 13–14 Vic., cap. LXV.
15 *Parl. Papers*, 1850, **XLIX**, p. 376.
17 Ibid., 1851, **XLVIII**, p. 202.

14 13–14 Vic., cap. XIII.
16 Ibid., 1850, **XLIX**, p. 336.

18 C.R.O., T.T./1/10, Carlisle–Eamont Bridge Trust, Vouchers and Accounts (1859–81), correspondence in connection with Mr Knatchbull Hugessen's Bill for the Abolition of Turnpike Trusts, Letter to Chris Fairer from the Clerk of the Worcester Turnpike Trust, 18 February 1868.

number of Trusts, asserting that Trust dissolution would throw the entire burden of road maintenance upon the landed interests in the adjacent townships, and

'that such a measure would be attended with great inconvenience and also be most unjust to the Landowners and Tenant Farmers. Your Petitioners respectfully submit that the plan proposed in the Bill referred to is not an equitable one, inasmuch as it throws the burden wholly on the land which is already subject to the greater portion of the local taxation of the country such as Poor Rates, County Buildings, Parish Roads, Lunatic Asylums, Police Rates and various other charges from which the merchant and capitalist are almost exempt.'[19]

The Penrith Clerk was in favour of this petition and considered its tone particularly apposite to the Penrith area, on the grounds that the

'Turnpike Roads immediately contiguous to the Town of Penrith and other Towns are used by Tradesmen and others more than by the Landowners or Tenant Farmers and that in the event, the cost of maintaining such roads being thrown wholly on the Parishes, such Parishes would be unfairly and unjustly taxed for the benefit of trade and towns, whereas under the present system of Tolls, the burden and benefit fall alike upon the persons using the road'.[20]

Therefore, 'Landowners and occupiers of land in the different Townships through which the road passes would prefer paying the small Tolls to which they are now subject, to undertaking the repairs of the road which will devolve upon them at the expiration of the Local Act'.[21]

The townships to the north of Carlisle, along the Glasgow Road, had a similar grievance in so far as this section of road was being 'subject to extraordinary wear and tear, arising chiefly from a very large traffic in bricks manufactured within about two miles of Carlisle and carted along to that city for use and transport'.[22]

[19] Ibid.   [20] Ibid.
[21] K.R.O., Ambleside Trust Minutes, 27 September 1862.
[22] P.R.O., MH 28 No. 14, Letter from Trustees of Carlisle–Glasgow Road to Whitehall, 20 March 1880.

Nevertheless, in spite of petitions and recriminations, the Cumbrian Trusts, in common with other such organisations elsewhere, were facing dissolution by the early 1870s. In view of this, the apportioning of responsibility for the repair of the Ambleside Turnpike Road was of particular importance, since by this time it carried by far the heaviest volume of 'through' traffic of any Cumbrian road. Thus local ratepayers had a two-fold grievance. In the first place, the wear and tear upon the road surface was excessive by contemporary standards, and second, the greater part of this damage was created by 'through' traffic controlled by outsiders and conveying outsiders who made no contribution to local rates.

At first, in 1870, a compromise was suggested by the Ambleside Trust which recommended that, since the bulk of the traffic using the section of road between Kendal and Windermere was local, the Plumgarths and Staveley Gates along this line of road could be conveniently dismantled. The heavily-used section of Trust road between Windermere and Keswick was recognised to be in a quite different category, however, since it carried a high proportion of 'through' traffic. It was considered, therefore, that the repair of this latter portion of road

'would in the event of the abolition of the Tolls of both the last mentioned Gates (Ambleside and Grasmere) press very heavily upon the occupiers of rateable property in the Township through which the road passes, who use the road very little. This meeting is unanimously of the opinion that the Toll at Grasmere which would be retained at a cost disproportionate to its value should be abolished; but that the Toll Gate at Ambleside should be continued but that the Tolls to be hereafter received should be reduced in amount half.'[23]

Nevertheless, in spite of these assurances, the dissolution of the Ambleside Trust was felt to be inevitable by the neighbouring townships and in May 1871 the Kendal Farmers' Club held a meeting on this subject; a full account of which appeared in the *Westmorland Gazette* for 27 May 1871 under the heading, 'The Highways and Byeways: who's to mend them?'[24]

This was treated as a general problem, but it was made abundantly clear in this Report that the dissolution of the Ambleside Trust would be particularly undesirable unless there was some provision for equalising parochial highway rates. The

[23] K.R.O., Ambleside Trust Minutes, 3 December 1870.
[24] *Westmorland Gazette*, 27 May 1871.

meeting began by drawing attention to the variation in the amount of wear and tear of the different highways within the region. The example of Helsington parish was selected to illustrate this disparity

'where the rate-payers have at one and the same time the privilege of paying Toll and repairing over three miles of Turnpike at a cost utterly out of proportion to the use they make of it, but which cost is rendered necessary by the heavy public traffic passing over it, and compare this for example with the Township of Whinfell where there is no Toll to pay, and where the Highway Rate and public traffic are equally light. It stands to reason that such an inequality as this can't be fair, and the remedy which naturally suggests itself is that everyone should contribute to the repairs of the roads just as in proportion he uses them.'

The Trust clerk then proceeded to draw attention to the high rates which would be imposed upon the surrounding townships following the dissolution of the Ambleside Trust. For instance, it was estimated that the township of Strickland Ketel would be obliged to raise an additional rate of $5\frac{1}{4}$d in the £ if the toll gates were removed. 'True the Ratepayer will get rid of the Toll but that is really a case of thank you for nothing, as by far the greater majority never go through the Plumgarths Gate at all, or at any rate very seldom, and I don't suppose they often indulge themselves in a trip to the Lakes.'

Table 4. Estimated increase in township rates which would follow the dissolution of the Ambleside Trust.

Township	Additional rates in £	Annual cost of repair
Nethergraveship	$\frac{1}{4}$D.	£2
Strickland Ketel	$5\frac{1}{4}$D.	£100
Crook	$3\frac{1}{2}$D.	£25
Undermillbeck	$\frac{3}{4}$D.	£30
Nether Staveley	$3\frac{1}{4}$D.	£30
Over Staveley	$1\frac{1}{2}$D.	£15
Hugill	4D.	£40
Applethwaite	$5\frac{1}{2}$D.	£160
Troutbeck	$6\frac{1}{2}$D.	£75
Ambleside	5D.	£200
Rydal and Loughrigg	$3\frac{1}{2}$D.	£50
Grasmere	$3\frac{1}{2}$D.	£75

The meeting concluded that, on balance, the Turnpike Trusts should be eventually dissolved but that this should be conditional on 'the extension of the area of rating', on the grounds that a single township was a quite inadequate unit for road administration and repair.

The townships adjoining the Ambleside Trust road had justifiable cause for complaint, but in one respect they were more fortunate than most of their counterparts elsewhere in Cumbria. They were not likely to be faced with a backlog of road repairs in the event of Trust dissolution. The Ambleside Trust made substantial profits until the end of its life and hence could afford to maintain its roads in reasonable condition. Other Cumbrian Trusts which devoted a significant proportion of their funds to road maintenance throughout their history included the Cockermouth–Penrith, Cockermouth–Maryport and Alston Trusts. All three gave road repairs priority over interest and principal debt repayments when allocating their annual expenditure. Significantly, none of these Trusts was over-exposed to railway competition during this period. The Cockermouth–Penrith railway was not opened until 1865, whilst the Cockermouth–Maryport and Alston Trusts never faced direct competition from a parallel railway line at any period of their history.

Most Trusts, as we have noted, could not afford to be so prodigal, nor were they allowed to be. By the 1850s, Whitehall was exercising closer control over Trust expenditure, and reminding Trustees when they overstepped the mark in this respect. For instance, when the Brough-Eamont Trustees applied for a Renewal Act in 1856, they were asked to account for an expenditure of £1,600 on road improvements since 1835, and an apparent neglect of all opportunities to repay their debts during this same period.[25] The Northern Division of the Carlisle–Eamont Trust was likewise warned by Whitehall in 1867 to limit its road expenditure,[26] and this warning was repeated in 1873. 'The Clerk is requested to state why the provisions of the local Act are not adhered to in respect of the amount laid out in repair of the road—the sum expended in 1873 and in previous years appearing to have greatly exceeded the amount allowed for that purpose.'[27] Even the Ambleside Trust could not spend money with complete impunity, and in 1862, the Secretary of State, Sir George Grey,

[25] *Parl. Papers*, 1856, **LVIII**, p. 178.
[26] C.R.O., Carlisle–Eamont Trust (Northern Division), Minutes 26 January 1867.
[27] Ibid., 30 January 1875.

expressed his 'regrets that part of the Trust Funds have been expended in improvements in lieu of paying off the debt'.[28] It was also usual after about 1850 for a clause to be inserted into Trust Renewal Acts prohibiting, or at least severely limiting, further borrowing by the Trust in question. Thus the Appleby Trustees were not allowed to contract further loans after 1851.[29]

Therefore the Government was giving scant encouragement to road improvements, whilst also showing a corresponding lack of interest in enforcing Trust amalgamation and other needful administrative reforms. Official recognition of the need to eliminate Trust debts and to replace the various Turnpike authorities by a new administrative organisation, had completely obscured the necessity for making adequate provision for road repair during the intervening period when Trust debts were being repaid. Thus a very considerable strain was thrown upon the various townships which were called upon to repair the roads of insolvent Trusts. Most Trust officials could not fairly be blamed for this situation. In general, they seem to have made conscientious efforts to maintain their roads, but a combination of declining receipts coupled with the demands of creditors and pressure from Whitehall, greatly limited the scope of their repair work.

Most Trusts were paying interest upon their debts during the middle years of the nineteenth century; the only Cumbrian exceptions to this being the Carlisle–Westlinton[30] and Carlisle–Temon Trusts.[31] These interest payments were proving a considerable embarrassment to many Trusts following the onset of railway competition. Therefore, an Act of Parliament was passed in 1850 by which 'Trusts in the very last stages of bankruptcy might possibly find some advantage by obtaining the power to rid of accumulated Interest and part or all of the percentage on the debt without the expense of going to Parliament'.[32] A good many Cumbrian Trusts took advantage of this Act to reduce their interest rates and obliterate arrears during the next decade. For instance, the Heron Syke Trust, after recapitulating its financial difficulties following the opening of the competing Lancaster–Carlisle railway line, concluded in its Renewal Bill that 'under these circumstances the only remedy appears to be such a reduction in the rate of interest as will allow, after the payment of

---

[28] K.R.O., Ambleside Trust, Misc. Correspond., Letter to Thomas Harrison from Whitehall, 3 October 1862.

[29] L.P.A. 13–14 Vic., cap. XIII.

[30] *Parl. Papers*, 1840, XXVII, p. 80.

[31] Ibid., p. 78.   [32] L.P.A. 14–15 Vic., cap. 38.

such interest annually, a surplus to be applied in reduction of the debt, which surplus will be gradually increased as the payment of interest becomes lessened, so as to extinguish the debt as early as possible'.[33] Two years later, the Alston Trust appealed to the Secretary of State for leave to extinguish interest arrears amounting to £50,852 11s 6d.[34] It was usual for such petitions to be granted; the Alston Trust paid no interest after 1852 and its arrears were likewise extinguished.[35] Similarly, the Heron–Syke Trust's rate of interest was reduced from $4\frac{1}{2}$ to $2\frac{3}{4}$ per cent as a result of its petition, and a further reduction to $2\frac{1}{2}$ per cent was achieved in 1873.[36]

Despite the weight of this evidence, however, some Trusts were disinclined to antagonise their creditors and, like the Ambleside Trust in 1862, considered 'that it would involve a great and uncalled for injustice to the Mortagees and Creditors of the road to ask them to reduce the rate of interest guaranteed to them by their Securities'.[37] This statement was made by the clerk of the Ambleside Trust in response to pressure from Whitehall for the Trust to discontinue its present high rate of interest ($4\frac{1}{2}$ per cent) on pain of suspension of the Trust's Continuance Act. Finally, in the following year, the Trust was obliged to compromise with governmental policy and its interest rate was reduced from $4\frac{1}{2}$ to 4 per cent.[38]

Trust creditors were in a difficult position. In view of the financial embarrassments of the majority of contemporary Trusts, they could hardly have been sanguine that their loans would be repaid rapidly or in full. On the other hand, they valued the regular payment of a substantial rate of interest upon the principal which they and their predecessors had advanced to the various Trusts. They were thus forced to choose between two unwelcome alternatives: they must either accept a lower rate of interest and forfeit all claims to arrears, in the hope that the Trusts concerned would accumulate a surplus to pay off their principal debt, or, alternatively, they could press for a continued high rate of

[33] *Parl. Papers*, 1850, XLIX, p. 337.
[34] Ibid., 1853, XCVII, p. 504.
[35] See Appendix C for details of sources from which Trust Accounts were obtained.
[36] Other Trusts which began to pay a lower rate of interest during the 1850s and 1860s included the Ulverston–Carnforth, Brampton–Longtown, Cockermouth–Workington, Milnthorpe–Levens, Carlisle–Eamont Bridge and Kirkby Stephen–Hawes Trusts.
[37] K.R.O., Ambleside Trust Minutes, 27 September 1862.
[38] *Parl. Papers*, 25 November 1862.

interest payments and thereby risk a more protracted and less certain principal repayment.

At first, most creditors were more ready to accept the second alternative. The Ulverston–Carnforth mortgagees, for example, deprecated any proposed reduction in their interest rate,[39] as did their Brough–Eamont counterparts in 1856.[40] The Kirkby Stephen–Hawes creditors had taken up a similar position in 1851,[41] but were advised by James McAdam to accept the Secretary of State's recommended reduction in their interest payments to 2 per cent on the grounds that 'nothing larger than 2 per cent could be paid by the Trust so as to allow a surplus for a Sinking Fund under its present circumstances'.[42] Likewise, the creditors of the Brampton–Longtown Trust were obliged to countenance a similar reduction,[43] although some of them continued to hold reservations on this point in so far as it might set a precedent for further reductions by the Trustees. Other creditors objected to this arrangement, on account of the Trust having in the past paid interest to some more readily than others. For instance, the creditors of the Cockermouth–Workington Trust noted that 'The Trust affairs are not so bad as to require so great a sacrifice on the part of the more easy creditors, and they trust you will not require them to sacrifice the arrears'.[44]

The repayment of the Trust's principal debt was also accelerated by giving priority to those creditors who were prepared to accept a lower composition in lieu of full repayment of their original subscription. Thus, the Ambleside Trustees advertised to this effect in 1851[45] and their example was followed by the Ulverston–Carnforth Trustees who declared that they were only prepared to pay off individual debts, on condition that the creditors concerned should accept a dividend of not more than 10s in the £.[46]

In these circumstances, it became increasingly important for Trusts to capitalise upon short distance traffic and to prevent toll evasions where possible. However, this policy proved difficult to apply in many cases, as previous discussion has shown. The most

[39] *Parl. Papers*, 1850, **XLIX**, p. 376.

[40] Ibid., 1856, **LVIII**, p. 180.

[41] K.R.O., Kirkby Stephen–Hawes Trust, miscellaneous correspondence; Letter from Thomas Browne to John Flower, 4 October 1851.

[42] Ibid., Letter from James McAdam to John Flower, 28 November 1851.

[43] C.R.O., Brampton–Longtown Trust, Misc. Accounts.

[44] *Whitehaven News*, 12 November 1863.

[45] K.R.O., Ambleside Trust Minutes, 18 January 1851.

[46] P.R.O., MH 28 No. 4, Letter from Trustees of Ulverston–Carnforth Road to Whitehall, 31 October 1877.

that a Trust could do as a rule was to erect side gates on the busier road junctions in order to tax traffic at these points. On the other hand, if vehicles were prepared to follow more circuitous routes along probably inferior roads, it was usually possible for them to evade at least some of these toll gates however carefully they were positioned. Since Trust roads were now used mainly by local traffic, such travellers were all the more likely to be knowledgeable about the topography of the area and the scope for evading local toll gates. Where such knowledge was lacking, it could usually be obtained at a price, as one local writer has noted. 'Toll free by-roads were in request and a class of local guides with the knowledge of such travel came into existence. The Bannisdale and Shap Toll Bars, for instance, could be cut out by riding up Longsleddale valley and going either by Mardale to Bampton, or by Mosedale to Shap Abbey, and joining the western road north of or about the Village of Thrimby.'[47]

On account of these toll evasions, most Trusts attempted to increase rates of toll and reduce the number of exemptions at their Gates. For instance, in 1856 the Cockermouth–Penrith Trustees sought permission 'to have a small toll granted upon horses and carts carrying lime, which they have not had under their former Acts, as there are a great number of carts carrying lime, many of which pass nine or ten miles along the road and cut it up very much without at present contributing anything towards its repair'.[48] The Trust was successful in this application, and the Ambleside Trust was equally successful in removing exemptions on coal traffic in 1870.[49]

In spite of opposition from townships and road users, these measures did make a considerable contribution towards the repayment of the Trusts' debts and their subsequent dissolution; the majority of the Cumbrian Trusts being dissolved during the 1870s and early 1880s. The Carlisle–Eamont Trust survived longer than most, but on 17 August 1881 the Trust clerk received his final instructions from Whitehall.

'I am directed by the Local Government Board to inform you that, by virtue of "The Annual Turnpike Acts Continuance Act 1881;" the Local Act for the above named Trust will be repealed

[47] William Palmer, *The Verge of Lakeland* (1938), p. 91.

[48] C.R.O., Bleaymire and Shepherd Collection, Minutes of Select Committee of H. of C. on Cockermouth–Penrith Road Bill of 1856.

[49] K.R.O., Ambleside Trust Minutes, 3 December 1870.

on the 1st Day of November next; and they request that the Trustees will make the necessary arrangements for pulling down and removing the several Toll Gates, Bars, etc., and, if required, the Toll Houses also, and for disposing of the Trust property previous to this date.'[50]

It was also usual for a Trust to compensate its officers at this stage out of its remaining funds, and to obtain a certificate from two Justices 'that the road was at the time it became a Highway in complete and effectual repair'.[51] Any further balance remaining out of the Trust's revenues was then to be distributed amongst the various townships and highway districts upon whom would fall the immediate liability for repairing the Turnpike road in question.

Not all Trusts were fortunate enough to possess a balance of income. In spite of previous official reassurances, some creditors had still not been repaid in full or even in part by the time their Trust was dissolved. Thus, out of fourteen Cumbrian Trusts for which statistics are available in the years immediately prior to their dissolution, at least three had not cleared their debts.[52] If a creditor had not been reimbursed by the time a Trust was dissolved he was unlikely to get any satisfaction subsequently. There was no formal continuity between Turnpike Trusts and any subsequent administrative bodies, and so no one could be said to be responsible for making any payment of this sort. Certainly, I have not been able to find any instances in subsequent newspaper records of creditors being paid retrospectively by any other authority.

The responsibility for the repair of disturnpiked roads was likely to impose a severe strain upon the resources of the various parishes and highway districts, but their responsibilities were reduced after the passage of the 'Highways and Locomotives Amendment Act of 1878'. This Act stipulated that all roads disturnpiked since 1870 should become 'Main Roads' and that the county should pay half the cost of their maintenance; the other half being divided between the district in which the road lay and the central Government.

However, in practice, the Quarter Sessions in both Cumberland and Westmorland, were not prepared to grant main road status

[50] C.R.O., 1/13: Correspondence re winding-up of Carlisle–Eamont Trust (Southern Division).   [51] Ibid.
[52] These Trusts were: Brampton Longtown (Debt £3,100 at dissolution); Heron Syke (Debt £2,272 at dissolution); Alston (Debt £24,673 at dissolution).

to any highway or disturnpiked road unless it conformed to certain standards. In the first place, the road must carry a considerable volume of non-local traffic; thus giving it a more than parochial importance. Also, the road in question must be inspected by the county surveyor and pronounced by him to be in a satisfactory state of repair, before the Quarter Sessions would agree to control it and to subsidise its future maintenance.

In view of the declining revenues of the majority of Cumbrian Trusts and their consequent lack of expenditure on road repairs, the majority of dissolved Trust roads were likely to prove a heavy burden to the various parishes, until such time as they were deemed by the Quarter Sessions to be in a sufficiently good state of repair to be accepted as "Main Roads". Thus, when the Cumberland road surveyor had made his initial inspection of the counties' disturnpiked roads in 1879, he reported that, with the exception of the Alston and Whitehaven regions, 'the roads in the other districts showed such unmistakable signs of recent neglect, that with due regard to the interests of the County ratepayers, and the proper discharge of my duties, I could not recommend certificates (main road) to be given to any of them'.[53]

It is hardly likely that the highway districts relished being burdened with such heavy expenditure, but they appear to have accepted the responsibility. In fact, they had little option but to do so. Recognising this, they doubtless decided that the sooner they repaired the disturnpiked roads, the sooner they would be able to shift part of the burden on to the shoulders of the Quarter Sessions and the county surveyor. Consequently, the county officials met with a fairly good response from the various highway districts in Cumbria, and the Cumberland road surveyor, George Bell, was soon able to report that 'Improvement is visible in nearly every part and the willingness has been expressed by all the local officials I have met to put their disturnpiked roads into thorough repair with as little delay as possible'.[54]

Bell was less happy, however, about the response of the parochial authorities, and he concluded his report by noting that

'In the case of roads managed by parishes, only some of the parishes have kept their roads up to the necessary standard, although it cannot be said that too much has been asked of the parish surveyors. The reason of this, in my opinion, is that

---

[53] C.R.O., CCH3/1, Cumberland Highway Committee Papers (1879–84), County Surveyor's Report, 21 May 1879.
[54] Ibid., County Surveyor's Report, 25 March 1880.

whereas in each Highway District there is a Surveyor whose sole business is to look after the proper management of the highways, and he has under him a full staff of well trained workmen who can be concentrated upon any particular part of his district to execute all necessary repairs at the shortest notice, and in the least costly and most satisfactory manner; whereas in parishes, the area is too small in most cases to keep even one good surfaceman constantly at work upon the roads. Hence the necessary work is neglected, until it costs twice as much to put the roads right again and then it is usually done in a most imperfect manner.'[55]

Thus, Bell in this report reiterates the familiar appeal for larger units of administration to supervise road maintenance.

During the 1880s, the Quarter Sessions of both counties were flooded with local applications for main road status and, although these were not always granted, the majority of the Cumbrian disturnpiked roads had become recognised as main roads by 1890. Nevertheless, both counties continued to examine each application with care, and as late as 1894, former Turnpikes linking Kendal with Appleby and Kirkby Stephen, respectively, were still not deemed to be in sufficiently good condition to justify main road status.[56]

Local parishes and highway boards were naturally particularly anxious for the county to contribute to the repair of disturnpiked roads within their boundaries but, in addition, a good many roads which had never been turnpiked also became recognised as 'main roads' during this period. By the end of the century, out of a total Cumberland main road mileage of 508½ miles, 206 miles had never at any time been turnpiked.[57] This is a surprisingly high proportion of the whole, and does suggest that by this period, traffic in Cumberland had become somewhat more wide-ranging and was no longer confined to the familiar long established routes.

There is little doubt that during the 1880s, road and bridge administration in Cumbria was becoming more integrated than it had been at any time previously. Nevertheless, both counties still contained a proliferation of local administrative sub-

[55] C.R.O., CCH3/1, County Surveyor's Report, 25 March 1880.

[56] K.R.O., Westmorland County Council Accounts, 1894–5.

[57] C.R.O., CCH/1/4 Cumberland Highway Commission, Minutes (1896–9), 13 July 1896.

divisions: parishes, highway districts, urban and rural sanitary authorities, to which the Quarter Sessions tended to delegate a large measure of responsibility for road and bridge repairs. In the first place, unless a highway was approved by the county as a main road, the entire responsibility for, and expense of, its maintenance still rested with the local highway board or the corresponding parochial authority. This responsibility could, on occasions, be quite an onerous one. Certain roads might carry a good deal of local traffic which could involve the appropriate local authority in quite heavy maintenance commitments. The parishioners could expect no help from the county unless they could prove that a fair proportion of this traffic had come from outside the area. The Egremont Rural District Council appears to have had a particularly heavy burden of road maintenance in the 1880s, and made several applications to the Quarter Sessions for the registration of certain heavily used sections of highway as 'main roads'. However, each application was turned down on the grounds that the traffic concerned was predominantly local.[58]

Other local roads might be heavily used for a fairly small portion of the year; notably those carrying tourist traffic. The Quarter Sessions did not always consider these circumstances to be adequate grounds for accepting a highway as a main road. For instance, in July 1899, the Cockermouth Rural District Council appealed to the County Council for a contribution to the cost of repairing Honister Pass 'on account of the very heavy expenditure incurred by the Rural District Council in the upkeep of this road owing to the large tourist traffic over it'. The county did not give any assistance on this occasion either.[59]

The county authorities were, of course, more directly involved in the maintenance and administration of recognised main roads, but even here, prior to the passage of the 1888 Local Government Act, the highway districts and parishes were still expected to contribute part of the cost of any repairs. In addition, both counties usually delegated all detailed repair work on main roads and bridges to the local highway surveyor in return for an agreed annual grant from the county to the highway authority concerned. All repairs which were expected to exceed £50 in cost were to be inspected by the county road surveyor before any additional grant to the locality could be sanctioned. Thus, during this period the county surveyor was unlikely to be involved in the actual

[58] C.R.O., CCH/3/1 Cumberland Highway Commission Papers (1879–4).
[59] C.R.O., CCH/1/4 Cumberland Highway Commission Papers, 15 July 1899.

G

repair of main roads unless the work was of too technically difficult a nature for the local surveyor to handle. He could instead devote the greater part of his attention to major bridge repairs, and to the continuous assessment of the annual county grant to the various local authorities. This latter responsibility entailed the inspection of work completed and, on occasions, making a more detailed assessment of the likely cost of intended road improvements. By these means, the county was able to check that their local authority grant had not been squandered, and that any additional claim for extraordinary repairs would be scrutinised in advance by their own surveyor.

Thus, although the county was in the habit of delegating the bulk of detailed repair work to local authorities, the position of county road surveyor was an important one. Cumberland and Westmorland were well served in this respect. Both George Bell, the Cumberland county road surveyor, and Joseph Bintley, his Westmorland colleague, gave long and distinguished service to their respective counties. Bell was appointed in 1879 and continued to serve in this capacity until after the turn of the century. Bintley had an even longer term of office, being appointed in 1866 and not retiring until 1919.

Although on paper there was a wide diversity of administrative areas in both counties following the 1878 Act, in practice a fair degree of uniformity prevailed. This was mainly because both county road surveyors insisted on high standards of work from the various local highway authorities and were meticulous in inspecting all completed repairs to roads and bridges. The Quarterly Reports of both men reveal their close attention to detail and their careful assessment of costs during this period. When, in 1895, Bintley was requested by the South Westmorland Rural District Council to prepare a Report on the state of their highways, his final offering extended over sixty closely written foolscap pages.[60] Both surveyors were particularly active in the years immediately following the passage of the 1878 Highways and Locomotives Act; there were a large number of disturnpiked roads to examine and, in general, a multitude of local authority claims for main road status. In addition, the local magistrates were not prepared at first to delegate automatically all main road repairs to the Highway District concerned. Consequently, detailed repair work might be retained in the hands of the county road surveyor if it was felt that the locality concerned had not,

60 K.R.O., Westmorland Highways Committee Papers (1888–1905).

as yet, the experience to cope with their day to day work of main road and bridge maintenance. In fact, as late as 1894, the Cumberland road surveyor participated directly in repair work when a section of the popular tourist route skirting Lake Ullswater required particularly extensive repairs. This was considered to be 'a piece of work beyond the powers of a small parish like Soulby to cope with to advantage'.[61] Bell's greatly increased duties during this period were recognised by the Cumberland authorities when, in 1884, they raised his salary from £200 to £350 'in consequence of the great increase in his duties owing to so many miles of disturnpiked roads now being brought under his care'.[62] In 1890, Bell's salary was again raised: from £350 to £400 on this occasion. He was also allowed an additional sum of £200 to cover his travelling expenses.[63] This was an unusually high salary by contemporary standards and it testifies to Bell's acknowledged ability and to his growing responsibilities within the county.

It is significant also to note that the county still held the option of resuming the direct repair of any main road if the Highway District concerned proved to be ineffective. For instance, as late as 1895 the Highways Committee of the Cumberland County Council noted that it would continue to delegate road repair responsibilities to local authorities 'Provided always that in the event of a new Surveyor being appointed by the Board, the Council shall not be bound to continue this agreement but shall have the option of terminating the same forthwith'.[64] However, by this time there is no evidence to suggest that the county refused to delegate road and bridge responsibilities in any particular case.

In general, therefore, despite administrative sub-division and the extensive delegation of detailed repair work in the various Highway Districts, both counties were in a position to exercise close control over main road and bridge maintenance. Power was centralised in the person of the county road surveyor who was in turn responsible to the Highways Committee of the County Council after 1888. There was also growing pressure by this time to simplify the administration in both counties. The appointment of Bell as the first 'County Road Surveyor' of Cumberland in

---

[61] C.R.O., CCH1/3, Cumberland Highway Committee Minutes (1893–6) 24 February 1894.

[62] C.R.O., CCH3/1, Cumberland Highway Committee Papers (1879–84).

[63] C.R.O., CCH3/4, Cumberland Highway Committee Papers (1890).

[64] C.R.O., CCH/1/3, Cumberland Highway Committee Minutes (1893–6) 23 November 1895.

1879, reflects the county's awareness of its new supervisory powers over road administration and repair following the passage of the 1878 Act. Two years later, in 1881, Bell also took over responsibility for the repair of the county bridge roads and by 1887 he had further extended his authority to include most of the major county bridge repair work. This allowed the resident surveyor, John Cory, to concentrate more fully upon the maintenance of the various county buildings without detriment to any of the bridges.

This marks a noteworthy advance in administrative specialisation within the county. For the first time, bridges, bridge roads and main roads were under the control of the same official. The passage of the Local Government Act of 1888 gave a further impetus to administrative re-organisation within both counties. This Act relieved the Highway District of the need to contribute to main road repair. Thus, the newly created County Council now carried the entire financial responsibility for main road and bridge maintenance outside certain areas.

In response to these new responsibilities the Westmorland County Council carried out a notable overhaul of their administration. Following the passage of the 1878 Act the county had been divided up into a number of Highway Districts: Kendal, Shap, Brough and Warcop, Brougham and Clifton, Windermere and Rydal, Luneside, Kirkby Stephen, Kirkby Thore, Natland, Crosby, Ravensworth and Crackenthorpe. In 1892, the number of Highway Districts was reduced to four, each of which was under the control of a main road-superintendent who was in turn directly responsible to the county surveyor.[65] This marked a considerable advance upon any previous administrative system in the county.

The Cumberland authorities showed a corresponding readiness to encourage greater administrative uniformity within their boundaries. In 1889 it was suggested that the county be divided up into a number of regions, each under a 'District Surveyor' who would in turn employ competent local men as foremen. 'In this way uniformity of management all over the County would be secured instead of the present changing system of parish management; varying from year to year with the change of Surveyor.'[66] The same guiding principle is evident when, in the following year, the County Council 'resolved that it is expedient that as far as

[65] K.R.O., Westmorland Highway Committee Papers (1888–1905).
[66] C.R.O., CCH/1/1, Cumberland Highway Committee Minutes, 1 April 1889.

practicable, with the consent of the District ratepayers, all bridges on main roads in the Lordship of Millom and the parishes of Crosthwaite, Dalston and Holme Cultram, after being put into proper repair, be taken over by the County and thus secure uniform management, and that the said Lordship and parishes be henceforward liable to the County Bridge Rate'.[67] By 1892 these proposals had, in practice, been adopted. The twelve Highway Board surveyors were renamed 'Main Road Superintendents', and where no Highway Board existed, full-time 'working foremen' were appointed. All these officials were directly supervised by, and responsible to, the county road and bridge surveyor.

Lancashire provides something of a contrast to Cumberland and Westmorland in that its County Council does not appear to have had any clearly defined relations with the various local authorities within its boundaries. Arrangements between the County Council and local surveyors were reported in 1892 to be only 'tentative'.[68] No doubt, the presence of so many working authorities within Lancashire complicated its administration to a considerable degree.

The 1894 legislation gave a further stimulus to administrative uniformity within Cumbria. The Act of that year sub-divided all counties into Urban and Rural District Councils. These bodies superseded pre-existing parish councils, Highway Boards and Rural sanitary authorities as units of administration for the less important roads and bridges. This legislation was not put into practice immediately in all areas but by 1900 it is fair to say that larger units of administration were universal. The County and County Borough Councils had assumed complete financial responsibility for the main roads and bridges, whilst Rural District and Urban District Councils had taken charge of the remaining road and bridge repairs. This new sub-division of the county had a twofold advantage over the old system. In the first place, the newly created Rural District Council covered a larger area than did most of the old parishes and Highway Boards. Also, unlike the latter, they were created simultaneously and, as a result, formed a much tidier and more coherent administrative network.

Thus, although the dissolution of the various Turnpike Trusts disrupted existing administrative practices, on the whole it can be said that, by 1900, the regulation of road and bridge repair in

[67] C.R.O. CCH/1/1, Cumberland Highway Committee Minutes, 18 April 1890.
[68] C.R.O., CCH/4/26, Papers of County Surveyors' Society (1890).

Cumbria was more centralised and efficient than at any time previously. The County Council was a larger and more prosperous body than the old Turnpike Trusts, and the county rate for road repair proved to be a more flexible and potentially more remunerative source of income than the pre-existing tolls. It was certainly less disruptive to traffic. Furthermore, the County Councils provided a unitary authority for both road and bridge repair, whereas under the turnpike system the two categories had been kept quite separate.

Most County Councils appear to have been conscientious in administering their new responsibilities, and national expenditure on road and bridge repair increased steadily throughout the 1890s. The Webbs calculated that the total sum spent on main roads in England and Wales, outside the County Boroughs, had increased from £947,182 in 1890 to £2,231,962 by 1902. The various Rural District Councils and Urban District Councils were correspondingly active, since expenditure on non-main roads increased from £2,019,797 to £3,254,804 during the same period.[69] Expenditure on road and bridge repair in Cumbria increased at a rate which was somewhat below the national average. Nevertheless, the region's total outlay still showed a substantial increase. In 1889 the Cumberland County Council spent £14,100 on repairs to their main roads and bridges;[70] by 1900 this figure had risen to £29,000.[71] The increase in Westmorland was of roughly the same proportion: from £7,473 in 1889[72] to £12,876 by the end of the century.[73] The latter figure is particularly noteworthy in that the total expenditure of the Westmorland County Council on all items was as little as £30,000 during the last few years of the 1890s. The total annual Cumberland County Council expenditure during these years usually averaged out at about £90,000. Thus road and bridge expenditure was a slightly higher proportion of the total county outlay in Westmorland than in Cumberland.

The increased expenditure of both counties reflects their growing responsibilities. It also reflects the increasing volume of traffic which was now using the region's main roads. A high proportion of this increased traffic can be accounted for by continued

[69] S. & B. Webb, p. 259.

[70] C.R.O., CCH1/1, Cumberland Highway Committee Minutes, 29 March 1890.

[71] C.R.O., CCH1/4, Cumberland Highway Committee Minutes, 14 October 1899.

[72] K.R.O., Westmorland Highway Committee Papers (1888–1905).

[73] Ibid.

suburban growth on the fringes of the various towns in Cumbria. Thus, there was a further expansion of short distance commuter and market traffic into the town centres. This was no surprise to contemporaries since it marked the continuation of a pre-existing trend. However, local authorities were much less prepared for another road transport development which had become manifest by the end of the century: the re-emergence of 'through' traffic. Through traffic had previously been confined to isolated routes which lacked a competitive railway, but the increasing use of bicycles for holiday and general travel during the 1890s and, finally, the invention of the motor car, promised to revolutionise the whole picture within a very short space of time.

Very few motor cars were using the Cumbrian roads as early as 1900, but the writing was quite definitely on the wall.[74] Traditional types of loosely consolidated road surfaces were quite unsuitable for motor traffic. The wheels of the first motor cars were usually studded with iron in order to reduce the danger of skidding, and these wheels soon tore up the road surface making it virtually unusable and raising dust storms in the process. The dust created by passing motor vehicles was to give rise to increasingly bitter comment during the first decade of the twentieth century especially from the owners of property adjacent to main roads.

Thus, in order to engineer and implement the necessary technical breakthroughs in road building and repairs which would be necessary to remedy these deficiencies, a further overhaul of the existing administration would be necessary. Improvements in the administration of roads and bridges since 1878 had been useful if not spectacular, but new traffic revealed new limitations in the existing machinery.

In the first place, increased traffic on the main roads leading into the towns was likely to accentuate the already existing confusion as to the exact responsibility for road repair in suburban areas. By 1889 the average cost per mile of maintaining urban main roads in Cumberland was £106 15s compared with a corresponding figure of £40 16s 6d for the rural main roads.[75] Hence disputes over road maintenance expenditure continued.

[74] The first car to be registered in Cumberland (following the Motor Car Act of 1903 which compelled the registration of all motor vehicles) was a 5 hp Baby Peugeot owned by William Parkin Moore of Wigton. By the end of 1904 there were 281 car registrations in the county.

[75] C.R.O., CCH/1/4, Cumberland Highway Committee Minutes, 14 October 1899.

County Councils, County Borough Councils and Urban District Councils each tried to foist responsibility off on to the other.

The Westmorland County Council appears to have had good relations with the various urban authorities within its boundaries, but its Cumberland counterpart became involved in several long disputes during the 1890s. It was in keeping with tradition that Carlisle and Penrith should be most active in these matters. In April 1890 the Carlisle Town Council asked the county authority to subsidise the repair of certain 'main roads' within the city boundaries.[76] The County Council was not sympathetic. In the following year, the Town Council reiterated their claim; this time in more specific terms, claiming a grant of £1,320 9s 4½d from the county towards the repair of the suburban roads in question.[77] Finally, in 1894, the Local Government Board was asked to arbitrate and it was decided in October of that year that the county should pay the Carlisle Town Council a total of £718 1s 4d for the year ending March 1892, and a further £676 0s 5d to cover the following year.[78] A similar dispute between the county and the Penrith Urban District Council dragged on from 1893 until 1898. On this occasion, the roads at issue had already been accepted by the county as 'main roads', in 1892, but the two authorities could not agree as to the annual grant which the Urban District Council should be allowed by the county for repairing the roads.

Thus the lessons of the earlier part of the century had not yet been completely learnt. There were still too many statutory authorities for road repair and this was almost bound to lead to disputes over the responsibility for the maintenance of certain stretches of road. The powers of the County Councils were still too limited, and, even where they did control road administration, their habit of delegating actual repairs to the various Rural District Councils and Urban District Councils was always liable to lead to disputes over costs. The Webbs, in their study of highway administration, were quick to point out the anomaly of a situation where the locality undertook the maintenance of a stretch of road, whilst the county paid the bill.

Although in general, one can say that the administrative system for road and bridge repair in England and Wales at the end of the nineteenth century was an improvement upon any

[76] C.R.O., CCH1/1, Cumberland Highway Committee Minutes 24 April 1890.   [77] Ibid., 23 May 1891.
[78] C.R.O., CCH1/3, Cumberland Highway Committee Minutes 11 October 1894.

previous arrangement, it was only likely to be adequate if the volume of traffic within a particular region remained fairly constant. This, as we have seen, was far from being the case. In fact, by 1900, it was fairly clear that, in view of the potential increase in motor traffic and the consequent need to undertake widescale alterations to both the surface and alignment of main roads, even a County Council with enhanced powers would be unable in the long run to cope with these new demands. The state would have to play a much more positive part in road administration and repair. Up until this time, the Exchequer had provided occasional grants and loans for local authorities to undertake major road and bridge repairs, but, during the early 1900s, there was a growing demand for a central government department to assume executive control of road and bridge building and administration. It was felt that such a department would ensure a tidier and more coherent system of administration and would furthermore help to ensure that all existing highway legislation was implemented in full; no local authority being allowed in future to evade its responsibilities through a lack of central administrative supervision. A Transport Department would also, it was argued, be able to advise County Councils on technical and administrative problems and also provide larger grants than under the existing 'ad hoc' system.

The Government's response to this pressure, the setting up of the Road Board in 1909,[79] and finally, a Ministry of Transport in 1919, falls outside the scope of this study, but the pattern of future developments had already begun to emerge by the end of the nineteenth century.

[79] For further details see W. Rees Jeffreys, *The King's Highway* (1949).

Chapter 7

CONCLUSION

The main purpose of this study has been to consider road transport with close reference where possible to nineteenth century social and economic changes within Cumbria. This has first of all involved an assessment of the motives, methods and achievements of the various organisations and individuals responsible for administering and subsidising road and bridge construction. A second related consideration concerns the volume and nature of traffic using the Cumbrian roads and the extent to which, in the pre-railway period at least, road improvements stimulated and sustained an increasing quantity of traffic. A third aspect of this survey has entailed comparing roads with other forms of transport, notably railways. The final and most difficult task has been to assess the contribution which road improvements made to the region's economic and social development in this period.

One of the most striking features of this survey has been the increased attention which the various authorities, notably Turnpike Trusts, devoted to road and bridge maintenance during the first four decades of the nineteenth century. These activities appear to have been especially marked between about 1815 and 1835; a period which saw the inauguration of seven new Turnpike Trusts in the Cumbrian counties, as well as increased expenditure on road repairs by some of the older established Trusts in the area. Similarly, the road building activities of the Enclosure Commissioners during the early years of the century provided a useful guide and supplement to parochial efforts in this direction. Expenditure on bridge repairs by the respective Quarter Sessions of Cumberland and Westmorland also seems to have risen considerably during this period, although the absence of comparable statistics for eighteenth century bridge expenditure makes any accurate comparison impossible.

It is, of course, rather more difficult to build up a qualitative picture of Cumbrian roads and bridges in this period. Increased expenditure in itself does not necessarily entail higher standards of workmanship. It may simply reflect the increasing wear and tear of the road surface by a growing volume of traffic. However, a detailed appraisal of the items of expenditure by a good many road and bridge authorities, accompanied by evidence of their more rigorous selection of officers, does suggest that higher standards were being set. This entailed the construction of wider and more substantial bridges and the building of wider and straighter roads with reduced gradients where necessary.

These improvements, along with developments in vehicular construction, were stimulated in the first place by the demands of an increasing volume of wheeled traffic. There is little doubt also that by ameliorating the hardships and uncertainties of travel, improved road conditions added further to the amount of traffic using the various Cumbrian roads. Certainly the evidence of toll receipts and expanding stage and mail coach services between about 1820 and the mid 1840s all points to a continued expansion of road traffic in this period.

The growth of tourism in the Lake District provides a particularly good illustration of this connection between road improvements and increased traffic. Early visitors to the area were sometimes impressed by the intrinsic qualities of its scenery but rarely by its roads. It seems unlikely therefore that the initial stages of tourism owed very much to improved road conditions. However, if the Lake District was to cater for more than an adventurous few, it was important that its roads should receive more attention and better publicity. It appears that by the end of the eighteenth century, visitors to the area were more disposed to comment favourably upon the road conditions which they encountered. This favourable publicity, added to the restrictions which the Napoleonic Wars had imposed upon overseas travel, led to a considerable increase in the volume of tourists visiting the area by the beginning of the nineteenth century. By the 1820s, this traffic had reached considerable dimensions, as evidenced by the receipts of the well-documented Ambleside Trust. This Trust was obliged to devote a high proportion of its increasing Toll receipts to road maintenance and the available evidence for the 1820s and 1830s suggests that this duty was most competently discharged. As a result, the condition of the roads between Kendal and Keswick underwent further improvement and hence were well equipped to cater for further increases in tourist traffic during the 1840s by which time the railway had reached Windermere.

The ambitious programmes of road improvement carried out by a number of Cumbrian Trusts during this period were often well beyond their current resources and hence were financed by external loans. The apparent readiness of people to lend money on the required scale also suggests a general confidence that the turnpikes would, in the future, attract more traffic and hence more toll receipts. This would enable such Trusts to repay their creditors handsomely. It is likely, however, that some of the most prominent local families such as the Lowthers had an additional motive for lending money in this fashion. They anticipated that better roads would give a desired boost to the regional economy in which they had a considerable stake.

It is clear that for a short time at least the expectations of the first group of creditors were satisfied in that Trust receipts continued to rise. It is more difficult, however, to tell whether the second set of creditors gained comparable satisfaction. In other words, did road improvements in fact contribute very much to regional economic developments in the nineteenth century?

This is an important line of enquiry for most historians of transportation and it seldom provides precise answers. The historian of rail or canal transport does, however, possess one advantage which is not shared by the student of roads in this period. The former usually knows the year in which individual railways or canals were first open to traffic. This kind of knowledge, needless to say, is a useful starting point in an enquiry of this kind, but the history of road transport in Cumbria during this period does not provide such definite landmarks. The inauguration of new Trusts usually precipitated a spate of road improvements, but rarely led to the building of completely new sections of road over substantial areas of countryside. Hence even the most ambitious programmes of road improvements rarely created a completely new situation, since the old road may well have carried a substantial body of traffic in the first place. It was also usual for major road repairs to take a number of years to complete. Often a Trust would carry out such repairs in a series of phases with periods of inactivity in between to allow for the accumulation of toll receipts to meet its repair bills. The gradual nature of road rebuilding makes it all the more difficult to pinpoint its impact upon the economy of the area.

A further point to note is that the major road improvements in Cumbria during the early decades of the nineteenth century were accompanied by parallel developments in coastal shipping and canal building. West Cumberland in particular benefited from an expansion of coastal shipping facilities in this period, whilst South Westmorland, Furness and North West Cumberland had access to newly opened canals. These developments clearly had a complementary influence on the region's economic growth in the first half of the nineteenth century and it is often difficult to isolate the particular contribution of road transport in this context.

The expansion of agricultural activities in Cumbria during the late eighteenth century and in the first half of the nineteenth century, provides in some ways the clearest indications of the economic utility of improved roads. Throughout this period the bulk of farm produce was carried by road and as farmers expanded the scope of their activities easy access to local and regional markets was becoming essential. This need was recognised from the start by the Enclosure Commissioners, many of whom regarded road improvement as an integral part of their land re-organisation programmes. This is not to say that improved roads were a prime cause of agricultural expansion in this period. The opportunities and incentives offered by the price inflation of the Napoleonic War period clearly did more than any other contemporary factor to stimulate the more intensive cultivation of farmland. However, an improved and more flexible system of road communications was an essential instrument in furthering this process.

On the whole, it is more difficult to assess the contribution which roads made to the development of mining in Cumbria during this period. The Alston lead mines were exclusively dependent upon road transport during the first half of the nineteenth century, but with this exception the bulk of the region's mineral wealth was concentrated in the coastal belt of West Cumberland and in Furness. This meant that local mining magnates attached more importance to the expansion of coastal shipping and harbour facilities in the pre-railway period. Nevertheless, improved roads represented an important link in the chain of increased productivity in this area. The port of White-haven had benefited from improved communications with its hinterland as far back as the beginning of the eighteenth century, and in subsequent years road improvement received a fair amount of attention from local mining magnates. The increased traffic which the West Cumberland Turnpikes were carrying during the first half of the nineteenth century, provides a further indication of the usefulness of improved road communications between the various mines and their respective ports. It is probable also that the inauguration of new Turnpike Trusts between Carlisle and Cockermouth, and between Cockermouth and Maryport during the 1820s both reflected and stimulated a greater flow of traffic along these particular routes. An important element in this traffic was a stage and mail coach service. West Cumberland was increasingly well served in this respect by the 1820s, and this in itself provides a striking indication of the extent to which improved roads helped to reduce the landward isolation of West Cumberland.

Carlisle and Kendal were the major regional centres of population away from the coast. Both had become focal points for an expanding system of turnpike roads during the early nineteenth century and the question arises to what extent improved roads contributed to the growth of these two towns and their respective industries? It is reasonable to suppose, although difficult to prove, that the fairly rapid expansion of both towns as market and manufacturing centres in the late eighteenth and early nineteenth century was in part due to local road improvements. They must both have benefited considerably from the expansion of north-south traffic during the period, whilst the construction of the 'Military Road' linking Carlisle with north-east England appears to have had some bearing upon the progress of manufacturers in this particular city. Kendal had a long-standing importance as a market and woollen manufacturing centre. At first, the town relied more upon cross-country pack horse traffic than upon road communications, but there is little doubt that the construction of improved roads linking Kendal with the Pennine towns and also with Lancashire and Furness helped it to retain its traditional importance within Westmorland. By the 1820s Kendal was an important centre for stage coach and carrier services just as it had previously been a centre for pack horse traffic.

It is probably fair to say, however, that although improved roads might have laid the basis for the establishment of industries within both Kendal and Carlisle, they could not provide adequately for their further expansion during the nineteenth century. In particular, the developing industries of both towns needed large supplies of coal, and these could not be provided by the local carrying services on the requisite scale or at acceptable prices. This helps to explain the demand for the building of canals to link Kendal and Carlisle with the respective coalfields of South Lancashire and West Cumberland. The Lancaster canal, linking Kendal with industrial Lancashire, was finally opened in

1819, and from the start it seems to have satisfied the expectations of its promoters by providing considerable quantities of coal for industrial and household needs. Carlisle was not quite so fortunate in this respect. Its proposed canal link with West Cumberland never quite materialised, and the city had to be satisfied with a shorter canal to Port Carlisle. However, this setback was of no great long-term significance in view of the emergence of Carlisle as a major railway centre. This latter development permitted local industries to expand and multiply at a rate considerably in excess of anything which had been possible under previous transport conditions. Road carriage services were particularly ill equipped to carry heavy commodities such as coal, but there is little doubt that, on the whole, improved standards of road maintenance enabled carrying firms to provide a quicker and more flexible service. It is also reasonable to suppose that this service would be less costly on average than in the past. Carriers would be able to make more journeys in the same amount of time and this saving would more than offset any additional toll charges they might have to pay as the Turnpike system expanded.

It is worth noting also that the majority of Turnpike Trusts in the Cumbrian counties made their own contribution to price reductions, by allowing certain of the more basic commodities such as milk to travel toll free, 'because on account of the health of the inhabitants, all possible encouragement ought to be given to farms to sell their milk'.[1] Similar exceptions were made with regard to items of fuel, both turf and coal.

However, the cost of carriage was only one of a number of complex and interrelating factors which together determined the market price of a given commodity. This has made it difficult to demonstrate and impossible to quantify the connection between road improvements and price levels in Cumbria during the early decades of the nineteenth century. Local newspapers provide the main source of information on price levels during this period; most editions providing a weekly summary of market prices in the various towns, with additional comments upon price fluctuations where appropriate. This evidence suggests that food prices in particular followed a rather erratic course in these years, although the general tendency was for prices to rise during the Napoleonic War years and then to fall gradually during the next

---

[1] C.R.O., Carlisle–Eamont Trust, miscellaneous papers relating to the Trust Bill of 1808. Letter to Bleaymire and Shepherd, 27 March 1808.

three decades. This pattern corresponds to national price trends in the period and as such does not suggest that reduced carriage rates were having much effect upon the course of war-time inflation. Similarly, price reductions in the post-war period were an inevitable aftermath of the war and likewise do not, in themselves, necessarily point to road transport as a factor in producing this altered situation.

Nevertheless, it would seem reasonable to infer that in both cases reduced carriage costs would benefit the consumer indirectly, even though these benefits might not have been apparent during the war years due to the operation of other more powerful factors. Furthermore, the road improvements in many parts of Cumbria during the early decades of the century, helped both the consumer and the producer by enabling local markets to cater for a wider area and draw their produce from a wider circle of farmers and tradesmen. Equally, these enlarged markets gave the more ambitious farmers every incentive to improve the quality and quantity of their yields and to reduce their prices where possible in order to undercut a growing number of competitors. However, major road improvements usually took a number of years to complete and for this reason amongst others one would not expect them to have an immediate and easily identifiable impact upon local price levels. As a result, transport was rarely mentioned as a relevant factor by contemporary commentators upon local market prices. Such critics were more concerned with discussing weekly and seasonal fluctuations in price levels and hence usually attributed price reductions to good weather or more general favourable market trends.

Contemporaries were much more impressed by the impact of rail transport upon Cumbrian society. There is no doubt that railways by virtue of their speed, relative cheapness and vastly greater carrying capacity gave an unprecedented stimulus to economic activities and social changes within the area. Probably the main economic function of the railways within Cumbria was to make possible the growth of larger industries by bringing together in one place the necessary raw materials and power resources, whilst at the same time linking these industries more effectively with their respective markets.

A recapitulation of the later nineteenth century growth of the West Cumberland and Furness economy illustrates this point particularly well. In the first place, roads had facilitated the mining of coal and iron ore; the output of haematite from the various Furness mines increasing from about 20,000 tons in

1793[2] to 300,000 tons in 1851.[3] Mining was then given a further impetus following the construction of the Furness, Whitehaven–Furness Junction and Ulverston–Carnforth railways.[4] These lines, together with the Whitehaven Junction, Whitehaven–Cleator–Egremont and Cockermouth–Keswick–Penrith railways, made possible the most important single economic development of the railway period in Cumbria: the growth of an iron industry with centres at Barrow in Furness, Millom, Whitehaven and Workington. The building of these railways and the discovery of high grade haematite ore, coincided with the development of the Bessemer process which made particular use of these high quality ore reserves. At first, both Furness and West Cumberland exported most of their iron, but the position was transformed in the early 1860s by the opening of two invaluable railway links. The first line, linking Barnard Castle with Tebay, was opened on 4 July 1861, whilst an associated branch line from Kirkby Stephen to Clifton Junction was opened in December of the same year.

Both areas were now able to exploit Durham coke in order to develop their own iron industries. In 1864, J. T. Smith established a new steel company at Barrow, combining the Bessemer process with rail-rolling upon a large scale, and making extensive use of Durham coke, haematite from local mines at Park and Hodbarrow, and local limestone from the quarries at Stainton.[5] The next three years marked a turning point in the history of the Furness iron-field; it was ceasing to be an exporter of raw haematite and was beginning to smelt its own ores upon a large scale. In 1863 about one-third of Furness haematite went into local furnaces;[6] by 1865 the proportion had risen to nearly half,[7] and by 1868 it was nearly five-eighths.[8] Similarly, West Cumberland iron production had expanded considerably by the 1870s as a result of the opening of rail communication from Durham to Workington and Whitehaven, following the completion of the Cockermouth–Penrith Railway in 1864. By 1882, Cumberland had produced its maximum output of pig iron,

[2] J. D. Marshall, *Furness and the Industrial Revolution* (1958), p. 35.

[3] H. W. Schneider, 'On the Haematite Iron Mines of Low Furness', C.W.A.L.S. (1884–5), p. 106.

[4] By 1871 the Furness haematite mines were producing over 1 million tons.

[5] J. D. Marshall, op. cit., pp. 252–3.

[6] Ibid., p. 251.

[7] Ibid., p. 257.

[8] Ibid.

amounting to 1,001,181 tons, 12 per cent of the total output for Great Britain.[9]

This large scale development of an iron industry in West Cumberland and Furness, and the accompanying growth of Barrow, was almost entirely due to the building of railways in this region, and, as such, illustrates the limitations of road transport. Good roads were able to provide for individual sectors of the economy, but were unable to cope with sustained heavy traffic. They could not give the speedy and well-integrated service which would be necessary in order to transport coal from distant mines to smelt the local ore. Similarly, although Barrow was the only Cumbrian town which owed its being to the railways, its growth provides a powerful illustration of the impact which an ambitious Railway Company could make upon a particular region. The Furness railway was opened in 1845 and, under the initiative of the Duke of Buccleuch, Lord Burlington, H. W. Schneider and James Ramsden, Barrow expanded rapidly. At first, it owed its existence to the traffic using the Furness railway' but gradually it developed railway workshops and haematite steel works which were producing a total of 250,000 tons of pig iron by 1873.[10] There was a corresponding development of ship building in this period; the Barrow yards being capable of building simultaneously five vessels of 4,000 tons capacity by 1873.[11] During this period, the population of Barrow had risen from a mere 150 in 1843 to a total of 8,176 by 1864,[12] and the town possessed one of the most efficient Bessemer plants in the world, in addition to one of the best equipped shipyards in the British Isles. The emergence of Barrow as an iron manufacturing town was paralleled on a smaller scale by the contemporaneous growth of Millom, across the Duddon estuary from Barrow in south-west Cumberland. This area had been largely neglected during the eighteenth and early nineteenth centuries and its economy remained undeveloped in consequence. In the absence of turnpikes its road conditions were not such as to encourage many visitors and it was not until the construction of the White-haven and Furness Junction railway that its communities were effectively linked with other parts of Cumbria. Subsequently, its

[9] Oliver Wood, 'Development of the Coal, Iron and Shipbuilding Industries of West Cumberland, 1750–1914 (unpublished PhD. thesis, Univ. London, 1952), p. 264.
[10] Sidney Pollard, 'Barrow in Furness and the Seventh Duke of Devonshire', *Economic History Review* (1955–6), p. 215.   [11] Ibid.
[12] J. D. Marshall, op. cit., p. 198.

iron ore resources were exploited more effectively and formed the basis for an iron industry in the Millom area. Hence, in this particular case railways not only fulfilled a valuable economic function but were of great social usefulness in reducing the isolation of a section of Cumbria which had clearly not shared in many of the benefits of earlier road improvements.

However, on the whole the main role of rail transport within Cumbria was as an accelerator of social and economic changes. It is worth reiterating that, with the exceptions of Barrow and Millom, the majority of Cumbrian towns experienced their most rapid period of growth in the pre-railway period of the nineteenth century. Certain of these towns also expanded the range of their economic activities quite markedly during this same period. Railways, of course, made a great contribution to the economy of the region but in many respects they were building upon foundations already laid. Similarly, if one examines the pattern of travel within the area, it is clear that the volume of local and through traffic increased considerably in the decades immediately preceding the building of railways. Hence, although railways carried far more people at less cost, a pattern of increased travel had already been set. This is particularly well illustrated by the expansion of tourism. The tourist trade was already well under way before the first railways reached the fringes of the Lake District. Thereafter the main contribution of railway excursions was to enable a wider cross-section of the public to visit the Lakes.

Roads were inevitably overshadowed by railways during the second half of the nineteenth century, but they still formed an essential link in the region's transport network. Previous discussion, reinforced by surviving toll gate receipts, has served to illustrate the very considerable extent to which local traffic used the turnpikes at this time, and the way in which the turnpike trustees and carrying services adjusted their business to exploit to the full this increased short-distance feeder traffic to towns and railway stations. It is also worth paying attention to the administration of bridges during this same period. Bridge repair was financed by an annual county rate and, as such, was not affected by railway competition in the same way. Therefore, both counties continued to spend a high proportion of their total annual income on bridge maintenance throughout the nineteenth century. It appears that the two county authorities devoted approximately the same proportion of their revenues to this purpose: just under one-sixth of the total county rate in each case. Thus, between 1839 and 1875 Cumberland spent approximately £465,000, of which £72,000 was devoted to bridge repair; this represented an average annual expenditure of £1,946 upon bridges. Westmorland utilised its smaller resources in a similar way, and spent £21,000 out of a total county rate of £135,000 upon bridge repairs between 1839 and 1875; an average annual bridge expenditure of £622.[13] It is particularly interesting to note that bridge expenditure in both counties did not decline very substantially after 1855.[14] Although it is unrealistic to compare county expenditure with that of the various Turnpike Trusts in view of the Trusts' greatly depleted income, it is still notable that the county authorities should continue to pay so much attention to bridge repair at a time when railways were absorbing an ever-increasing proportion of the region's traffic.

This latter period also provides a new slant on what is one of the most interesting facets of this survey: the clash between the urban and commercial interests on the one hand and the rural interests on the other, over the imposition of tolls in the neighbourhood of expanding towns. This is in some respects analogous to earlier disputes preceding Trust inauguration: between agriculturalists who preferred low rates to improved road conditions, and their more enterprising neighbours who were prepared to endure high tolls in order to facilitate road repairs and thus aid the marketing of their surplus farm and mineral produce. However, the later disputes are more complex. The clash of urban and rural interests had become increasingly marked as towns expanded and the Trusts' revenues declined. In addition, the impending dissolution of the various Trusts and the demands of their creditors, emphasised the growing gulf between 'outside' speculators and the Cumbrian rural interests.

By the close of the nineteenth century, the area's road and bridge authorities were facing problems which bore some similarity to those which confronted their predecessors a century earlier. On the first occasion, the pressures of industrialisation and the demand for increased business and leisure travel, reflected and stimulated improvements in vehicular construction and in road making and administration. Now, the advent of the motor car was to pose a fresh challenge and to necessitate a further breakthrough in road making techniques and in administrative practice.

[13] See Appendix D for further details.
[14] Cumberland annual bridge expenditure 1839–54—£2,163; 1855–75— £1,781; Westmorland annual bridge expenditure 1839–54—£631; 1855–75— £518.

Cumbria had altered greatly during the nineteenth century. Its economy was more complex, its social structure more varied and its people less backward by the end of the century. In this respect, it resembles most parts of England and Wales during this period. Nevertheless, Cumbria is in some respects unusual in that it was becoming increasingly isolated economically during the nineteenth century. Industry was now concentrated in larger units than before, and local initiative and mineral resources were no longer sufficient to maintain a really large scale industrial society. An economically productive hinterland, large reserves of capital and proximity to markets were now becoming of paramount importance. Towns such as Whitehaven were successful in an age when economic units were smaller and more localised, but the West Cumberland ports could not hope ultimately to compete on equal terms with Glasgow and Liverpool, both of which were outlets for a highly populated and industrialised hinterland. Similarly, Carlisle and Kendal, despite improved communications, were too far removed from large industrial centres. Barrow, admittedly, suggests an exception to this generalisation but, despite its spectacular development during the middle decades of the century, its advantages of mineral resources, port and railway facilities, still proved insufficient in the long run to offset the handicap of its distance from other centres of industry. Therefore, the town's future potential was limited and by the end of the 1870s 'it was clear that Barrow would never become a great port for general commerce'.[15]

Thus one can justifiably maintain that, whilst Cumbria was now increasingly productive, its economic importance, relative to the rest of the country, had somewhat declined. Nevertheless, in considering this paradox one must not lose sight of the great benefits which road and rail improvements conferred upon the Cumbrian community during these years, and the immeasurable difference which they had made and were to make to the lives of individual people living in the area.

[15] Melville and Hobbs, 'Early Railway History in Furness', C.W.T. *Tract Series*, **XIII** (1951), p. 64.

Appendix A

DATES OF INAUGURATION AND DISSOLUTION OF THE VARIOUS CUMBRIAN TURNPIKE TRUSTS

Trust	Inauguration	Dissolution
Whitehaven	1739	1870
Newcastle–Carlisle (Military Road)[1]	1747	1877
Brough–Eamont Bridge	1753	1882
Cockermouth–Workington	1753	1883
Kendal–Kirkby Lonsdale–Milnthorpe	1753	1877
Carlisle–Eamont Bridge[2]	1753	1883
Heron Syke–Eamont Bridge	1753	1882
Appleby–Kendal	1760	1872
Cockermouth–Keswick–Kendal[3]	1761	1883
Sedbergh	1761	1874
Kendal–Ireleth	1763	1872
Carlisle–Skillbeck	1767	1828
Longtown	1793	1876
Milnthorpe–Levens Bridge	1801	1874
Kingstown–Westlinton	1806	1872
Brampton–Longtown	1807	1876
Brougham Bridge	1812	1877
Carlisle–Glasgow	1815	1883
Ulverston–Carnforth	1818	1877
Carlisle–Cockermouth	1824	1883
Alston	1824	1875
Kirkby Stephen–Hawes	1825	1874
Cockermouth–Maryport	1825	1885
Carlisle–Brampton	1828	1876

[1] The Cumberland section of the Road formed a separate Trust in 1811 and was subsequently referred to as the Carlisle–Temon Trust.

[2] Divided into Two Divisions in 1830.

[3] A separate Trust was formed in 1824, the Ambleside Trust constituting the road between Kendal and Keswick.

Appendix B

DATES OF OPENING OF CUMBRIAN RAILWAY LINES

1838[1]	Newcastle–Carlisle
1840	Maryport–Aspatria
1844	Carlisle–Wigton
1846	Remainder of Maryport–Carlisle line
1846	Furness Railway (piel to Kirkby Ireleth)
1846	Lancaster–Carlisle
1846	Maryport–Workington
1847	Cockermouth–Workington
1847	Kendal–Windermere
1847	Whitehaven Junction Line (Whitehaven to Maryport)
1848	Extension of Furness Railway (Kirkby Ireleth to Broughton)
1849	Whitehaven–Ravenglass
1850	Whitehaven and Furness Junction line (Whitehaven to Broughton)
1852	Alston–Lambley
1854	Dalton–Ulverston
1855	Carlisle–Port Carlisle
1856	Port Carlisle–Silloth
1857	Whitehaven–Cleator–Egremont
1857	Ulverston–Carnforth
1859	Broughton–Coniston
1861	South Durham and Lancashire Union Line (Darlington to Tebay)
1862	Eden Valley Line (Kirkby Stephen to Clifton)
1864	Egremont–Lamplugh
1865	Cockermouth–Keswick–Penrith
1867	Ulverston–Newby Bridge
1868	Newby Bridge–Lakeside
1869	Egremont–Sellafield
1876	Settle–Carlisle

[1] The dates mark the opening of passenger traffic on the line in question.

Appendix C

SOURCES OF AVAILABLE TURNPIKE RECEIPTS

Trust	Years covered	Source
1. Alston	1822–34	Q.S.P. Rolls
	1834–52	*Cumberland Pacquet*
	1852–74	Q.S.P. Rolls
2. Ambleside	1775–81	Trust Misc. Papers
	1806	*Carlisle Journal*
	1824–75	Trust Minutes
3. Appleby–Kendal	1815–16	*West Advertiser*
	1821–33	Q.S.P. Rolls
	1834–49	Parl. Papers
4. Brampton–Longtown	1823–32	Q.S.P. Rolls
	1834–41	Trust Misc. Papers
	1843	Q.S.P. Rolls
	1845	Q.S.P. Rolls
	1849	Trust Misc. Papers
	1853	Trust Misc. Papers
	1857	Trust Misc. Papers
	1861–3	Trust Misc. Papers
	1865	Trust Misc. Papers
	1867–70	Trust Misc. Papers
	1875–6	Trust Misc. Papers
5. Brougham Bridge	1851	Trust Misc. Papers
6. Brough–Eamont Bridge	1798–1801	*Cumberland Pacquet*
	1812–15	*West. Advertiser*
	1821–33	*West. Gazette*
	1833–54	Parl. Papers
7. Carlisle–Brampton	1828–76	Trust Minutes
8. Carlisle–Cockermouth	1823–44	Q.S.P. Rolls
	1852–5	*Cumberland Pacquet*
	1857–62	*Cumberland Pacquet*
	1865–6	*Cumberland Pacquet*
	1868	*Cumberland Pacquet*

Trust	Years covered	Source
9. Carlisle–Eamont Bridge (N)	1823–30	Q.S.P. Rolls
	1830–83	Trust Minutes
10. Carlisle–Eamont Bridge (S)	1823–59	Trust Account Books
	1859–83	Trust Minutes
11. Carlisle–Skillbeck	1790–1827	Trust Minutes
12. Carlisle–Temon	1823–54	Q.S.P. Rolls
	1854–76	Trust Minutes
13. Cockermouth–Maryport	1825–44	Q.S.P. Rolls
	1852–5	*Cumberland Pacquet*
	1857–61	*Cumberland Pacquet*
	1865–6	*Cumberland Pacquet*
	1868	*Cumberland Pacquet*
14. Cockermouth–Penrith	1799–1802	*Cumberland Pacquet*
	1804–24	Trust Minutes
	1824–34	Q.S.P. Rolls
	1834–54	Parl. Papers
	1854–6	Trust Minutes
	1858–62	*Cumberland Pacquet*
	1866–70	*Cumberland Pacquet*
	1872–8	Trust Minutes
15. Cockermouth–Workington	1804–19	*Cumberland Pacquet*
	1823–44	Q.S.P. Rolls
	1848	*Cumberland Pacquet*
	1850	*Cumberland Pacquet*
	1852–5	*Cumberland Pacquet*
	1857–62	*Cumberland Pacquet*
	1865–6	*Cumberland Pacquet*
	1868	*Cumberland Pacquet*
16. Heron Syke	1816	*West. Gazette*
	1819	*West. Advertiser*
	1822–38	Q.S.P. Rolls
	1839–49	Parl. Papers
	1851–71	Trust Misc. Papers
	1875	Trust Misc. Papers
	1876–82	Q.S.P. Rolls

Trust	Years covered	Source
17. Kendal–Ireleth	1822–70	Trust Misc. Papers
18. Kingstown–Westlinton	1830	Q.S.P. Rolls
	1834–72	Q.S.P. Rolls
19. Kirkby Lonsdale– Kendal–Milnthorpe	1834–52	Parl. Papers
20. Kirkby Stephen–Hawes	1847	Hallam MSS
	1855	Hallam MSS
	1857	Hallam MSS
21. Longtown	1823–30	Q.S.P. Rolls
	1830–2	*Cumberland Pacquet*
	1832–7	Q.S.P. Rolls
	1840–7	Q.S.P. Rolls
	1850–1	*Cumberland Pacquet*
22. Milnthorpe–Levens	1828–34	Q.S.P. Rolls
	1860–75	Q.S.P. Rolls
23. Sedbergh	1797–1822	Q.S.P. Rolls
24. Ulverston–Carnforth	1822	*West. Advertiser*
	1826–76	Trust Misc. Papers
25. Whitehaven	1806	*Cumberland Pacquet*
	1808–9	*Cumberland Pacquet*
	1811–13	*Cumberland Pacquet*
	1815–19	*Cumberland Pacquet*
	1823–69	Q.S.P. Rolls

Appendix D

THE RELATIONSHIP OF BRIDGE EXPENDITURE
TO TOTAL COUNTY EXPENDITURE
IN CUMBRIA

CUMBERLAND

Year	Total county expend. £	Total bridge expend. £	Percentage of whole
1839	8,923	1,826	20·5
1840	9,921	3,506	35·4
1841	12,516	6,178	49·4
1842	10,507	3,234	30·9
1844	11,896	2,156	18·1
1848	10,493	1,617	15·4
1849	12,648	1,496	11·9
1850	10,548	1,183	11·3
1851	8,999	1,140	12·7
1852	8,244	1,246	15·2
1853	8,628	1,214	14·1
1854	9,462	1,162	12·2
1855	11,074	1,834	16·5
1856	10,716	1,596	15
1857	10,813	2,385	22
1859	10,407	1,838	17·7
1862	13,307	2,452	18·4
1863	13,830	1,877	13·7
1864	12,168	1,881	15·4
1865	13,037	1,866	14·4
1866	13,633	1,670	12·3
1867	13,406	1,737	13
1868	14,697	1,753	12
1869	16,071	1,750	11
1871	16,563	1,390	8·3
1872	16,890	1,671	9·9
1873	17,862	1,564	8·7
1874	18,973	1,705	9
1875	18,598	1,307	7

WESTMORLAND

Year	Total county expend. £	Total bridge expend. £	Percentage of whole
1827	2,734	387	14·4
1828	3,106	645	20·8
1829	3,015	411	13·4
1830	2,100	385	18·3
1831	2,003	382	19·1
1832	2,772	212	7·6
1833	2,835	335	12
1834	2,907	215	7·4
1835	3,293	1,720	52·1
1836	3,281	900	27·3
1837	3,262	783	23·7
1838	4,497	2,133	47·4
1839	4,275	1,175	27·3
1840	3,536	1,321	37·7
1841	3,409	1,225	36
1842	3,211	599	18·7
1843	2,985	475	15·8
1844	2,810	406	14·5
1845	3,534	674	19·3
1846	3,536	629	18
1847	3,019	577	19·2
1848	3,388	385	11·3
1849	3,729	706	19·1
1850	3,334	428	13
1851	2,996	311	10·3
1852	3,273	330	10
1853	3,126	536	17·3
1854	3,216	327	10·2
1855	2,763	539	19·3
1856	3,723	383	10·3
1857	3,078	301	9·7
1858	3,342	466	14·2
1859	3,254	292	8·8
1860	4,117	219	5·3
1861	2,298	174	7·6
1862	3,762	353	9·3
1863	3,698	230	6·2
1864	3,981	511	12·8
1865	3,483	209	6
1866	3,642	254	7
1867	4,517	909	20·2

Year	Total county expend. £	Total bridge expend. £	Percentage of whole
1868	5,299	1,081	20·4
1869	4,251	487	11·6
1870	5,827	1,965	33·9
1871	3,820	216	5·4
1872	4,707	583	12·4
1873	4,566	585	12·9
1874	4,111	285	7
1875	4,954	828	16·6
1876	6,736	398	6
1877	8,550	1,315	15·5
1878	8,184	744	9·1

Appendix E

TURNPIKE TRUST OFFICIALS AND THEIR YEARS OF OFFICE

1. Alston Trust[1,2]

Nature of Office	Official(s)	Dates
Clerk	Robert and William Bainbridge	1829–35
	John Ruddock and Robert Bainbridge	1835–55
	Robert and Utrick Bainbridge	1855–75
	J. G. Mellican	1875–
Treasurer	Jonathan Walton	1835–56
	Thomas Cook	1856–75
Surveyor	David William Rome	1835–41
	William Buck	1841–67
	George Cunningham	1867–70
	Hugh Mackenzie	1870–5

2. Ambleside Trust

	Official(s)	Dates
Clerk	John Braithwaite	1801–22
	John Collinson	1822–53
	William Petty	1853–9
	Thomas Harrison	1859–83
Treasurer	John Braithwaite	1801–25
	Thomas Reveley	1825–39
	William Thompson	1839–83
Surveyor	John Braithwaite	1801–25
	Edward Bolt	1825–36
	George Theobalds	1836–47
	William Robinson	1847–53
	Crayston Webster	1853–83

[1] An asterisk following the name of an early trust official, indicates that his term of office began in the year listed. In all other cases, the date alongside the earliest named official of any particular trust, simply refers to the earliest time in which the person is known to have held the office in question.

[2] An asterisk following the last-named of any group of officials indicates that the date of his leaving office is unknown. In all other cases, the official in question relinquished his office at the time the particular trust was dissolved.

Nature of Office	Official(s)	Dates
3. Appleby–Kendal Trust		
Clerk	John Milner*	1822–46
	Robert Wharton*	1846–
Treasurer	Robert Gibson	1822–33
	Thomas Reveley	1833–46
	James Bouefield*	1846–
Surveyor	Robert Gibson and	
	William Hastwell	1822–33
General Surveyor	John Loudon McAdam	1833–6
Superintendent Surveyor	James Townsend	1833–6
Surveyor	James Townsend	1836–46
	Robert Taylor*	1846–
4. Brampton–Longtown Trust		
Clerk	Robert Norman	1829–36
	William Carrick	1836–76
Treasurer	John Norman	1829–36
	John Bowman	1836–49
	Henry Halton	1849–76
Surveyor	James Walker	1836–76
5. Brough–Bowes Trust		
Clerk	John Heelis*	1833–
Treasurer	George Thompson	1833–7
	Henry Hopes*	1837–
Surveyor	Mitchell Ewbank*	1833–
6. Brougham Bridge Trust		
Clerk	George Hutchinson	1827–53
	William Hutchinson	1853–77
Treasurer	George Hutchinson	1852–77
Surveyor	George Hutchinson	1852–77
7. Brough–Eamont Bridge Trust		
Clerk	Thomas Harrison*	1801–
	Edward Heelis	1878–82
8. Carlisle–Brampton Trust		
Clerk	Robert Norman*	1828–34
	Chris Wannop	1834–43
	John Norman	1843–76
Treasurer	Peter Dixon*	1828–47
	Henry Halton	1847–76
Surveyor	Chris Hodgson*	1828–9
	Emmanuel Demain	1829–37
	Andrew Patterson	1837–65
	Philip Nicholson	1865–73
	Alex Ormiston	1873–6

Nature of Office	Official(s)	Dates

9. *Carlisle–Eamont Bridge Trust*
A. *Whole Trust*

Clerk	John Thompson	1808–
Treasurer	George Blamire	1778–
Surveyor	Joseph Moss	1823–

B. *Northern Division*

Clerk	Chris Wannop	1841–3
	John Norman	1843–83
Treasurer	John Bowman	1841–7
	H. J. Halton	1847–83
Surveyor	Andrew Patterson	1841–65
	Philip Nicholson	1865–73
	Alex Ormiston	1873–83

C. *Southern Division*

Clerk	John Pattinson	1823–41
	John Bowman	1841–58
	Chris Fairer	1858–83
Treasurer	Thomas Atkinson	1823–83
Surveyor	Thomas Turnbull	1829–51
	David Davis	1851–4
	James Mitchell	1854–83

10. *Carlisle–Skillbeck Trust*

Treasurer	George Blamire	1804–20
	J. Graham	1820–7

11. *Carlisle–Temon Trust*

Clerk	Chris Wannop	1835–42
	John Norman	1842–77
Treasurer	John Bowman	1835–47
	H. J. Halton	1847–77
Surveyor	Andrew Patterson	1835–65
	Philip Nicholson	1865–73
	Alex Ormiston	1873–77

12. *Cockermouth–Carlisle Trust*

Clerk	Edward Steel	1853–80
	Edward Waugh	1880–3

13. *Cockermouth–Maryport Trust*

Clerk	Edward Steel	1854–65
	Edward Waugh	1865–83

Nature of Office	*Official(s)*	*Dates*
14. *Cockermouth–Penrith Trust*		
Clerk	John Fisher	1803–26
	J. W. Fisher	1826–32
	Richard Fisher*	1852–
Treasurer	John Fisher	1803–23
	Jonathan Otley	1823–6
	W. James	1826–42
	G. Hebson*	1842–
Surveyor	Timothy Todburster	1792–1807
	Samuel Culling	1807–18
	John Fisher	1818–35
	George Watson	1835–
15. *Cockermouth–Workington Trust*		
Clerk	John Fisher	1799–1804
	Joseph Steel[3]	1804–64
	Edward Waugh	1864–82
	R. Broatch	1882–3
16. *Heron Syke Trust*		
Clerk	Nathan Tyson	1815–33
	Thomas Reveley	1833–57
	Roger Moser	1857–82
Treasurer	Thomas Reveley	1819–33
	William Satterthwaite	1833–50
	William Petty	1850–71
	Henry Hoggarth	1871–82
Superintendent Surveyor	Hugh Blackwood	1833–7
	Robert Reid	1837–58
	James Liddell	1858–71
	James Buck	1871–3
General Surveyor	John Loudon McAdam	1833–5
	John Loudon McAdam and John McConnell	1835–6
	John McConnell	1837–58
	Crayson Webster	1858–73
17. *Kendal–Ireleth Trust*		
Clerk	Henry Remington*	1844–
Treasurer	William Petty and John Postlethwaite	1834–66
	John Jackson	1866–72

[3] Probably father and son with same name.

H

Nature of Office	Official(s)	Dates

18. Kendal–Kirkby Stephen Trust

Clerk	Thomas Harrison*	1808–

19. Kingstown–Westlinton Trust

Clerk	Chris Wannop	1834–42
	John Norman	1842–72
Treasurer	John Bowman	1834–47
	H. J. Halton	1847–72
Surveyor	Robert Sewell	1834–5
	Andrew Patterson	1835–65
	Philip Nicholson	1865–72

20. Kirkby Lonsdale–Kendal–Milnthorpe Trust

Clerk	William Romaine Gregg	1863–77
Treasurer	Richard Roper	1863–77
Surveyor	William Talbot	1863–77

21. Kirkby Stephen–Hawes Trust

Clerk	Middleton Hewitson	1847–51
	John Flower	1851–73
	William Wilson	1873–4
Treasurer	Robert Gibson	1825–41
	Thomas Mason	1841–74

22. Longtown Trust

Clerk	James Holmes	1835–6
	S. Ewart	1836–40
	James Mounsey*	1840–
Treasurer	Robert Armstrong	1835–47
	Henry Graham*	1847–
Surveyor	John Yule	1835–43
	James Walker*	1843–

23. Milnthorpe–Levens Trust

Clerk	Thomas Reveley	1834–60
	Roger Moser	1860–74
Treasurer	William Satterthwaite	1823–52
	Henry Hoggarth	1852–74
Superintendent Surveyor	Hugh Blackwood	1834–
General Surveyor	John Loudon McAdam and John McConnell	1834–6
Surveyor	Crayston Webster*	1860–74

Nature of Office	Official(s)	Dates
24. Sedbergh Trust		
Treasurer	James Davis	1800–22
Surveyor	Joshua Smithson and Arthur Croxton	1800–15
	John Rigg and Matthew Coulton*	1815–
25. Ulverston–Carnforth Trust		
Clerk	James Johnson*	1818–50
	Edward Hutton	1850–65
	Gardiner Thompson	1865–77
Treasurer	James Briggs	1823–37
	John Kitching	1837–77
Surveyor	John Postlethwaite	1820–37
	Thomas Townson	1837–41
	Thomas Robinson	1841–64
	Crayston Webster	1864–77
26. Whitehaven Trust		
Clerk	P. H. Younger	1816–33
	Edward Carr Knubley	1833–50
	Peter William Sherwen	1850–66
	John Fox	1866–70
Treasurer	P. H. Younger	1816–33
	John Longmire	1833–50
Treasurer	Charles Halton	1850–9
	R. Brown	1859–70
Superintendent Surveyor	A. McKinley	1833–5
	R. Newton	1835–41
	Henry Wright	1841–7
	A. Robertson	1847–50
	John McConnell	1850–7
	J. Ross	1857–61
	R. Pickering	1861–70
General Surveyor	John Loudon McAdam	1833–6
	John McConnell	1836–50
	Alex Robertson	1850–70

Appendix F

NAMES OF LESSEES OF
VARIOUS TOLL GATES

1. *Ambleside Trust*

A. *Waterhead Gate*

1798–1800	William and John Newton	1829–30	Joseph Wood
1801–6	William and John Newton and John Grunn	1831–7	John Long (Sedbergh) (Joseph Wood, Tom Long)[1]
1807–9	Thomas Jackson, James Backhouse, James Jackson	1840–1	Joseph Wood
		1842–3	Charles Winn
		1844–50	George Foster
1813–15	John and Jonathan Scott, Robert Walker	1851–3	Joshua Bower
1816–21	John Scott and Robert Walker	1854–6	George Foster
		1857–8	Charles Winn
1822–4	Richard Backhouse and Thomas Partain	1859	Joshua Bower and Charles Winn
		1860	James Willing (?)
1825	John Scott	1861–70	Charles Winn
1826–8	Richard Backhouse	1871–3	Richard Bailey
		1874	Thomas Bower

B. *Grasmere Gate*

1798–1807	Stephen Thompson and Thomas Eccles	1842–3	Charles Winn
		1844–51	George Foster
1807–10	Stephen Thompson and William Hartley	1851–3	Joshua Bower
		1854–6	George Foster
1813–24	Thomas Thompson and John Allinson	1857–8	Charles Winn
		1859	Joshua Bower and Charles Winn
1825	Henry Sutcliffe	1860	James Willing (?)
1826–32	Thomas Thompson	1861–70	Charles Winn
1833–8	John Long	1871–4	Richard Bailey
1838–9	Joshua Bower	1875	Thomas Bower
1840–1	Joseph Wood		

C. *Plumgarths*

1798–1800	George Birkett and George Airey	1801–7	Chris Hind, James Jackson, Thomas Eccles

[1] Sureties bracketed after lessee where known; also place of residence of lessee named *if* he a *non-local man*.

1807–9   George Beecham and Richard Taylor

1810–12   Thomas Jackson, George Beecham, Richard Taylor

1813–15   George Beecham and Richard Taylor

1816–18   William Bainbridge (Heysham) and Thomas Clark

1819–21   Henry Sutcliffe and John Barcliff

1821–4   John Scott and Robert Walker

1825   George Beecham and Richard Taylor

1826–8   George Beecham

1829   Joseph Wood

1830–2   George Beecham

1833–7   John Long

1838–9   Joshua Bower (Glass Manufact. of Hunslet) (Joseph Wood and John Long)

1840–53   George Foster

1854–6   George Elleray

1857   George Foster

1858   Joseph Wood

1859   Joseph Wood and George Elleray

1860   Joseph Wood

1861–70   Charles Winn

1871–4   Richard Bailey (Preston)

1875   Thomas Bower (Enoch Blackburn of Hunslet and Richard Bower of Harrogate—both Toll Contractors)

D. *Staveley*

1798–1800   George Birkett and George Airey

1800 et seq.   *See* Plumgarths names (gates let together)

2. *Brampton–Longtown Trust*

A. *Kirkby Moor*

1836   Robert Fawkes

1837   James Grieves

1863–4   Aaron Moses

1866–70   Alex Armstrong

B. *Lineside*

1863–1870   David Brow

3. *Carlisle–Brampton Trust*

A. *Botcherby*

1829   Elizabeth Seilby

1830–1   Henry Varty

1832   John Wood

1833–4   Henry Varty

1835   Edward Calvert

1836–7   Henry Varty

1838   Chris Wilson

1839   Chris Wannop

1840–1   Chris Wilson

1842–3   Thomas Winthrop

1844   Joseph Cowper

1845   Thomas Gibson

1846   Edward Calvert

1847–54   Joseph Cowper

1855   William Wilson

1856   Alex Armstrong

1857   Matthew Pattinson

1858–61   Joshua Bower

1862   Francis Mitchinson

1863–9   Joshua Bower

1870–3   Charles Winn

1874   Joshua Bower

1875   Thomas Bower

B. *Corby Hill*

1829–30 John Calvert	1839 David Graham
1831 Edward Calvert	1840–1 Chris Wilson
1832 William Wood	1842–3 Joseph Cowper
1833 William Ellis	1844–9 Thomas Winthrop
1834 William Nicholson	1850–7 Joseph Cowper
1835 John Armstrong	1858 Matthew Pattinson
1836 Thomas Winthrop	1859–74 Joseph Cowper
1838 John Long	1875 Thomas Bower

C. *Geltside*

1830 Elizabeth Seilby	1840–1 Chris Wilson
1831 Joseph Smith	1842–73 Joseph Cowper
1832 John Calvert	1874 John Hogg
1833–6 Edward Calvert	1875 Thomas Bower
1837– Thomas Graham	

4. *Carlisle–Eamont Trust* (*Northern Division*)

A. *Harraby*

1841 John Long	1861–8 Joshua Bower
1842 John and Edward Calvert	1869–70 Marion Tate
1845 John Walton	1871 John Varty
1851 Joshua Bower	1872 Marion Tate
1852 Joshua Bower	1873 John Varty
1853 William Cavill	1874 Robert Varty
1854 William Towers	1875–6 John Varty
1855 Jacob Rowlands	1877 Joshua Bower
1856 John Varty	1878 Moffat Hetherington
1857 Alex Armstrong	1879 Thomas Bower
1858 Thomas Bower	1880 Moffat Hetherington
1859 Joshua Bower	1881 Ebenezer Anderson
1860 Gavin Tait	1882 John Harrison

B. *Hesket*

1841 John Calvert	1860 Thomas Nixon
1843–4 John Walton	1861–2 Thomas Ivison
1845 Charles Bell	1863 John Nixon
1851–2 Thomas Gibson	1864–70 Thomas Ivison
1853 Thomas Long	1871–75 Thomas Stevenson
1854–5 Thomas Gibson	1876 John Harrison
1856 John Varty	1877 Joshua Bower
1857 Thomas Thompson	1878–9 Thomas Bower
1858–9 Thomas Ivison	1880–2 Benjamin Hoofe

5. *Carlisle–Eamont Trust (Southern Division)*

A. *Townhead (or Milehouse)*

1823–7	John Monkhouse	1878	William Bocock
1827–30	Nicholas Noble	1879	George Bocock
1830–3	Joseph Rayson		(Newcastle) (John Bower,
1834–6	John Calvert		Toll Collector of
1837–43	John Long		Harrogate and Robert
1844–6	James Wood		Bower, Toll Collector of
1847–50	No lessees		Hunslet, and Enoch
1851–3	Joshua Bower		Blackburn)
1854–5	John Nixon	1880	John Shackleton (John
1856–8	Charles Winn		Thompson of Cumberland,
1858–68	Joseph Mounsey		Yeoman, and Robert
1869–75	John Varty		Bower of Hunslet)
1876–7	Thomas Stephenson		

B. *Kempley Bank*

1808	George Workman	1858–60	Joseph Mounsey
1809–12	Isaac Longrigg	1861–3	Charles Winn
1823–33	Joseph Kendal	1864	John Varty (Gentleman of
1834–6	Rebecca Hobson		Newcastle) (Robert Varty
1837–9	Joseph Kendal		and William Varty both
1840–3	John Long		Drapers of Newcastle)
1844	Thomas Gibson	1865–73	Charles Winn
1845–6	William Long	1874	Richard Metcalfe
1847–50	No lessees	1874–8	William Bocock (John
1851	William Long		Bower of Harrogate and
1852–3	Joshua Bower		Enoch Blackburn of
1854	William Long		Hunslet (Toll
1855	Joseph Peascod		Collectors))
1856	John Nixon	1879	John Hornsby (miller of
1857	Charles Winn		Stainton)
1857–8	John Varty and		
	Dennison		

6. *Carlisle Skillbeck Trust*

A. *Warnell Fell*

1790s	(For most of decade at	1804–8	John Noble
	least) Joseph Dobson	1823–7	Francis Carruthers

B. *Cummersdale*

1795	Joseph Frizzle	1808–11	Peter Brugh
1802–3	William Frizzle	1826	J. Irwin

7. *Carlisle–Temon Trust*

A. *Crosby*

1855   Thomas Ivison
1856–1860   John Nixon
1861   Gavin Tait
1862   John Nixon

1863   Thomas Ivison
1864–1875   John Nixon
1876   John Hogg

B. *Low Row*

1855   James Murray
1856   James Robson
1857–1859   James Murray
1860   John Robson

1861   Thomas Pelter
1862–1863   James Murray
1864–1876   John Robson

8. *Cockermouth–Penrith Trust*

A. *Penrith*

1808   Joseph Kendal

B. *High Hill*

1808   James McGowan
1814   Thomas Forster
1854   Charles Winn
1855   Thomas Bell (Maryport)

1878   R. R. Lowthian
1879–80   Mrs Bell
1881–3   George Forster

C. *Brow Top*

1808   John Scott
1814   Thomas Mawley

1854–5   Isaac Wren (Keswick Labourer)
1878–83   Geoffrey Johnston

D. *Brigham*

1808   Thomas Forster
1814   Thomas Forster

1854–5   Isaac Wren
1878–83   Geoffrey Johnston

E. *Kirkgate*

1808   George Tallantine
1814–16   Fleming Birkitt
1854   Anthony Fletcher
(Hensingham miner)

1855   Gate not let
1878   Mr Coulthard
1879–83   George Forster

F. *Cockermouth Town Head*

1808   John Ingham

G. *Castlegate*

1878   Charles Winn and George Forster

1878–83   George Forster

H. *Skirsgill*

1854–5	Charles Winn	1879–83	George Forster
1878	Charles Winn and George Forster		

I. *Saint Helens*

1854	Mary Bennett	1879	Mrs Blain
1855	Not let	1880	George Forster
1878	Charles Winn and George Forster	1881	J. Robinson
		1883	M. Norman

J. *Scales*

1854–5	James Bainbridge	1883	M. Airey
1878–81	J. Robinson		

K. *Woodend*

1854–5	John Cowper	1878–83	William Nicholson

L. *Wythburn*

1854–5	John Hawkrigg	1880–3	George Forster
1878–9	Mr Rigg		

M. *Brackenrigg*

1854–5	John Dodd	1879	John Varty
1878	Charles Winn and George Forster	1880–3	Mrs Blair

N. *Whinlatter*

1854–5	William Tickers	1879–83	Mrs Vickers
1878	Mr Vicer		

9. *Heron Syke Trust*

A. *Burton*

1860	R. Baxter	1875	Thomas Richardson

B. *Netherbridge*

1860	George Forster	1875	George Forster

C. *Bannisdale*

1860	Philip Cooper	1875	Robert Mattinson

D. *Shap*

1860   George Forster   1875   Charles Baker

E. *Clifton*

1860   Elizabeth Bourman   1875   Richard Bailey (Preston)

10. *Kirkby Stephen–Hawes Trust*

A. *Apperset*

1847–8   William Mason

B. *Bollam Gate and Riggs Bar*

1847–8   William Robinson

11. *Ulverston–Carnforth Trust*

A. *Wilson House*

1826–8   Joseph Wood, Joseph Burns and John Long

1840   Thomas Scholick, William Pawley, William Scholick and John Halliwell

1845   George Elleray and Joseph Wood

1846   Joseph and William Simpson

1856–7   Joseph and James Wood

1858   Joseph Wood and George Elleray

1859   Richard and Martin Bailey and Simon Charnley (Preston)

1860   Joseph Wood (George Elleray)

1861   Joseph and William Simpson

1862   William and John Hodgkinson

1863–4   Joseph Wood, Septimus Rawes (Kendal Coal Merchant) and Richard Rawes (Coal dealer)

1865   Joseph Wood, John Wood and Thomas Long

1867   George and Richard Roberts and James Deane

1868   John Herbert, John Kirkby (both Innkeepers)

1869   Richard Bailey (Fullwood Toll Gate), Martin Bailey and John Ray (Preston Butcher)

1870–4   John Herbert, Martin and Richard Bailey

1875   Richard and Martin Bailey and John Ray

1876   George Forster

B. *Beetham*

1843   Thomas Schollick and James Mackereth

1845   William Hodgkinson and Joseph Wood

1846   John Mackereth

1856   William and Richard Hodgkinson and Richard Thistlethwaite

1857   Richard and Martin Bailey

1858 William and Richard
      Hodgkinson
1860 William Hodgkinson and
      George Forster
1861-2 Joseph and William
      Taylor
1863 Joseph Taylor and Joseph
      Steele
1865-8 Richard and Joseph
      Taylor and Joseph
      Steele

1869 Richard and Martin
      Taylor and John Ray
1870-3 Joseph and Richard
      Taylor and Joseph
      Steele
1876 Thomas Bower and
      George Forster

C. *Beethwaite Green*

1840 Thomas Scholick
1845 George Elleray and
      Joseph Wood
1846 Joseph Simpson and
      William Simpson
1856-7 Joseph and James
      Wood
1858-9 Joseph Wood and
      George Elleray
1860 Edward Long
1861-2 Joseph Wood and
      George Elleray
1863 Joseph Wood

1865-7 George Roberts (near
      Preston), Richard
      Roberts (Swinton) and
      James Dean (Gentleman
      of Manchester)
1868 William Scholick
1869 Roger Park
1870-3 John Herbert, Martin
      and Richard Bailey
1875 Thomas and William
      Wearing, John Pawley
1876 Thomas Bower and
      George Forster

D. *Underfield*

1840 Miles and William
      Simpson
1843 Joseph and William
      Simpson
1846 Joseph Wood and George
      Elleray
1856-1857 James and Joseph
      Wood
1858 Joseph Wood and George
      Elleray
1859 Charles Winn (Joshua
      Bower, Enoch Blackburn)
1860 Richard Bailey
1861 George and John Forster
      and Edward Long

1862-6 Charles Winn
1867 Richard Bailey
1868 Charles Winn
1869 Joseph Wood, George
      Elleray
1870 Richard Bailey
1871 George Elleray
1872 Grace Elleray, George
      Forster, Joseph Elleray
1873 Richard Bailey
1875 Richard Bailey
1876 Thomas Bower and
      George Forster

Appendix G

LIST OF MORTGAGEES OF THE COCKERMOUTH–PENRITH TURNPIKE TRUST IN 1856

(INCLUDING DETAILS OF THEIR LOAN)

Earl of Lonsdale	£4,201 5s
William Marshall	£1,000
James Parkin	£1,000
Robert Pease	£700
Sir John Walsh	£650
A. Fisher	£300
John Simpson	£300
Thomas Harrison	£295
Henry Curwen	£250
Mrs Hartley	£200
Thomas Hartley	£200
Representatives of the late Rev. Josh Steel	£200
Sir John Lowther	£200
Stanley Dodgson	£200
Sir Henry Ralph Vane	£200
Robert Clark	£150
Colonel Green Thompson	£150
Thomas D. Spedding	£150
Executors of the late Josh Robinson	£141
Henry Howard	£100
Executors of the late Eliz. James	£100
F. W. Hazell	£100
Rev. Hilton Wybergh	£100
David Bell	£100
John Harrison	£100
Mary Goodall	£100
Trustees of Lorton School	£100
Richard Watts	£100
Miss Hodgson	£100
Trustees of the Keswick Dissenting House	£100
Mrs Drummond (of Glasgow)	£100
John Wilson	£100
Mrs Iredale	£100
Mrs Dykes	£100
Trustees of Huntingdon's Charity	£100
Sir Wilfrid Lawson	£100

Robert Jefferson	£100
William Lewthwaite	£97
Rebecca Crosthwaite	£75
Lieut. General James Jones	£75
Colonel James Steel	£50
Robert Jepson	£50
Richard Bowman	£50
John Norman	£50
Executors of the late John Hudson	£50
Trustees of the Cockermouth Dispensory	£50
Catherine Harper	£50
Rev. James Ward	£50
St John's Chapel	£30
Wardens for the Poor of St John's	£25
Mary Rome	£25
Jonathan Otley	£25
William Sisson	£25
John Dixon	£20

Bibliography

MANUSCRIPT MATERIAL

PUBLIC RECORD OFFICE

A. *Greenwich Hospital MSS (Northern Estates)*
1. ADM 65/79   In Letters, 1801–31
2. ADM 66/127   Out Letters, 1800–4
3. ADM 66/90   Out Letters, 1819–22
4. ADM 66/137   Out Letters, 1823–5
5. ADM 66/138   Out Letters, 1825–7
6. ADM 66/93   Out Letters, 1828–30
7. ADM 66/146   Out Letters, 1851–8
8. ADM 70/38   Ledgers, 1824–5
9. ADM 79/62   Report on the Northern Estates, 1870

B. *Details of winding up of the various Turnpike Trusts*
1. MH 28 (1873) No. 3 Kirkby Stephen–Hawes Trust
                     No. 4 Ulverston–Carnforth Trust
                     No. 6 Kirkby Lonsdale–Kendal–Milnthorpe Trust
                     No. 7 Alston Trust
                                     Brampton–Longtown Trust
                     No. 8 Alston Trust
                                     Kirkby Stephen–Hawes Trust
                     No. 10 Kirkby Stephen–Hawes Trust
                                     Carlisle–Brampton Trust
                     No. 14 Carlisle–Glasgow Road
                     No. 15 Newcastle–Carlisle Road
2. MH 28 (1877) No. 1 Milnthorpe–Levens Trust
                                     Kirkby Stephen–Hawes Trust

HOUSE OF LORDS RECORD OFFICE

1. Contractors for the Carlisle–Newcastle Military Road, 1753
2. Accounts for the Carlisle–Newcastle Military Road, 1753–9

CARLISLE RECORD OFFICE

A. *Turnpike Trust Material*
1. *Carlisle–Eamont Bridge Trust*
    (*a*) Minute Book (N. Div.), 1840–59
    (*b*) Minute Book (N. Div.), 1859–83

(c) Minute Book (S. Div.), 1859–81

(d) Account Book (S. Div.), 1823–36

(e) Account Book (S. Div.), 1836–43

(f) Account Book (S. Div.), 1844–79

(g) Account Book (S. Div.), 1879–81

(h) Account Book (N. Div.), 1859–81

(i) Treasurer's Cash Book (S. Div.), 1823–41

(j) Treasurer's Cash Book (S. Div.), 1841–70

(k) Treasurer's Cash Book (S. Div.), 1871–81

(l) T.T.1/16: Mortgage Book (S. Div.), 1839–59

(m) T.T.1/10: Voucher and Accounts (S. Div.), 1859–81

(n) T.T. 1/7: Details of Toll Leases (S. Div.), 1858–80

(o) Misc. Papers re Road Bill of 1808.

(p) Report on Trust Road Improvements by J. L. McAdam, 1825

(q) Misc. Papers re Road Bill of 1830

(r) Correspondence re dispute over Toll payments by Patterdale Lead proprietors, 1844

(s) T.T.1/6: Correspondence re Stoneygate Toll Bar Dispute, 1859

(t) T.T.1/2: Brief for opposition to the 1859 Road Bill

(u) T.T.1/4: Correspondence re 1859 Road Bill

(v) T.T.1/5: Minutes of evidence before Select Committee of H. of C. on 1859 Road Bill, 29 and 30 March, 1859

(w) T.T.1/13: Correspondence re winding-up of Trust 1880–2

2. *Carlisle–Brampton Trust*
   (a) Minute Book, 1828–63
   (b) Minute Book, 1863–76

3. *Carlisle–Temon Trust*
   (a) Minute Book, 1855–77
   (b) Account Book, 1855–73

4. *Cockermouth–Workington Trust*
   (a) Misc. Papers, Receipts and Letters

5. *Brampton–Longtown Trust*
   (a) Misc. Papers–Receipts and Letters
   (b) Minute Book, 1829–77

6. *Brougham Bridge Trust*
   (a) Misc. Papers, 1812–52—Receipts, Letters and Mortgage Agreements

7. *Carlisle–Skillbeck Trust*
   (a) Minute Book, 1776–1806
   (b) Minute Book, 1806–32

8. *Carlisle–Glasgow Trust*
   (*a*) Misc. Papers. re. The setting up of the trust

9. *Longtown Trust*
   (*a*) Misc. Papers

10. *Various plans of Turnpikes* (**P.D.**)

No.	Date of Deposit	Name of Plan
1.	1806	Moffat to Longtown
2.	1808	Cockermouth to Wigton and Carlisle
3.	1811	Appleby to Penrith
4.	1813	Longtown and Brampton
5.	1813	Longtown to Haithwaite Gate
6.	1813	Sark Foot and Allison's Bank
7.	1815	Glasgow to Carlisle
8.	1823	Keswick and Ambleside
9.	1823	Keswick and Penrith
10.	1823	Oldstone
11.	1823	Cockermouth and Carlisle
12.	1823	Keswick and Cockermouth
13.	1824	Cockermouth to Maryport, Allonby, Wigton and Carlisle
14.	1825	Comes Hill in Durham to Nenthead
15.	1826	Carlisle to Brampton by Warwick Bridge
16.	1826	Carlisle to Brampton by Warwick Bridge
17.	1826	Carlisle to Brampton by Warwick Bridge
18.	1827	Carlisle to Brampton by Warwick Bridge
19.	1828	Cocker Bridge
20.	1828	Brampton to Midgeholme
21.	1828	Longtown to Mulescroft by Hobbies Burn
22.	1829	Carlisle to Eamont Bridge
22a.	1831	Cockermouth to Workington
23.	1842	Calder Bridge to Bootle with alternative line over River Esk
24.	1842	Plan and Section of part of the Cockermouth and Maryport Turnpike Road from Westlands Farm to Birkby Common
25.	1853	Penrith and Cockermouth Roads
26.	1855	Penrith and Cockermouth
27.	1855	Carlisle to Sark Bridge
28.	1855	Turnpike Roads in Cumberland
29.	1878	Highways near Whitehaven
30.	1886	Petteril Bank Footpath Diversion
31.	1888	Whitehaven District Highways
32.	1889	Arlecdon and Frizington Main Roads

No.	Date of Deposit	Name of Plan
33.	1889	Egremont Main Roads
34.	1889	Whitehaven Roads
35.	1891	Cleator Moor Roads
36.	1891	Addingham Parish Roads
37.	1891	Hawksdale Main Roads
38.	1891	Workington Roads
39.	1891	Egremont Roads
40.	1891	Cleator Moor Roads
41.	1891	Dalston and Hawksdale Main Roads
42.	1891	Egremont Main Roads
43.	1891	Arlecdon and Frizington Main Roads
44.	1891	Holme Cultram Main Roads
45.	1891	Low Row Brampton Main Roads

B. *Cumberland Highway and Bridge Administration*
  1. Quarter Sessions Petition Rolls, (1800–78)
  2. F3: County Accounts, 1839–1900
  3. F5: County Treasurer's Vouchers
  4. F12: County Finance Committee Report Book, 1849–81
  5. Bridge Administration (AB):
     AB/1   Various Deeds re Bridges
     AB/7   Accounts for repair of Workington Bridge, 1774
     AB/8   Papers re rebuilding of Eden Bridge, 1805–16.
     AB/9   County Bridge Contract Book, 1834–8
     AB/12/1 Report of Joint Committee of Cumberland and Westmorland Justices re widening Eamont Bridge, 28 June 1874
     AB/12/2 Report of Joint Committee on inspection of work carried out on Eamont Bridge, 13 July 1875
     AB/13 Report of Committee on Cinderdale Bridge, Wasdale, 28 December 1876
     AB/14/1 Report on Bulgill Bridge by George Dixon, Mining Engineer, 18 June 1861
     AB/15 Documents relating to Bleng Bridge, Gosforth
  6. Highway Administration (AH):
     AH/2/6 Armathwaite Road Diversion Plan, 1803
     AH/2/7 Indictment of Nichol Forest Quarter in the parish of Kirkandrews on Esk for condition of their Highways (n.d. but about 1800)
     AH/6   Quarter Sessions Highway Papers, 1863–90
     AH/6/2 Report of the Committee on Highway Administration, 1863

AH/6/4   Letters from the Clerk of the Whitehaven Turnpike Trust to the Clerk of the Peace, re the Bridge at St Bees, 1862–3

AH/6/5   Certificate of the Justices, re roads made by the Maryport and Carlisle Railway Company, 18 March 1868

AH/6/7   Correspondence of the Whitehaven Highway District, 1871

AH/6/9   Returns of Highway District to the Local Government Board, 1875

AH/6/10   Correspondence of Leath Highway Board, 1877–8

AH/6/26   County Surveyor's Reports, 1857/80

7. Highway Committee Records

CCH1/1   Minute Book, 1874–91
CCH1/2   Minute Book, 1891–3
CCH1/3   Minute Book, 1893–6
CCH1/4   Minute Book, 1896–9
CCH3/1   Various Papers, 1879–84
CCH3/2   Various Papers, 1885–7
CCH3/3   Various Papers, 1888–9
CCH3/4   Various Papers, 1890
CCH3/5   Various Papers, 1891
CCH3/6   Various Papers, 1892–9
CCH4/26   County Surveyors' Society—Particulars of Management of the main roads in England and Wales, 1890

C. *Parish Records*

1. Dalston Parish Records
   (*a*) Bridge Repair Book, 1771–87
   (*b*) Account Book re repair of Union Bridge, 1812
   (*c*) Detailed specifications for the repair of Hawksdale Bridge, 1830–8
2. Holm Cultram Records
   (*a*) Surveyor's Account Book, 1777–1836
3. Leath Ward:
   (*a*) Highway Returns, 1852 and 1863
4. Sebergham
   (*a*) Surveyor's Account Book, 1837–50
5. Staffield:
   (*a*) Highway Rate Books, 1797–1858
6. Brampton Rural District Council
   (*a*) Misc. Papers, 1892–3

D. *Hodgson MSS*

1. Various Eighteenth Century Road Indictments

2. Dispute between County Surveyor and Workington parish over the non-repair of Cocker Bridge, 1822
3. Dispute between County and the Parish of Crosthwaite over their respective responsibilities for bridge repair in Crosthwaite Parish, 1836
4. Details of the Rebate allowed to certain Districts in Cumberland which maintained their own Bridges, viz: Millom, Holme Cultram Crosthwaite and Dalston
5. Surveyor's Report for Dalston Parish, 1840
6. Litigation re Workington Bridge, 1840 and 1845
7. Report of the Committee to inquire into and revise the Salaries and Expenditure of the County of Cumberland, 1850
8. County Surveyor's Schedule of new Roads made by Maryport–Carlisle Railway Company, 1856
9. Details of dispute between the County Surveyor and the Maryport–Carlisle Railway Company over damage done to Ullock Bridge, 1867
10. Dispute between the County Surveyor and the Whitehaven–Cleator–Egremont Railway Company, 1868
11. Report of the Committee on County Expenditure, 1869
12. Details of road diversions in Dalston Parish, 1874

E. *Senhouse MSS*
   1. Papers re Highway administration in Township of Ellenborough, 1789–1873
   2. Details of Newcastle–Maryport Canal project:
      (a) Report of William Chapman, 1795
      (b) Report of William Jessop, 1795
      (c) Second Report of Chapman, 1807
      (d) Various Letters re the proposed Canal, 1794–1807
   3. Letters re the appointment of the Maryport Postmaster, 1801
   4. Letters re Netherhall Bridge, 1810
   5. Plan of new roads built by Humphrey Senhouse at Maryport, 1816
   6. Mortgage of Tolls of Cockermouth–Maryport Turnpike Trust to Humphrey Senhouse, 7 October 1828
   7. Plan of new road from Maryport to Allonby, 1834
   8. Various Correspondence re Maryport–Carlisle Railway Company, 1834–7

F. *Lowther MSS*
   1. Various Letters re Roads (1745–53)
   2. Various Road Plans:
      (a) Stanwix to Westlinton, n.d. c. 1754
      (b) Esk to Scotch Dyke, n.d. c. 1750
      (c) Longtown Bridge to Sark Bridge, n.d. c. 1750

(d) Two sketch plans of a proposed Turnpike Road from Appleby to near Shap with a branch road from Highgate near Tebay to Brough, n.d., c. 1750

(e) Plan of Keighley to Kendal Turnpike Road, c. 1750

(f) Plan of roads leading into Penrith, n.d. c. 1750

(g) Plan of various proposals for the alignment of the Penrith to Keswick Turnpike Road, n.d. c. 1750

3. Carriers Accounts of Robert Dawson, 1750–8
4. Carriers Accounts of John Jackson, 1758–60
5. Whitehaven Harbour Trustees Minutes, 1782–1812
6. Election Correspondence, 1796–1832
7. Vouchers for Election Expenditure, 1796–1832

G. *Curwen MSS*
1. D/CU/5/199: Account Book of Charles Uldale (Principal Curwen Agent), 1788–1801
2. Tonnage Book, 1804–16

H. *Howard of Greystoke MSS*
1. D/HG/126: Printed Acts for enclosing lands in Bassenthwaite, Inglewood Forest and the Barony of Penrith, 1770–1813
2. D/HG/157: Misc. papers re roads in Newbiggen, 1777–1872

I. *Mounsey–Heysham MSS*
1. Case and opinion as to repair of roads on Carlisle and Cummersdale Moor, 1828, II, 306
2. Statute Work on Highways in Caldewgate Quarter, 1775, III, 185

J. *Rheda Estate MSS*
1. DF 5/88: Details of Howgate Road Deviation over Lingla Beck, Frizington, 1876

K. *Egremont MSS*
1. Details of traffic carried along the Whitehaven–Cleator–Egremont Railway, 1858–60

L. *Bleaymire and Shepherd Collection*
1. Correspondence re the Cockermouth–Penrith Trust Road Bill, 1856

M. *Documents Deposited by S. Raine*
1. 14—Memorial from the Mayor and Corporation of Carlisle to the Lords of the Treasury, re a grant for a road from Carlisle to Port Patrick, 10 February 1808

N. *Records of the City of Carlisle*
   1. 17(*b*): Carlisle Gas Company Minute Book, 1818–28
   2. Ferguson Letter Book, 1847–82 (relating to Gingham manufacture in Carlisle)

TULLIE HOUSE, CARLISLE

A. Account Book of George Blamire, Treasurer of the Carlisle–Skillbeck Road, 1767–1829
B. Military Road Minute Book, 1761–91

KESWICK MUSEUM

A. *Material re Cockermouth–Penrith Turnpike Trust*
   1. Minute Book, 1804–1824
   2. Minute Book, 1853–1856
   3. Minute Book, 1877–1884

PRIOR'S KITCHEN, DURHAM UNIVERSITY

A. *Howard of Naworth MSS*
   1. 630, No. 5—Details of Carriage of Sheep along the Carlisle Canal, n.d., c. 1820
   2. 630, No. 71—Reference to Cattle Drives to Brough Fair

KENDAL RECORD OFFICE

A. *Turnpike Trust MSS*

   1. *Ambleside Trust*
      (*a*) Minute Book, 1762–1810
      (*b*) Minute Book, 1824–75
      (*c*) Treasurer's Account Book, 1784–1806
      (*d*) Treasurer's Account Book, 1827–39
      (*e*) Books relating to appointment of Trustees:
         i. 1824–32
         ii. 1839–72
      (*f*) Details of Leases of Toll Gates, 1813–74
      (*g*) Various Miscellaneous Papers (1765–74)—these include:
         i. Vouchers for road repairs, 1779–1861
         ii. Minutes of Trust meetings
         iii. Correspondence with local landowners
         iv. Correspondence with the Secretary of State
         v. Papers re Toll Traffic, 1855–6

   2. *Heron Syke–Eamont Bridge Trust*
      (*a*) Treasurer's Account Book, 1823–43
      (*b*) Treasurer's Account Book, 1846–55

    (c) Treasurer's Account Book, 1855–82
    (d) Mortgage Book, 1845–50
    (e) Miscellaneous Papers—these include:
        i. Mortgage Agreements, 1821–30
        ii. Toll Gate Receipts: 1843–9, and 1861–83

3. *Milnthorpe and Levens Trust*
    (a) Treasurer's Account Books:
        i. 1823–48
        ii. 1848–70
        iii. 1871–5
    (b) Treasurer's Cash Book: 1842–8
    (c) Account Book, 1837–47
    (d) General Statements of Trust Receipts, 1852–75
    (e) Details of Mortgage Agreements, 1799–1869
    (f) Misc. Correspondence, 1855–74

4. *Appleby-Kendal Trust*
    (a) Accounts, 1820–40

5. *Kirkby Stephen–Hawes Trust*
    (a) Correspondence re Trust Road Bill, 1851–2
    (b) Plan of Turnpike 1824

6. *Sedbergh Trust*
    (a) Accounts, 1803–11

B. *Westmorland Highway and Bridge MSS*
    1. Quarter Sessions Petition Rolls, 1800–78
    2. County Accounts, 1826–78
    3. Quarter Sessions Order Books:
        (a) 1669–96
        (b) 1697–1724
        (c) 1725–37
    4. Details of Highway Diversions, 1825–72
    5. Misc. Quarter Sessions Papers
    6. Crosby Ravensworth Township Account Book, 1804–36
    7. Crosthwaite Parish Day Book, 1856–1921
    8. Kirkby Lonsdale Parish, Surveyor's Account Book, 1843–44
    9. Ravenstonedale Parish, Surveyor's Payment Book, 1779–1800
    10. County Highway Committee: Various Papers, 1878–1900

C. *Family MSS*

    1. *Browne MSS*
        (a) i, 221—Survey of the Bridges in Kendal Ward, 1713
        (b) i, 220—Survey of the Highways in Kendal Ward, 1730
        (c) ii, 384—Account of the Expense of conveying vagrants
            through the County of Westmorland, 1714
        (d) ii, 389—Ibid., 1721

2. *Carriers Accounts of Walter Berry and Son*
  (*a*) Carters Accounts:
    i. 1840–5
    ii. 1842–6
    iii. 1846–54
  (*b*) Salt Accounts:
    iv. 1847–59
    v. 1855–61
    vi. 1848–51
    vii. 1850–2
3. *Hallam MSS*—Misc. Accounts

D. *Other Items*
  1. Lancaster Canal Minute Book, 1818–35

KENDAL PUBLIC LIBRARY

A. *Appleby–Kendal Trust*
  1. Receipts, 1817

B. *Kirkby Stephen–Hawes Trust*
  1. Receipts, 1826–7

LEVENS HALL

A. *Lancaster Canal MSS*
  (*a*) Box No. 3, No. 30—Papers re the Canal prior to its construction
  (*b*) Box G—No. 12—Vouchers and Papers re Canal, 1821

LANCASHIRE RECORD OFFICE

A. *Turnpike Trust Material*
  1. *Kirkby Kendal–Kirkby Ireleth Trust*
    Q.D.T. Trust Accounts, 1822–37, 1840–45, 1847–51, 1857–72
  2. *Ulverston–Carnforth Trust* (T.T.K)
    (*a*) TTK 1/1—1/3—Maps of the proposed Turnpike
    (*b*) TTK 1/4—1/6—Details of Bridge Repair Contracts
    (*c*) TTK 1/9—Details of Toll Mortgages, 1820–44
    (*d*) TTK 1/10—Details of Toll Leases, 1826–76
    (*e*) TTK 1/12—1/15—Details of Litigation arising from disputes between the various Trust Creditors
    (*f*) TTK 1/21—Trust Account Book, 1847–55
    (*g*) TTK 1/22—Trust Cash Book, 1860–78
    (*h*) TTK 1/23—Various papers re Toll receipts; 1823–4, 1855, 1862 and 1864

    (*i*) TTK 1/26—1/34—Various Letters re the condition of the Turnpike Road

    (*j*) TTK 1/37—Correspondence of Trust with James McAdam

B. *Lancashire Highway and Bridge Administration*

  1. Q.S.P.—Quarter Sessions Petition Rolls (North Lonsdale Hundred), 1800–78

  2. QJ—Quarter Sessions Indictment Rolls (North Lonsdale Hundred), 1800–78

  3. Q.S.O./2—Quarter Sessions Order Book, 1822

  4. Q.A.R.—Highway Committee Minutes, 1878—81

  5. Q.A.R. 6/8—Plans of Bridges repaired in Hundred of North Lonsdale, 1777

  6. Q.A.R. 7/4—Returns of Minor Bridges in North Lonsdale, 1801–2

  7. Q.A.V. 3/1—Report of Special Committee on Public Bridges, 1849

  8. H.B.C. 1/1—Cartmel Highway Board Minutes, 1877–90

C. *Miscellaneous*

  1. Cartmel Enclosure Commissioner's Minutes, 1796

  2. DDLO–Records of the Lowood Gunpowder Company, Colton:

    (*a*) Cash Cooks, 1798–1839

    (*b*) Cartage Accounts, 1829–34

OTHER SOURCES

A. Various Letters lent by Mrs Titterington of Stainton—relating to travel along the Lancaster Canal

B. Diary of a Kendal man (in the possession of Mr R. G. Plint of 'Townview', Kendal)

C. Report on the proposed Deviation from the Brough–Bowes Turnpike Road at Maiden Castle, 1835 (in the possession of Heelis, Solicitors, Appleby)

D. Visitors' Book of the 'Salutation Hotel', Ambleside, 1858–74 (in the Armitt Library, Ambleside)

PRINTED MATERIAL

British Museum (*State Paper Room*)

A. *Parl. Reports re Transport*

  1. *Parl, Papers*, 1808, II, p. 333, et seq.—Report on the State of the Highways of the Kingdom

  2. *Parl. Papers*, 1811, III, p. 707 et seq.—Report from the Select Committee on Mail Coach Exemption from Toll

  3. *Parl. Papers*, 1811, III, p. 789 et seq.—Report from the Select Committee upon the Roads between Carlisle and Port Patrick

4. *Parl. Papers*, 1815, III, p. 333 et seq.—Report from the Select Committee on the Carlisle–Glasgow Road
5. *Parl. Papers*, 1821, IV, p. 343 et seq.—Report on the State of the Highways of the Kingdom
6. *Parl. Papers*, 1824, XX, p. 1 et seq.—Statement of Income and Expenditure of the Turnpike Trusts in England and Wales
7. *Parl. Papers*, 1830, X, p. 189 et seq.—Report of the Select Committee on the State of the Northern Roads
8. *Parl. Papers*, 1833, XV, p. 400 et seq.—Report of the Select Committee on Turnpike Trusts
9. *Parl. Papers*, 1834, XIV, p. 193 et seq.—Report of the Select Committee on County and Highway Rates in England and Wales
10. *Parl. Papers*, 1836, XIX, p. 335 et seq.—Report of the Select Committee on Turnpike Trusts
11. *Parl. Papers*, 1837, XX, p. 295 et seq.—Report from the Select Committee on Internal Communication Taxation
12. *Parl. Papers*, 1837, XX, p. 343 et seq.—Report from the Select Committee on the Highway Rates Bill
13. *Parl. Papers*, 1839, IX—Report from the Select Committee to ascertain how far the formation of Railways may affect the interests of Turnpike Trusts
14. *Parl. Papers*, 1839, XLIV, p. 1 et seq.—Survey of the Expenditure of County Rates on Bridge Maintenance
15. *Parl. Papers*, 1840, XXVII, p. 1 et seq.—Report of the Committee of Inquiry into the state of the Roads in England and Wales
16. *Parl. Papers*, 1848, LI, p. 355 et seq.—Return of the Total Receipts, Expenditure and Debts of the Turnpike Trusts in England and Wales (1834–45)
17. *Parl. Papers*, 1850, XLIX, p. 335 et seq.—Report on the Heron Syke–Eamont Bridge Turnpike Trust Road Bill.
18. *Parl. Papers*, 1850, XLIX, p. 375 et seq.—Report on the Ulverston–Carnforth Turnpike Trust Road Bill
19. *Parl. Papers*, 1851, XLVIII, p. 201 et seq.—Report on the Appleby–Kendal Trust Road Bill
20. *Parl. Papers*, 1853, XCVII, p. 500 et seq.—Report on the Alston Trust Road Bill
21. *Parl. Papers*, 1854, LXIV, p. 296 et seq.—Report on the Kirkby Lonsdale, Kendal and Milnthorpe Trust Road Bill
22. *Parl. Papers*, 1856, LVIII, p. 178 et seq.—Report on the Brough–Eamont Bridge Trust Road Bill
23. *Parl. Papers*, 1856, LVIII, p. 146 et seq.—Report on the Cockermouth–Penrith Trust Road Bill
24. *Parl. Papers*, 1859, XIII, p. 715 et seq.—Report on the Carlisle and Eamont Bridge Trust Road Bill
25. *Parl. Papers*, 1863, XXVIII, p. 291 et seq.—Report on the Newcastle–Carlisle Trust Road Bill
26. *Parl. Papers*, 1864, IX, p. 331 et seq.—Report from the Select Com-

mittee appointed to inquire into the expediency and practicability of abolishing Turnpike Trusts

B. *Local and Personal Acts—Road Acts*

1. *Alston Turnpike Trust*
   (*a*) 55G3 cap. viii
   (*b*) 1–2G4 cap. x
   (*c*) 5G4 cap. xxxiv
   (*d*) 16–7V. cap cxii
   (*e*) 38–9V. cap. cxciv
2. *Ambleside Trust*
   (*a*) 44G3 cap. xx
   (*b*) 5G4 cap. xiv
   (*c*) 26–7V. cap. 98
   (*d*) 34–5V. cap. 115
3. *Appleby–Kendal Trust*
   (*a*) 44G3 cap. lx
   (*b*) 5G4 cap. xv
   (*c*) 13–4V. cap. xiii
4. *Brampton–Longtown Trust*
   (*a*) 47G3 Sess 2. cap. xv
   (*b*) 10G4 cap. lxxxii
   (*c*) 27–8V. cap. 79
   (*d*) 39–40V. cap. 39
5. *Brough–Eamont Bridge Trust*
   (*a*) 41G3 cap. lxxxii
   (*b*) 19–20V. cap. lxxii
   (*c*) 41–2V. cap. 62
6. *Brougham and Penrith Trust*
   (*a*) 52G3 cap. cxxii
   (*b*) 3–4W4 cap. lxxx
   (*c*) 37–8V. cap. 95
7. *Carlisle–Brampton Trust*
   (*a*) 9G4 cap. xx
   (*b*) 39–40V. cap. 39
8. *Carlisle–Cockermouth Trust*
   (*a*) 4G4 cap. vii
   (*b*) 38–9V. cap. cxciv
9. *Carlisle–Eamont Bridge Trust* (*Northern and Southern Divisions*)
   (*a*) 48G3 cap. xxviii
   (*b*) 11G4 and W4 cap. cx
   (*c*) 22–3V. cap. xxv
10. *Carlisle and Mulaside Trust*
    (*a*) 50G3 cap. vi
11. *Carlisle–Temon Trust*
    (*a*) 51G3 cap. xiv

12. *Cockermouth–Maryport Trust*
    (*a*) 6G4 cap. lxxxv
    (*b*) 6–7V. cap. xv
    (*c*) 38–9V. cap. cxciv

13. *Cockermouth–Workington Trust*
    (*a*) 41G3 cap. xx
    (*b*) 4G4 cap. xxiii
    (*c*) 2–3W4 cap. xxix
    (*d*) 27–8V. cap. 79

14. *Heron Syke–Eamont Bridge Trust*
    (*a*) 55G3 cap. xxxvii
    (*b*) 13–4V. cap. lxiv
    (*c*) 35–6V. cap. C.85

15. *Kirkby Kendal–Kirkby Ireleth Trust*
    (*a*) 1G4 cap. xviii

16. *Kirkby Lonsdale, Kendal and Milnthorpe Trust*
    (*a*) 59G3 cap. xviii
    (*b*) 17–8V. cap. cxlv
    (*c*) 39–40V. cap. 39

17. *Kirkby Stephen–Hawes Trust*
    (*a*) 6G4 cap. xii
    (*b*) 15–6V. cap. lxxxix
    (*c*) 37–8V. cap. 95

18. *Longtown Trust*
    (*a*) 54G3 cap. cxxii
    (*b*) 11G4 and 1W4 cap. ix
    (*c*) 34–5V. cap. 115

19. *Milnthorpe and Levens Trust*
    (*a*) 41G3 cap. xxxvi
    (*b*) 3G4 cap. xii
    (*c*) 14–5V. cap. cxvii
    (*d*) 36–7V. cap. 90

20. *Penrith–Cockermouth Trust*
    (*a*) 44G3 cap. xx
    (*b*) 5G4 cap. iv
    (*c*) 19–20V. cap. lxiv
    (*d*) 41–2V. cap. 62

21. *Sedbergh Trust*
    (*a*) 45G3 cap. xxvii
    (*b*) 7G4 cap. lxvii
    (*c*) 34–5V. cap. 115

22. *Ulverston–Carnforth Trust*
    (*a*) 58G3 cap. lxx
    (*b*) 13–4V. cap. lxv
    (*c*) 37–8V cap. 95

23. *Whitehaven Trust*
    (*a*) 46G3 cap. cxxvii
    (*b*) 9G4 cap. x
    (*c*) 33–4V. cap. 73

C. *Railway Acts*
  1. Newcastle and Carlisle–10G4 cap. lxxii
  2. Maryport and Carlisle—7W4 and 1V cap. ci
  3. Furness—7–8V cap. xxii
  4. Lancaster and Carlisle—7–8V cap. xxxvii
  5. Whitehaven Junction—7–8V cap. lxiv
  6. Whitehaven and Furness Junction—8–9V cap. c.
  7. Ulverston and Lancaster—14–5V cap. cii
  8. Whitehaven—Cleator and Egremont—17–8V cap. lxiv
  9. Coniston—20–1V cap. cx
10. Cockermouth, Keswick and Penrith—24–5V, cap. cciii

House of Lords Record Office

A. *Select Committees on Railway Bills*
  1. Lancaster and Carlisle Railway, 14 February 1844
  2. Kendal and Windermere Railway, May 1845
  3. Whitehaven and Furness Junction Railway, 30 May 1845
  4. Ulverston and Lancaster Railway, 13 May 1851

Newspapers

  1. *Agreeable Miscellany*
  2. *Carlisle Journal*
  3. *Carlisle Patriot*
  4. *Cumberland Pacquet*
  5. *Kendal Chronicle*
  6. *Maryport Locomotive and Monthly Advertiser*
  7. *Ulverston Advertiser*
  8. *Ulverston News*
  9. *Westmorland Gazette*
10. *Whitehaven Gazette*
11. *Whitehaven Herald*
12. *Whitehaven News*

BOOKS AND PAMPHLETS

Albert, William, *The Turnpike Road System in England 1663–1840* (1972)
Allen, C. J., *An Account of the Maryport and Carlisle Railway* (1909)

Allison, J., *A Descriptive Sketch of Penrith and its Neighbourhood* (1836)

Allison, J., *Allison's Northern Tourists Guide to the Lakes of Cumberland, Westmorland and Lancashire* (1837)

Armitt, M. L., *Rydal* (1916)

Ashton, T. S., *Iron and Steel in the Industrial Revolution* (1951)

Ashton, T. S., and Sykes, Joseph, *The Coal Industry of the Eighteenth century* (1929)

Bailey, J., and Culley, G., *A General View of the Agriculture of the County of Cumberland* (1794)

Bailey, J., and Culley, G., *A General View of the Agriculture of the County of Westmorland* (1794)

Ballen, Dorothy, *Bibliography of Road-Making and Roads in the United Kingdom* (1914)

Bateman, J., *The General Turnpike Road Acts* (1854)

Bayldon, R., *Turnpike Road Traffic and Tolls* (1847)

Bird, William, *Gilsland and Neighbourhood—Description and History* (1913)

Birkett, Henry F., *The Story of Ulverston* (1949)

Black, *Black's Guide to the Lakes* (1841)

Blake, Brian, *The Solway Firth* (1955)

Bogg, *Five Thousand Miles of Wandering in the Border Country—Lakeland and Ribblesdale* (1898)

Bouch, C. M. L., *Prelates and Peoples of the Lake Counties* (1948)

Bouch, C. M. L., and Jones, G. P., *A Short Economic and Social History of the Lake Counties, 1500–1830* (1961)

Bradley, A. G., *Highways and Byways in the Lake District* (1901)

Bradley, Thomas, *Old Coaching Days in Yorkshire* (1889)

Briggs, John, *Letters from the Lakes* (1825)

Brown, J. W., *Round Carlisle Cross* (1922)

Bulmer, J., (Ed.), *Directory of East Cumberland* (1884)

Bulmer, J., (Ed.), *History, Topography and Directory of Furness and Cartmel* (1911)

Burn, Peter, *Brampton as I have known it* (1893)

Caine, Caesar, *Cleator and Cleator Moor, Past and Present* (1916)

Caird, James, *English Agriculture, 1850–1* (1852)

Camden, William, *Britannica*, II (1753 ed.)

Carrick, T. W., *History of Wigton* (1949)

Cary, John, *Cary's New Itinerary or an Accurate Delineation of the great roads . . . throughout England and Wales* (11 ed., 1798–1828)

Chippindall, W., *History of the Township of Ireby* (1935)

Clapham, J. H., *An Economic History of Modern Britain* (3 vols, 1926–38)

Clarke, James, *A Survey of the Lakes of Cumberland, Westmorland and Lancashire* (1787)

Clear, Charles R., *John Palmer (of Bath) Mail Coach Pioneer* (1955)

Cobbett, William, *Rural Rides in England during the years 1821–6*, (2 vols, 1914 ed.)

Coleridge, S. T., *Diary of a Tour to the Lake District August 1802* (printed in *Inquiring Spirit*—Kathleen Coburn (ed.), 1951)

Collingwood, W. G., *The Lake Counties* (1902)

Collingwood, W. G., *Lake District History* (1925)

Cook, E. T., and Wedderburn, Alexander, *The Works of John Ruskin* (39 vols, 1903–12)

Cooke, G. A., *Topographical and Statistical Discription of the County of Cumberland* (1814)

Copeland, John, *Roads and Their Traffic, 1750–1850* (1968)

Cossons, Arthur, 'The Turnpike Roads of Nottinghamshire', *Historical Assoc. Pamphlet*, No. 97 (1934)

Cowper, H. S., *Hawkshead* (1899)

Creighton, Mandell, *Carlisle* (1899)

Crowe, John, *Cycling In The Lake District* (1945)

Crump, W. B., *Huddersfield Highways Down the Ages* (1949)

Curwen, J. F., *Kirkbie Kendall* (1900)

Curwen, J. F. (ed.), *Records relating to the Barony of Kendale* (C.W.T. Record Series, 1923)

Curwen, J. F., *The Ancient Parish of Heversham with Milnthorpe* (1930)

Curwen, J. F., *The Later Records relating to North Westmorland* (C.W.T. Record Series, VIII, 1932)

Defoe, Daniel, *Tour of England and Wales*, III (1748)

de Quincey, Thomas, *The English Mail Coach*

Dickinson, William, *Essay on the Agriculture of West Cumberland* (1850)

Dickinson, William, *Essay on the Agriculture of East Cumberland* (1853)

Dickinson, William, *Further Essay on the Farming of Cumberland* (1853)

Dickinson, William, *Reminiscences of West Cumberland* (1882)

Eden, F. M., *The State of the Poor*, I (3 vols, 1797)

Eliot, George, *Middlemarch* (1959, Everyman ed.)

Fell, A., *The Early Iron Industry of Furness and District* (1908)

Ferguson, Richard S., *A History of Cumberland* (1890)

Ferguson, Richard S., *A History of Westmorland* (1894)

Fiennes, Celia, *The Journeys of Celia Fiennes* (Christopher Morris (ed.), 1949)

Fleming, Sir Daniel, *Description of the County of Cumberland, 1671*, R. S. Ferguson (ed.), Kendal, 1889)

Furness, William, *History of Penrith from the Earliest Record to the Present Day* (1894)

Garnett, Frank W., *Westmorland Agriculture—1800–1900* (1912)

Garnett, J., *Guide to the Highways of the Lake District of England* (1891)

Gibb, Alexander, *The Story of Telford* (1935)

Gilpin, William, *Observations Relative Chiefly to Picturesque Beauty made in the year 1772, in several parts of England, particularly the Mountains and Lakes of Cumberland and Westmorland* (2 vols, 1786)

Gradon, W. McGowan, *Furness Railway: Its Rise and Development, 1846–1923* (1946)

Gradon, W. McGowan, *A History of the Ravenglass and Eskdale Railway* (1947)

Gradon, W. McGowan, *A History of the Cockermouth–Keswick and Penrith Railway* (1948)

Gradon, W. McGowan, *The Track of the Ironmasters–A History of the Cleator and Workington Junction Railway* (1952)

Green, William, *The Tourist's New Guide to the Lakes* (1819)

Hadfield, Charles, *British Canals* (1950)

Hague, John, *Report on the Morecambe Bay Embankment* (1838)

Haldane, A. R. B., *The Drove Roads of Scotland* (1952)

Harper, Charles G., *Stage Coach and Mail in Days of Yore* (2 vols, 1903)

Harper, Charles G., *The Manchester and Glasgow Road* (2 vols, 1907)

Harper, Charles G., *The Great North Road* (2 vols, 1922)

Harris, Stanley, *The Coaching Age* (1885)

Hodgson, John, *A Topographical and Historical Study of the County of Westmorland* (1820)

Holden, William, *Holden's Triennial Directory* (1805–7)

Holdgate, Martin, *A History of Appleby* (1956)

Houghton, F. W., and Foster, W. H., *The Story of the Settle–Carlisle Line* (1948)

Housman, John, *A Topographical Description of Cumberland, Westmorland, Lancashire and part of the West Riding of Yorkshire* (1800)

Housman, John, *A Descriptive Tour and Guide to the Lakes, Caves and Mountains . . . in Cumberland, Westmorland, Lancashire and a Part of the West Riding of Yorkshire* (1802)

Howes, John B., *The Solway Junction Railway*

Hudson, John, *Handbook of the Lake District* (1860)

Hughes, Edward, *North Country Life in the Eighteenth Century*, **II** (1965)

Hutchinson, William, *An Excursion to the Lakes in Westmorland and Cumberland in 1773 and 1774* (1776)

Hutchinson, William, *History and Antiquities of Cumberland* (2 vols, 1794)

Jackman, W. T., *Transportation in Modern England* (1962)
Jefferson, Samuel, *The History and Antiquities of Carlisle* (1838)
Jefferson, Samuel, *The History and Antiquities of Leath Ward* (1840)
Jefferson, Samuel, *The History and Antiquities of Allerdale Ward above Derwent* (1842)
Jeffreys, W. Rees, *The King's Highway* (1949)
Jewkes, John, and Winterbottom, Allan, *An Historical Survey of Cumberland and Furness* (1933)
Jollie, F. *Cumberland Guide and Directory* (1811)

Kellett, J. R. *The Impact of Railways on Victorian Cities.*
Kelly, Edward, *Kelly's Guide to Westmorland and Cumberland, Northumberland and Durham* (1858).
Kirkpatrick, Margaret, *The Story of Wetheral* (1956)

Leigh, Samuel, *Leigh's Guide to the Lakes and Mountains of Cumberland, Westmorland and Lancashire* (1830)
Linton, J., *A Handbook of the Whitehaven and Furness Railway* (1852)
Little, Elizabeth, *Chronicles of Patterdale* (1961)
Loftie, Arthur, *A History of the Parishes of Wetheral and Warwick* (1923)
Lysons, Daniel, *History of Cumberland* (1815)

MacCulloch, John Ramsay, *A Descriptive and Statistical Account of the British Empire*, II (1847)
McIntire, W. T., *Lakeland and Borders of Long Ago* (1948)
MacLean, John S., *The Newcastle and Carlisle Railway—1825—1862* (1948)
Mannex, P. J., and Whellan, William, *History, Gazetteer and Directory of Cumberland* (1847)
Mannex, P. J., *Directory of Westmorland* (1849)
Marshall, J. D., *Furness and the Industrial Revolution* (1958)
Martineau, Harriet, *Guide to Windermere* (1854)
Martineau, Harriet, *A Complete Guide to the English Lakes* (1855)
Maryport and Carlisle Railway, *Half Yearly Reports* (1839–1851)
Report of the Committee of Investigation into the Maryport and Carlisle Railway Company, 4 September 1850
Maud, F. H., *Hockerill Highway* (1957)
Melling, Elizabeth, *Kentish Sources—Some Records and Bridges*, I (1959)
Melville, James, and Hobbs, J. L., *Early Railway History in Furness* (C.W.T. Tract Series No. 13, 1951)
Mingay, G. E., *English Landed Society in the Eighteenth Century* (1963)
Mitchell, Alex, *The English Lakes—An Excursion* (1862)

Morley, Edith (ed.), *The Correspondence of Henry Crabb Robinson with Wordsworth Circle 1808–66* (1927)
Morris, W. P., *The Records of Patterdale* (1903)

Nicholson, J. and Burn, R., *History of Cumberland* (1777)
Nicholson, J. and Burn, R., *History of Westmorland* (1777)
Nicholson, Cornelius, *The Annals of Kendal* (1835)
Nicholson, Norman, *The Lakers* (1955)

Palmer, William T., *The Verge of Lakeland* (1938)
Parker, C. A., *The Gosforth District—Its Antiquities and Places of Interest* (1904)
Parkinson, Richard A., *Parkinson's Guide and History of Kirkby Stephen and District*
Parsons and White, *History, Directory and Gazetteer of Cumberland and Westmorland, Furness and Cartmel* (1829)
Papers, Letters and Journals of William Pearson (1863)
Pennant, Thomas, *A Tour from Downing to Alston Moor* (1801)
Postlethwaite, John, *Mines and Mining in the Lake District—An Essay*, (1877)
Pratt, E. A., *A History of Inland Transport and Communication in England* (1912)
Pringle, Andrew, *General View of the Agriculture of the County of Westmorland* (1794)

Raistrick, Arthur, *Two Centuries of Industrial Welfare: The London (Quaker) Lead Company, 1692–1905* (1938)
Rawnsley, E. F., *Canon Rawnsley: An Account of His Life* (1923)
Rawnsley, H. D., *Ruskin and the English Lakes* (1901)
Redford, Arthur, *Labour Migration in England 1800–1850* (1926)
Robbins, R. Michael, *Middlesex* (1953)
Robbins, R. Michael, *The Railway Age* (1962)
Roberts, Charles J., *Directory of Barrow in Furness and the Furness District* (1886)
Robinson, Howard, *The British Post Office—A History* (1948)
Robinson, John, *A Guide to the Lakes* (1819)
Rolt, L. T. C., *Thomas Telford* (1958)
Rolt, L. T. C., *The Inland Waterways of England* (1956)
Rumney, A. W., *Cycling in The English Lake District* (1894)
Russell, Percy, *A Leicestershire Road* (1934)

Saville, John, *Rural Depopulation in England and Wales 1851–1951* (1957)
Scott, Daniel, *Bygone Cumberland and Westmorland* (1899)
Simmons, Jack, *The Maryport and Carlisle Railway* (1947)

I

Simmons, Jack, *The Railways of England—An Historical Introduction* (1961)

Slater, *Directory of Cumberland and Westmorland* (1869)

Smelser, N. J., *Social Change in the Industrial Revolution* (1959)

Somervell, Robert, *A Protest Against the Extensions of Railways in the Lake District* (1876)

Sopwith, Thomas, *An Account of the Mining Districts of Alston Moor, Weardale and le* (18*Teesda*33)

Sowerby, Richard R., *Historical Kirkby Stephen and North Westmorland* (1950)

Speight, H., *Romantic Richmondshire* (1897)

Stephenson, George, *Report on the Formation of a Railway between Lancaster and Carlisle—with observations on the mode of crossing Morecombe Bay* (1837)

Stockdale, James, *Annals of Cartmel* (1872)

Sugden, E. H., *A History of the Parish of Arlecdon and Frizington* (1897)

Thompson, F. M. L., *English Landed Society in the Nineteenth Century* (1963)

Topping, George, and Potter, John, *Memories of Old Carlisle* (1922)

Tovey, D. C. (ed.), *Letters of Thomas Gray* (3 vols, 1909)

Travers, Benjamin, *A Descriptive Tour to the Lakes of Cumberland and Westmorland in the Autumn of 1804* (1806)

Vale, Edmund, *The Mail Coach Men* (1960)

Walker, A., *Observations made in a Tour from London to the Lakes of Westmorland and Camberland in the Summer of 1791* (1792)

Walker, James, *The History of Penrith from the Earliest Times to the Present Time* (1858)

Wallace, William, *Alston Moor—Its Pastoral People, Its Mines and Miners* (1890)

Warner, R. D., *Tour through the Northern Counties of England and the Borders of Scotland* (2 vols, 1802)

Warriner, Frank, *The Millom District, A History* (1932)

Waugh, Edwin, *Oversands to the Lakes* (1860)

Webb, Sidney, and Beatrice, *The Story of the King's Highway* (1913)

Journals of John Wesley (Vols 4, 5 and 7, 1909 ed.)

West, Thomas, *A Guide to the Lakes* (1st ed. 1778)

West, Thomas, *The Antiquities of Furness* (1805)

Whellan, William, *History of Cumberland and Westmorland* (1860)

Whiteside, Joseph, *Shappe in Bygone Days* (1904)

Wilson, James, *A History of Dalston Bridges and Bridge Disputes* (1896)

Wilson, James, (ed.), *The Inclosure of the Moors, Commons and Waste Lands of Dalston, Cumberland* (1898)

Wilson, William, *Coaching Past and Present* (1885)

Wordsworth, Dorothy, *Journals of Dorothy Wordsworth* (1941), edit.
    by E. de Selincourt
Wordsworth, William, *Guide to the Lake District* (1835)
Wright, Frederick, *Leaves from Our Diary or Tales of a Tour of the
    English Lakes 1868–9*

Young, Arthur, *A Six months Tour through the North of England* (1770)
Young, G. M., *Early Victorian England 1830–1865*, (2 vols, 1951).

PERIODICALS

A. *Transactions of the Cumberland and Westmorland Antiquarian and
    Archaeological Society* (1873–1966)

1. Michael W. Taylor, 'An Account of Sockbridge Hall and Askham
    Hall West', II (O.S., 1874)
2. Miss Powley, 'Past and Present among the Northern Fells', II
    (O.S., 1874)
3. John Fell, 'The Guides over the Kent and Levens Sands, More-
    cambe Bay', VII (O.S., 1883)
4. T. Wilson, 'The Roman Road over Whinfell', VII (O.S., 1883)
5. W. Hall, 'Alston', VIII (O.S., 1884)
6. T. H. Hodgson, 'The Military Road in Cumberland', II (N.S.,
    1902).
7. T. H. B. Graham, 'The Townfields of Cumberland', X (N.S.,
    1910)
8. J. F. Curwen, 'The Lancaster Canal', XVII (N.S., 1916–17)
9. Caesar Caine, 'The Port of Ravenglass', XXII (N.S., 1922)
10. Rev. C. M. Lowther Bouch, 'Jonathan Boucher', XXVII (N.S.,
    1922)
11. W. T. McIntire, 'The Port of Milnthorpe', XXXVI (N.S., 1936)
12. W. T. McIntire, 'Arnside', XXXVII (N.S., 1937)
13. T. H. Bainbridge, 'Eighteenth Century Agriculture in Cumbria',
    XLII (N.S., 1942)
14. T. E. Casson, 'The Diary of William Fleming of Rowe Head
    Pennington, 1848–56', XLII (N.S., 1942)
15. T. H. Bainbridge, 'Land Utilisation in Cumbria in the mid
    Nineteenth Century', XLIII (N.S., 1943)
16. Rev. F. B. Swift, 'The Rev. John Barwis and his Journals', XLV
    (N.S., 1945)
17. T. H. Bainbridge, 'Some Factors in the Development of Cumbrian
    Agriculture, especially during the Nineteenth Century', XLIV
    (N.S., 1945)
18. J. Melville and J. L. Hobbs, 'Furness Travelling and Postal
    Arrangements in the Eighteenth and Nineteenth Centuries',
    XLVI (N.S., 1946)

19. T. H. Bainbridge, 'John Wesley's Travels in Cumberland', **XLVII** (N.S., 1947)
20. T. H. Bainbridge, 'John Wesley's Travels in Westmorland and Lancashire North of the Sands', **LII** (N.S., 1952)
21. Norman Dees, 'John Robinson, Turnpike Road Surveyor, 1772–92', **LII** (N.S., 1952)
22. Sidney Pollard, 'North-West Railway Politics in the Eighteen-Sixties', **LII** (N.S., 1952)
23. G. P. Jones, 'The Population of Broughton in Furness in the Eighteenth Century', **LIII** (N.S., 1953)
24. J. L. Hobbs, 'The Turnpike Roads of North Lonsdale', **LV** (N.S., 1955)
25. G. P. Jones, 'Some Population Problems Relating to Cumberland and Westmorland in the Eighteenth Century', **LVIII** (N.S., 1958)
26. Gordon G. Elliot, 'The Enclosure of Aspatria', **LX** (N.S., 1960)
27. J. L. Hobbs, 'The Journal of John Wilson Soulby of Rampside Academy, August–December 1847', **LX** (N.S., 1960)
28. B. G. Hutton, 'A Lakeland Journey, 1759', **LXI** (N.S., 1961)
29. F. Barnes and J. L. Hobbs, 'John Robinson's Book of Precedents. Part III—Miscellaneous Matters', **LXI** (N.S., 1961)

B. *Transactions of the Cumberland and Westmorland Association for the Advancement of Literature and Society (1875–92)*
1. H. W. Schneider, 'On the Haematite Iron Mines of Low Furness', x (1884–5)
2. W. Wilson, 'Former Social Life in Cumberland and Westmorland', xii (1886–7)
3. J. Fisher Crosthwaite, 'Recollections of the Keswick Post Office Past and Present', xiv (1888–9)
4. F. Harrison, 'Old Roads and Paths', xv (1889–90)

C. *Transactions of the Historical Society of Lancashire and Cheshire*
1. J. A. Dawson and T. A. Welton, 'On the Population of Lancashire and Cheshire and its Local Distribution during the Fifty years, 1801–51', x (1857–8)
2. A. Craig Gibson, 'Hawkeshead Parish', VI (N.S., 1865–6)
3. A. Craig Gibson, 'The Two Conistons', VII (N.S., 1866–7)

D. *Transactions of the Lancashire and Cheshire Antiquarian Society*
1. William Harrison, 'Commons Inclosures in Lancashire and Cheshire in the Eighteenth Century', VI (1888)
2. William Harrison, 'Ancient Fords, Ferries and Bridges in Lancashire', XIII (1895)
3. Sidney Pollard, 'Town Planning in the Nineteenth Century—The Beginnings of Modern Barrow in Furness', LXIII (1952–3)

E. *Journal of Transport History*
 1. Sidney Pollard and J. D. Marshall, 'The Furness Railway and the Growth of Barrow', **I**, No. 2 (November 1953)
 2. Peter L. Payne, 'The Bermondsey, Rotherhithe and Deptford Turnpike Trust, 1776–1810', **II**, No. 3 (May 1956)
 3. Robert H. Spiro, 'John Loudon McAdam and the Metropolis Turnpike Trust', **II**, No. 4 (November 1956)
 4. G. C. Dickinson, 'Stage Coach Services in the West Riding of Yorkshire between 1830 and 1840' (May 1959)
 5. Harold W. Hart, 'Some Notes on Coach Travel, 1750–1848' (May 1960)
 6. G. C. Dickinson, 'The Development of Suburban Road Passenger Transport in Leeds, 1840–95 (November 1960)
 7. J. T. Ward, 'West Riding Landowners and the Railways' (November 1960)
 8. T. S. Willan, 'The J.P.'s and the Rates of Land Carriage, 1692–1827', **V**, No. 4. (November 1962)
 9. Mervyn Hughes, 'Telford, Parnell and the Great Irish Road', **VI**, No. 4 (November 1964)
10. G. H. Martin, 'Street Lamps for Kendal', **VII**, No. 1 (May 1965)

F. *Economic History Review*
 1. M. W. Beresford, 'Commissioners of Enclosure', **XVI**, No. 2 (1946)
 2. C. W. Ashworth, 'British Industrial Villages in the Nineteenth Century', **III**, No. 3 (2nd series, 1951)
 3. Sidney Pollard, 'Barrow in Furness and the Seventh Duke of Devonshire', **VIII**, No. 2 (2nd series, December 1955)
 4. J. E. Williams, 'Whitehaven in the Eighteenth Century', **VIII**, No. 3 (2nd series, April 1956)
 5. David Spring, 'English Landownership in the Nineteenth Century —A Critical Note', **IX**, No. 3 (2nd series, April 1957)
 6. R. G. Wilson, 'Transport Dues as Indices of Economic Growth, 1775–1820', **XIX**, No. 1 (April 1966)

G. *Journal of Economic History*
 1. David Spring, 'The English Landed Estate in the Age of Coal and Iron, 1830–80', **XI** (1951)

H. *English Historical Review*
 1. Sidney Pollard, 'The Factory Village in the Industrial Revolution' (July 1964)

I. *History*
 1. Edward Hughes, 'North Country Life in the Eighteenth Century, (1940–1)

J. *Agricultural History*
  1. David Spring, 'A Great Agricultural Estate, Netherby Under Sir James Graham', **XXIX**

K. *Archaeologia Cambrensis*
  1. A. H. Dodd, 'The Roads of North Wales, 1750–1850', **LXXX** (7th series, 1925)

L. *Caernarvonshire Historical Society*
  1. R. T. Pritchard, 'Caernarvonshire Turnpike Trusts', Vol 22 (1961)

M. *East Yorkshire Local History Society*
  1. K. A. McMahon, 'Roads and Turnpike Trusts in East Yorkshire', (1964)

N. *Montgomeryshire Collections*
  1. R. T. Pritchard, 'Montgomeryshire Turnpike Trusts', **LVII** (Part 1, 1961)

O. *Scottish Geographical Magazine*
  1. Donald G. Moir, 'Statute Labour Roads', **LXXII** and **LXXIII** (September and December 1957)

P. *The Philatelist*
  1. R. C. Woodall, 'Postal History of Carlisle and Carlisle Mails— Early Transmission of Letters' (August and September 1950)

Q. *Country Life*
  1. Norman Jones, 'A Hundred Years of Windermere Steamers' (11 August 1960)

R. *Gentleman's Magazine*
  1. 'Extract of a Letter giving an Account of a Survey of the N, West Coast of England in August 1746' (January 1748)
  2. 'Observations on Improvements lately made in Cumberland', (June 1790)
  3. 'A Rambler's Revisit to Buttermere' (January 1800)

S. *Railway Magazine*
  1. C. J. Allen, 'An Account of the Maryport and Carlisle Railway' (October 1909)

General Index

Agriculture (*see also* Enclosures): Improvements in 22, 40, 83–4; Conservatism of many farmers 40, 41; Contribution of improved roads to 20
Allen, Ralph 109
Arnold, Matthew 158–9
Arnold, Thomas 118

Bell, George 126, 191–2, 194–6
Berry, Walter (Father and son) 99, 103–4, 135, 141
Bessemer process 209, 210
Bintley, Joseph 53, 194
Boots and shoes (manufacture of) 164
Botchergate (repair of) 170–2
Bower, Joshua 63
Bridges, 27, 50, 54, 80, 82, 85; Administration of 51–4, 74, 126, 211–12; Techniques of repair and construction, 79–81, 202–3
Buccleuch (Duke of) 210
Buttermere 159

Calico (manufacture of) 22
Camden, William 116
Canals, 37, 103, 134–5, 139–42, 206–7
Carlisle (Earl of) 98
Carrier Services: Cost of, 131–2, 136, 208; By pack horse 19, 24–7, 101; By carrier's cart 98–104, 136–8, 141, 153, 155, 161, 207; By carrier's wagon 102, 104–5
Cartmel 18, 26, 35, 44–5, 53, 111, 126–7, 135
Cattle Droving 24
Chapman, William 36
Coal: mining of 20, 23, 91–2; Carriage of 100, 133, 135–6, 138–41, 143–7, 153
Coastal Shipping 156; Duties levied upon 99, 138; Cost of travel by 132–4; Volume and nature of traffic 133–6, 138; Competition with road transport 136–8
Collinson, John 61

Coniston Lake 24, 156
Copper (Mining of) 24
Cory, John 54, 196
Cotton spinning 21, 164
Cumberland Pacquet 39
Curwen (family of) 20, 21, 23, 32
Curwen, John Christian 22, 57, 85
Cycling 199

Dalton, Doctor John 116
Dalton, John 38
Defoe, Daniel 29
Dickens, Charles 122–3

Education 38
Enclosures 22, 44, 45, 83, 97; Road building activities associated with 82, 86–8, 205
Ennerdale 97, 155, 157, 159
Eskdale 17, 34, 47

Field, William 53
Food prices 207–8
Furness 20, 126, 140, 156; Isolation of in eighteenth century 34–6; Mineral deposits within 20, 36; Stage and mail coach services to 106, 110, 111; Trade by sea 134–5; Impact of railways upon 127–8, 144, 152, 208–11

Gilpin, William 117
Glamorgan Agricultural Society 84
Graham (Family) 32, 70
Graham, Sir James 57, 83, 85, 167
Gray, Thomas 116, 119, 120
Greenwich Hospital Commission 60, 62, 69, 82, 93–5, 151
Greystoke Road 153, 172, 174–5
Guano 84, 99, 104, 141

Hardknott Pass 34
Holyhead Road 72–3, 78
Honister Pass 193
Honister Slate Quarries 159
Hostelries 30, 119, 120, 123, 157, 160
Hutchinson, William 117

Iron Ore: Mining of 20, 23, 92, 208–9; Carriage of 23, 92, 100–1, 140, 147, 155, 174–6; Manufacture of 37, 128, 209–11
Isle of Wight 68

Jessop, William 36

Lake District (*see also* Tourism): Appreciation of 116; Visitors to 116–17; Improvement of roads within 118–19, 203; Growing traffic within 119–21, 157; A Approach by rail 155–7; Steamship services to and within 156; Hotel facilities 119, 120, 161; Concern about tourist expansion 121, 158–9; Opposition to railways within 158–60; Western part less popular 157
Langdale 24, 34
Lead (mining of) 25, 92–4, 141–2, 153, 205
Leeds-Hunslet Turnpike Trust 165
London Lead Company 93–4, 102
Longsleddale 189
Lowther (family) 20, 32, 39, 57, 65, 66, 70, 96, 97
Lowther, Sir James 23, 29, 32, 33, 39, 68
Lowther, Sir John 21
Lowther, Sir William 84, 96
Low Wood Gunpowder Company 104, 135, 138

McAdam, James 47, 71, 149, 188
McAdam, John Loudon 59, 60, 69, 70, 78, 79, 81, 82, 85, 91, 93–5
McCulloch, J. R. 179

Mail Coaches: Expansion of 95, 109–11, 113, 206; Criticisms of 111–13, 115, 125; Cost of 130–2
Mardale 153, 189
Martineau, Harriet 161
Maychell, Thomas 45
Metcalfe, John 77, 78
Milton, Chris 53
Morecambe Bay (crossings of) 35, 109, 126–7
Mosedale 189
Motor car, 199, 201, 212

Mounsey (family) 70
Musgrave, Philip 57

Ogilby, John 19

Palmer, John 109
Population (growth of in Cumbria) 20, 163

De Quincey, Thomas 118, 122

Rail Transport 63, 100, 127, 143–7, 150–62, 166, 168–70, 173, 209–11; Early reactions to 150–1, 179; Cost of carriage by 132, 142–4; Speed of 143–4; Volume of traffic 144–7; Effect upon Turnpike Trust 145–9, 151–2, 154–5, 157, 161–2; Effect upon stage coach services 148–9, 152; Effect upon road carrier services 153, 161; Effect upon hostelries 149; Opposition to within Lake District, 158–60; Reduces isolation of parts of Cumbria 127–8, 210, 211; Stimulates growth of an iron industry 128, 208–10
Ramsden, James 210
Rawlinson, William 37
Rennie, John 73
Roads: Techniques of construction and repair 77–9, 202–3; Administration of, by the Parish 42–4, 46–8, 191–2; Administration of, by the highway district 48–9, 191–3; Administration of, by the county 27, 45, 49, 157, 193–201; Administration of, by turnpike trusts (*see* separate index for individual turnpike trusts) 55, 56–61, 68–72, 75, 76, 85, 88–91; Collection of tolls by 62–4, 97, 98, 165–77, 189, 207, 212; Debts of 32, 33, 65–7, 149, 173, 178–9, 181, 187–8, 190; Effects of railways upon, 145–58, 162, 165, 169, 170; Dissolution of 178–90; Condition of disturnpiked roads 191–2
Robinson, George 51, 53
Robinson, Henry Crabb 118
Ruskin, John 118, 158–9

Schneider, H. W. 92, 210
Schoose Farm 22
Scotland 68, 73
Scott Laird and Company 21,30
Senhouse (family) 21, 23, 32, 70, 85, 92
Senhouse, Humphrey 57
Sherman, Edward 145, 148
Slate (mining of) 135, 138, 140, 159
Smirke, Robert 80
Smith, J. T. 209
Somervell, Robert 159
South-West Cumberland 109, 133, 138; Isolation of 34–6, 124; Poor condition of its roads 124–6; Impact of railways upon 127, 210, 211
Stage coaches 26, 32, 38, 105–9, 114–16, 121–4, 133, 137, 152, 156, 160–1; Taxes imposed upon 129, 132–3; Cost of travel by 129, 130, 137, 139, 142–3, 158; Increasing speed of 38, 114; Competition amongst 114–15; Co-ordination of time-tables 115–16; Effect of railways upon 148, 152, 157, 161
Stagg, Joseph 93, 94
Stagg, Robert 93 102
Stainmore (or Great North Road) 25, 31, 32, 109, 110, 124, 146
State Policy: towards turnpike trusts 72, 74, 75, 180, 186–7; Grants

and loans to road and bridge authorities 74; Enquiries into road administration 67, 68, 74, 75, 145, 201; Establishment of a Ministry of transport 201
Steel, Edward 71
Stephenson, George 127
Styhead Pass 157

Telford, Thomas 73, 78–81
Temperance Movement 149
Theobalds, George 61
Tourism 116–24, 155–62, 193, 195, 203, 211

Ullswater Lake 155–6, 195

Warnell Fell 98
Wastdale 155, 157
Waugh, Edward 71
Wesley, John 34, 35
West, Thomas 117
Windermere Lake 156
Winn, Charles 63
Woollen Industry 18, 25, 30, 38, 97, 164
Wordsworth, William 39, 118, 122, 158–9
Wrynose Pass 34

Young, Arthur 30, 32

Index to Cumbrian Turnpike Trusts

Alston 60, 69, 70, 77, 94–6, 98, 145n., 179n., 185, 187, 191

Ambleside 46, 61, 63n., 70n., 72, 78, 89–91, 99, 100, 116, 118–21, 157–8, 160–2, 183–9, 203

Appleby–Kendal 30, 62n., 70, 70n., 180–1, 186, 192

Brampton–Longtown 96, 145–6, 150, 187n., 188

Brougham Bridge 57–8, 69, 70, 108

Brough-Eamont Bridge 108, 145–6, 149, 180, 185, 188

Carlisle–Brampton 63n., 71, 145, 154, 162, 166–7, 179, 180

Carlisle–Cockermouth 57, 63, 71, 145n., 147

Carlisle–Eamont Bridge 58, 61–4, 69, 70, 77–9, 85, 89, 107–8, 116, 146–9, 151, 154–5, 167–72, 174, 176–7, 180–2, 185, 187n., 189, 190

Carlisle–Glasgow 73, 78, 166, 182

Carlisle–Portpatrick 73, 79, 116

Carlisle-Skillbeck 59, 98

Carlisle–Temon (or 'Military Road') 30, 31, 36, 59, 70, 73, 145, 179, 180, 186

Cockermouth–Maryport 63, 70, 71, 97, 98, 100, 145n., 147, 175–6, 185

Cockermouth–Penrith 30, 58, 60, 63n., 65, 66, 68, 70, 77, 78, 85, 98, 121, 153–5, 162, 172–7, 179n., 185, 189

Cockermouth–Workington 63, 65, 71, 100, 145n., 147, 180, 187n., 188

Heron Syke-Eamont-Bridge 30, 62n., 65, 77–9, 81, 97, 106–7, 116, 141, 146–9, 152, 155, 179n., 181, 186–7, 189

Kendal-Kirkby Ireleth 33, 35

Kingstown–Westlinton 70, 179, 186

Kirkby Lonsdale-Kendal-Milnthorpe 30, 62n., 145n.

Kirkby Stephen-Hawes 33, 71, 72, 96, 187n., 188

Longtown 74

Milnthorpe-Levens 70n., 78, 106–7, 142, 146–7, 166

Sedbergh 59, 65, 71, 72

Ulverston-Carnforth 63n., 67, 77, 81, 106, 108, 111, 181, 187n., 188

Whitehaven 29, 30, 60, 70n., 77, 81, 97, 100–1, 124, 147–8, 155, 162, 179n., 191

Index to Places

Allonby 109
Alston 25, 49, 92–3, 95, 108, 110, 124, 205
Ambleside 19, 103, 109–10, 118–21, 156, 158, 160, 184
Appleby 17, 18, 24, 26, 104, 109, 110, 163
Applethwaite 184
Arnside 99, 103
Aspatria 144, 152

Backbarrow 37
Bampton 189
Bannisdale 189
Barnard Castle 26, 104, 209
Barrow in Furness 128, 135, 144, 209, 210, 211, 213
Bigland 86
Birmingham 113, 137, 148
Blencow 172
Boot 143
Bootle 35, 47, 109, 125–6
Boroughbridge 24
Bothel 19
Bowes 110
Bowness (Lake District) 110, 119, 161
Bowness (on Solway) 48
Bradford 106
Braithwaite 159
Brampton 18, 36, 49, 98, 143, 163
Bridgefoot 111
Brighton 137
Bristol 69
Brough 24, 104, 110, 148, 196
Broughton in Furness 20, 109, 127, 152, 155
Burgh by Sands 48
Burneside 97
Burton in Kendal 18, 111, 113

Caldbeck 32
Calder Bridge 125
Cambridge 28
Carleton 108, 168

Carlisle 18, 19, 21, 24, 30, 36, 73, 80, 85, 98, 99, 102, 104, 105, 109, 110, 113, 115, 116, 130, 133, 138, 141–4, 152–4, 163–4, 166–72, 177, 182, 200, 206–7, 213
Castle Carrock 19
Cleator 23, 92
Clifton Junction 209
Cockermouth 18, 19, 26, 80, 105, 109, 156, 158, 193
Colchester 28
Coniston 24, 111, 140, 155, 156
Corby 19
Crook 184
Crosthwaite 86, 197

Dalston 51, 199
Dalton 34, 35, 92, 144
Darlington 37
Dent 26
Drigg 143, 157
Duddon Bridge 125
Dumfries 115, 134, 137

Edinburgh 106, 109, 110, 113, 130
Egremont 18, 19, 20, 36, 109, 113, 124–5, 136, 193
Ellenborough 100
Exeter 69

Farleton 18
Fleetwood 135–6, 156
Flookburgh 111

Garrigill 49
Glasgow 23, 26, 106, 108–10, 113, 115, 130, 134, 143, 213
Glasson 103, 141
Grange over Sands 86, 155
Grasmere 117, 119–21, 156, 160
Greta Bridge 109

Harrington 21
Hawkshead 26, 110, 111, 156
Helsington 184
Hensingham 100
Hereford 69
Hertford 28

Hest Bank 127
Hexham 36, 94, 108
High Newton 43
Hincaster 18
Hodbarrow 209
Holderstone 18
Holker 86
Holme Cultram 51, 197
Hugill 184
Hull 106
Hunslet 63
Huntingdon 28

Ireleth 34–5

Kendal 18, 19, 25–7, 30, 35, 38, 65, 80, 82, 99, 105–6, 108–11, 119–21, 130, 135, 138, 139, 140, 143, 155, 163–4, 183–4, 196, 206, 213
Keswick 19, 22, 79, 109, 118–21, 155–8, 160, 163, 183
Kirkbampton 47–8
Kirkby Ireleth 135
Kirkby Lonsdale 24, 26, 106, 166
Kirkby Stephen 108, 196, 209
Knockmurton 20

Lakeside 155
Lancaster 35, 109, 111, 127, 140
Leeds 102, 106, 124, 151, 165
Leighton 37
Liverpool 82, 102, 109, 110, 112–13, 115, 133–7, 143–4, 148, 152, 213
Lockerbie 115
London 24–8, 104–6, 109–12, 115, 124, 130, 135, 137, 143, 148, 152
Longtown 47, 49
Lowca 37
Low Cark 43
Lower Holker 45, 126
Low wood 44

Manchester 102, 109, 110, 112–13, 124, 130, 137–8, 143–4, 148, 151–3,
Maryport 20, 21, 23, 24, 36, 80, 85, 92, 99, 106, 109, 137, 144–6, 152, 163
Millom 20, 37, 51, 126, 128, 133, 197, 209–11
Milnthorpe 99, 103, 111, 126, 134, 152

Natland 196
Netherbridge 80
Netherby 83
Nethergraveship 184
Nether Staveley 184
Newbiggin 172
Newby Bridge 86, 152
Newcastle 18, 19, 21, 25, 30, 95, 108–10, 144, 152–3
Northallerton 24
Norwich 115

Orton 26
Over Staveley 184

Park 209
Patterdale 141, 153
Penny Bridge 33
Penrith 19, 24, 26, 49, 69, 95, 102, 104–5, 108–13, 115, 142, 154–5, 163, 167–9, 172–5, 182, 200
Piel 135, 156
Pooley Bridge 155, 157
Port Carlisle 133
Portpatrick 110, 115
Preston 105, 137, 139, 152, 156

Ravenglass 35, 109, 125–6, 143, 152
Ravenstonedale 43
Richmond 24, 104
Ripon 24
Roseley 24
Rydal 119, 184

St Bees 20
Seascale 155, 157
Seathwaite (in Borrowdale) 157
Seaton 37
Sebergham 47
Sedbergh 17, 26, 108, 110
Sedgwick 18
Settle 24, 26, 106
Shap 18, 19, 31–2, 153, 155, 196
Sheffield 106, 124, 137
Skipton 24, 106
Soulby 195
Southampton 18
Sowerby 18
Stainton 172
Stribers 44
Strickland Ketel 184

Tebay 18, 209
Thrimby 189
Thwaite 89
Tilberthwaite 24
Troutbeck 155,184

Ulverston 20, 24, 26, 34–5, 106, 108, 109, 111–13, 125, 127, 134, 136, 138, 144, 152, 156
Undermillbeck 184
Upper Holker 45

Warton 140
Waterhead 156
Wetheriggs 84
Whinfell 184

Whitehaven 19, 21, 23, 26, 29, 30, 35–6, 91–2, 99, 102, 105–6, 109, 111–12, 115, 125, 127–8, 130, 133–8, 143–4, 152–3, 163, 205, 209, 213
Wigan 26
Wigton 22, 49, 69, 105, 109, 152
Windermere 121, 155–6, 161, 183
Witherslack 86
Worcester 181
Workington 19, 21, 23–4, 36, 81, 99, 105–6, 109, 111, 128, 138, 153, 163, 209

York 26, 102, 104, 106, 109, 124, 130, 151